Current Topics in Anaesthesia

General editors: Stanley A. Feldman
Cyril F. Scurr

6 Anaesthesia in Patients with Ischaemic Heart Disease

To my parents, M. S. Cheng and Y. Chung;
They have shown me the Way.
And to my wife, B. K. Wong;
She walks by my side.

Anaesthesia in Patients with Ischaemic Heart Disease

David C. Chung,
MD, FFARCS, FRCP(C)

Assistant Professor, Department of Anaesthesia,
University of Western Ontario;
Anaesthetist, Division of Cardiovascular and Thoracic Surgery,
University Hospital, London, Canada

Edward Arnold

First published 1982
by Edward Arnold (Publishers) Ltd.
41 Bedford Square, London WC1B 3DQ

British Library Cataloguing in Publication Data
Chung, David C.
  Anaesthesia in Patients with ischaemic
  heart disease. — (Current topics in
  anaesthesia, ISSN 0144-8684; 6)
  1. Anesthesia in cardiology
  I. Title II. Series
  617′.967412   RD598

ISBN 0-7131-4407-6

Set in Linoterm 10/11pt Times by Castlefield Press,
Northampton and printed in Great Britain by
Butler & Tanner Ltd., Frome and London

General preface to series

The current rate of increase of scientific knowledge is such that it is recognized that ' . . . ninety per cent of all the existing knowledge which can be drawn upon for the practice of medicine is less than 10 years old'.*

In an acute specialty, such as anaesthesia, failure to keep abreast of advances can seriously affect the standard of patient care. The need for continuing education is widely recognized and indeed it is mandatory in some countries.

However, due to the flood of new knowledge which grows in an exponential fashion greatly multiplying the pool of information every decade, the difficulty which presents itself is that of selecting and retrieving the information of immediate value and clinical relevance. This series has been produced in an effort to overcome this dilemma.

By producing a number of authoritative reviews the Current Topics Series has allowed the General Editors to select those in which it is felt there is a particular need for a digest of the large amount of literature, or for a clear statement of the relevance of new information.

By presenting these books in a concise form it should be possible to publish these reviews quickly. Careful selection of authors allows the presentation of mature clinical judgement on the relative importance of this new information.

The information will be clearly presented and, by emphasizing only key references and by avoiding an excess of specialist jargon, the books will, it is hoped, prove to be useful and succinct.

It has been our intention to avoid the difficulties of the large textbooks, with their inevitable prolonged gestation period, and to produce books with a wider appeal than the comprehensive, detailed, and highly specialized monographs. By this means we hope that the Current Topics in Anaesthesia Series will make a valuable contribution by meeting the demands of continuing educaton in anaesthesia.

Westminster Hospital   Stanley A. Feldman
London   Cyril F. Scurr

*Education and training for the Professions.
  Sir Frank Hartley, Wilkinson Lecture
  Delivered at Institute of Dental Surgery, 30.1.78
  University of London Bulletin, May 1978, No. 45, p. 3

Preface

Ischaemic heart disease is a malady more common in the affluent. Surgical patients who are also suffering from chronic myocardial ischaemia are at risk of having life-threatening cardiac complications during operation and in the postoperative period. Several major advances in the last decade have revolutionized the anaesthetic management of these patients. The first of many is the identification of subgroups of patients who are especially at risk. Another step forward is the evolution of the principles of protecting the ischaemic myocardium by lowering the blood pressure and depressing the myocardium, and yet improving the systemic circulation of the patient. At the same time new drugs have been developed to treat myocardial ischaemia, arrhythmias and congestive heart failure. The availability of monitoring equipment to follow the cardiovascular functions of the patient from moment to moment has allowed us to quantify and assess these newer drugs and techniques. In the chapters which follow, these current concepts are reviewed, with an emphasis on the application of these principles to the anaesthetic management of patients with ischaemic heart disease.

In order to present a comprehensive view of these topics, I have searched past and current literature and have consulted many of my colleagues with special interest in these areas. Naturally the opinions expressed also reflect my personal experience and interest. Although many of the chapters were originally prepared as lectures for the house staff in the Postgraduate Anaesthesia Programme, University of Western Ontario, this book should be a useful companion for all candidates preparing for examinations in the specialty of anaesthesia, to their teachers, to practising anaesthetists, and to physicians, surgeons, nurses and allied workers involved in the preoperative preparation and postoperative management of surgical patients with ischaemic heart disease.

London, Canada   1981   D.C.C.

Acknowledgements

I am greatly indebted to Dr D. E. A. Thompson of Women's College Hospital for her invaluable assistance since the inception of this project, to Professor R. A. Gordon for publishing Chapters 10 and 11 in the Canadian Anaesthetists' Society Journal and for reading and commenting on other parts of the manuscript, and to Dr R. R. Johnston, Dr E. I. Eger, II, Dr C. Wilson, *Anesthesia and Analgesia (Current Researches)* and Medtronic of Canada, Ltd for their permission to reproduce original illustrations.

Dr M. T. Cheung, Cardiologist at St Michael's Hospital, Dr P. T. H. Ko, Cardiology Fellow at University Hospital, and I have collaborated on Chapter 12. Their contributions are hereby acknowledged.

Many others have contributed generously to this monograph. In particular, I would like to thank Professor W. E. G. A. Spoerel for giving me leave to work on the manuscript, and all my colleagues for their helpful suggestions.

The diagrams in this book were drawn by Mr G. E. Moogk, Department of Instructional Resources, University Hospital, and the final draft was prepared by Mrs H. M. Burdach and Mrs W. L. Kassian. To them I am deeply grateful.

Glossary of drugs

Generic names		Common proprietary preparations
UK	Others	
Acebutolol		Sectral
Adrenaline	Epinephrine	
Alphadolone/ alphaxalone	CT1341	Alfathesin, Althesin
Atenolol		Tenormin
Bretylium tosylate		Bretylate, Darenthin
Cholestyramine		Cuemid, Questran
Chlorpromazine		Largactil, Thorazine
Diazepam		Valium, Vivol
Digitoxin		Crystodigin, Digitaline Nativelle, Digitox, Purodigin
Digoxin		Davoxin, Diganox, Lanoxin, Natigoxine Nativelle, Prodigox, Winoxin
Dimethyl tubocurarine	Metocurine	Metubine
Dobutamine		Dobutrex
Dopamine		Intropin, Revimine
Droperidol	Dehydrobenzperidol	Droleptan, Inapsine
Edrophonium		Tensilon
Enflurane		Ethrane
Fentanyl		Sublimaze
Fentanyl/droperidol		Innovar, Thalamonal
Gallamine		Flaxedil
Glucagon		Glucagon, Glucagon Novo
Glyceryl trinitrate	Nitroglycerin, trinitrin	Nitrostabilin, Nitrostat
Halothane		Fluothane, Somnothane
Hydrallazine	Hydralazine	Apresoline, Lopress
Isoflurane		Forane
Isoprenaline	Isoproterenol	Isuprel, Suscardia

Ketamine		Ketaject, Ketalar, Ketanest
Lignocaine	Lidocaine	Lidothesin, Xylocaine, Xylocard
Methoxamine		Vasoxine, Vasoxyl
Methoxyflurane		Penthrane
Methylphenidate		Methidate, Ritalin
Metoprolol		Betaloc, Lopresor
Nadolol		Corgard
Neostigmine		Prostigmin
Noradrenaline	Levarterenol	Levophed
Oxprenolol		Trasicor
Pancuronium		Pavulon
Pethidine	Meperidine	Demerol, Dolantin, Phytadon
Phentolamine		Regitine, Rogitine
Phenylephrine		Neo-Synephrine
Phenytoin	Diphenylhydantoin	Dilantin, Epanutin
Pindolol		Visken
Practolol		Dalzic, Eraldin
Procainamide		Pronestyl
Propranolol		Avlocardyl, Inderal, Sumial
Quinidine		Biquin Durules, Cardioquin, Quinate, Quinicardine, Rhythmidine
Sodium nitroprusside	Nitroprusside	Nipride
Sotalol		Beta-Cardone, Sotacor
Suxamethonium	Succinylcholine	Anectine, Brevidil M, Quelicin, Scoline, Sucostrin
Thiopentone	Thiopental	Intraval, Pentothal, Trapanal, Nesdonal
Timolol		Betim, Blocadren
Trimetaphan	Trimethaphan	Arfonad
Tubocurarine	d-Tubocurarine	Tubarine

Contents

Part I
Introduction

1

Ischaemic heart disease — the problems

According to the World Health Organizaton Task Force on Standardization of Clinical Nomenclature, *ischaemic heart disease* defines a spectrum of myocardial impairment due to the inadequacy of myocardial blood flow to meet the metabolic demand of the myocardium, which is caused by disease of the coronary circulation (Bernard *et al.*, 1979). While *coronary heart disease* is an acceptable synonym of ischaemic heart disease, other terms should no longer be used. Although an imbalance of myocardial blood supply and myocardial metabolic needs in the presence of normal coronary arteries — as in severe aortic stenosis, extreme ventricular hypertrophy and hypertension — will have a similar effect on the myocardium, the use of the term 'ischaemic heart disease' should be avoided in these conditions so that a standard terminology and universal diagnostic criteria can be established.

Atherosclerosis of coronary arteries is the most important cause of ischaemic heart disease in all developed countries. In Britain there is a large regional variation in mortality rate due to this disease. It is 438 per 100 000 among men between 35 and 64 years of age in Scotland; but it is only 356 per 100 000 in England and Wales (Fulton *et al.*, 1978). In Canada ischaemic heart disease accounts for nearly a third of all annual deaths (Lalonde, 1974). In the United States approximately 1.3 million patients have a myocardial infarction each year, and more than 675 000 patients die from chronic myocardial ischaemia and its complications (Hillis and Braunwald, 1977).

The effects of myocardial ischaemia

As a result of ischaemia the delivery of oxygen and substrates to myocardial cells fails to meet the metabolic demand of myocardial work, toxic metabolites of anaerobic metabolism cannot be removed, and abnormalities of electrical and mechanical functions of the myocardium follow. Since

1

myocardial ischaemia due to coronary artery stenosis is a regional process, the manifestation and the degree of disturbed functions depend on the site of arterial occlusion.

Abnormal electrical function can be seen on the surface electrocardiogram as changes in the repolarization of the heart, as ventricular irritability and as disturbances of impulse formation and impulse conduction. The early changes in repolarization seen in myocardial ischaemia are inversion of T waves and depression of ST segments. This can progress to elevation of ST segments in myocardial injury and appearance of Q waves in myocardial necrosis. The signs of ventricular irritability are ventricular arrhythmias. They are associated with a high incidence of sudden death. Other arrhythmias include sinus bradycardia, atrial tachycardia, atrial flutter and fibrillation, and all atrioventricular conduction disturbances.

Abnormal mechanical function is the result of a temporary or permanent loss of the contractile property of cardiac muscle. Ischaemia of the ventricular myocardium reduces the efficiency of the ventricle as a pump, while paradoxical ventricular wall motion (asymmetry and asynchrony) of ischaemic segments will decrease the effectiveness of ventricular ejection. If the papillary muscles are involved, mitral regurgitation can occur, and left ventricular pump function will be reduced even further.

Tachyarrhythmias as well as impairment of ventricular function will increase the work of the heart, and both will aggravate myocardial ischaemia. The interaction between arrhythmias and impaired ventricular function is also mutually aggravating. That is, arrhythmias will interfere with ventricular output, while ventricular impairment and enlargement, by stretching the automatic and conducting tissues, will cause arrhythmias. Therefore, the reciprocal interaction of myocardial ischaemia, arrhythmias and impaired ventricular function can form a vicious cycle to cause a rapid deterioration in cardiac function (Fig. 1.1).

Anaesthetic implications

Ageing and arterial hypertension, together with dietary, personal and social habits associated with affluence, have contributed to an increase in the prevalence of ischaemic heart disease during this century. At the same time, advances in the diagnosis and evaluation of the disease, together with aggressive medical therapy and coronary artery bypass operations, have improved the prospect of long-term survival of these patients. It can be expected that a significant number of surgical patients are also suffering from ischaemic heart disease.

These patients face many problems in the operating theatre. Tachycardia or hypertension, or both, precipitated by anxiety or painful stimuli, will increase the work and the metabolic needs of the heart, while an episode of hypotension or hypoxaemia will reduce myocardial blood flow or oxygen supply; and all these factors can set into motion the vicious cycle of myocardial ischaemia, arrhythmias and impaired ventricular function. Many anaesthetic agents are myocardial depressants and the ischaemic heart is particularly sensitive to their depressant action. On the other hand, agents

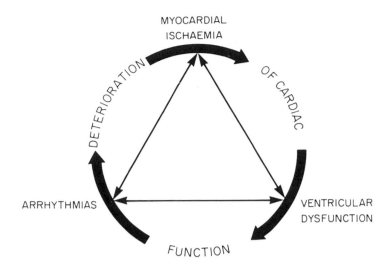

MYOCARDIAL
ISCHAEMIA

DETERIORATION

OF CARDIAC

ARRHYTHMIAS

VENTRICULAR
DYSFUNCTION

FUNCTION

Fig 1.1.   The reciprocal interaction of myocardial ischaemia, arhythmias and ventricular dysfunction. Any one of these factors can set into motion the vicious cycle leading to deterioration of cardiac function.

which have a stimulatory action on the circulation can be even more harmful because tachycardia and hypertension will increase the work of the heart and aggravate the discrepancy between coronary blood flow and metabolic needs. Anaesthetic agents which have arrhythmogenic properties pose another problem. They can interact with the unstable intrinsic rhythm of an ischaemic heart and with other cardiac and vasoactive drugs to precipitate serious arrhythmias.

The treatment of the disease also complicates anaesthesia: beta-adrenergic antagonists, cardiac glycosides and artificial pacemakers pose special problems. Beta-antagonists are common agents used for the treatment of myocardial ischaemia and hypertension. They are potent myocardial depressants. The combined depressant action of beta blockade and anaesthetic agents is always a cause for concern. Cardiac glycosides used for the treatment of heart failure are potentially toxic agents; there are many factors which will enhance their toxicity during anaesthesia and surgery. These include fluid, electrolyte and acid–base disturbances, hypoxaemia, abnormal renal and hepatic functions, and interaction with anaesthetic agents. Therefore patients being treated with digitalis deserve special attention during preoperative assessment. Patients with an implanted artificial pacemaker also require special consideration as it can fail to function properly and because electrosurgical instruments and electric equipment in the operating theatre can interfere with its proper function.

In the last decade, intensive basic and clinical research has begun to improve the prognosis of anaesthesia and surgery in these patients. Risk factors associated with postoperative cardiac complications have been identified. New drugs have expanded the scope of treatment of myocardial ischaemia, arrhythmias and heart failure. An appreciation of the factors regulating coronary blood flow, myocardial work, myocardial energy metabolism and ventricular ejection has made it possible to protect the myocardium compromised by ischaemia and to improve ventricular function. Advanced monitoring techniques have allowed close observation of myocardial, cardiac and circulatory functions. A better understanding of the circulatory effects of anaesthetic agents and their interaction with cardiac drugs has offered a genuine choice of these agents and anaesthetic techniques in special circumstances. The application of these principles to the preoperative assessment and preparation of patients with ischaemic heart disease and to the management of their problems during operation and in the postoperative period will be discussed in detail in the following chapters.

References

Bernard, R., Corday, E., Eliasch, H., Gonin, A., Hiait, R., Nikolaeva, L. F., Oakley, C. M., Oliver, M. F., Pisa, Z., Puddu, V., Rapaport, E., Strasser, T. and Wellens, H. (1979). Nomenclature and criteria for diagnosis of ischemic heart disease: report of the Joint International Society and Federation of Cardiology/World Health Organization Task Force on Standardization of Clinical Nomenclature. *Circulation* **59**, 607.

Fulton, M., Adams, W., Lutz, W. and Oliver, M. F. (1978). Regional variations in mortality from ischaemic heart and cerebrovascular disease in Britain. *British Heart Journal* **40**, 563.

Hillis, L. D. and Braunwald, E. (1977). Myocardial ischemia (first of three parts). *New England Journal of Medicine* **296**, 971.

Lalonde, M. (1974). *A New Perspective on the Health of Canadians: A Working Document.* Information Canada: Ottawa.

2

Coronary blood flow and myocardial energetics

The average human heart weighs 350 g, or 0.5 per cent of total body weight. Not only does it pump blood through the entire body, it is also in the unique position of being responsible for its own blood supply. Normal coronary blood flow is 80 ml/100 g per minute of cardiac tissue, or 6 per cent of cardiac output. This can be increased fourfold during strenuous exercise.

The normal working heart derives its energy totally from oxidative metabolism and consumes oxygen at the rate of 10 ml/100 g per minute of myocardial tissue. This amounts to the extraction of 14 ml of oxygen from each 100 ml of coronary arterial blood. This oxygen extraction ratio of 75 per cent is near maximum, and the only means to increase oxygen delivery to meet increased energy requirements is by increasing coronary blood flow. To satisfy this high and variable oxygen requirement, the normal coronary circulation regulates its blood flow according to metabolic needs so that supply and demand are always in balance.

When coronary arteries are narrowed, the ability of the heart to regulate its own blood flow and oxygen supply is compromised. During episodes of increased work, supply fails to satisfy demand and impairment of myocardial function follows. Ischaemic episodes can be controlled or even reversed by enhancing blood flow and oxygen transport to the ischaemic zone, by increasing the use of oxygen-sparing substrates for energy metabolism, and by improving the efficiency of myocardial work. A thorough understanding of the physiology of the coronary circulation, the energy metabolism of the heart, and factors determining the metabolic needs of the myocardium will lay the foundation for protection of the ischaemic myocardium.

The coronary circulation

Arterial supply and venous drainage

The heart derives its nutritional supply from two arterial channels which originate in the sinus of Valsalva situated behind the anterior and the left posterior cusps of the aortic valve (Anderson, 1978). Although the cardiac cavities are in direct contact with blood, there is little evidence to suggest that the myocardium obtains any nutrient or oxygen from this source.

The right coronary artery

Arising from the anterior sinus, this artery descends vertically in the right atrioventricular sulcus on the anterior surface of the heart. It turns posteriorly at the inferior border of the right ventricle to give off branches supplying the right atrium, the free wall of the right ventricle and, to a variable extent, the posterior one-third of the ventricular septum and the posterior wall of the left ventricle. In most instances the sinoatrial node and the atrioventricular node are supplied by branches of the right coronary artery.

The left coronary artery

The main stem of the left coronary artery originates in the left posterior sinus. It divides close to its origin into the left anterior descending branch and the circumflex artery. While the left anterior descending branch is embedded in adipose tissue of the anterior interventricular sulcus, the circumflex artery runs in the left atrioventricular groove. They supply the left atrium, the left ventricle and the anterior two-thirds of the inter-ventricular septum.

The coronary artery is said to be dominant if it gives rise to the posterior descending artery and supplies the posterior aspect of the interventricular septum and the posterior wall of the left ventricle. The right coronary artery is dominant in about 50 per cent of the human hearts, the left coronary artery is dominant in another 20 per cent, and the pattern of distribution is equally balanced in the remaining 30 per cent (Schlesinger, 1940).

Coronary venous blood returns to the heart by three major systems (Anderson, 1978): the coronary sinus, the anterior cardiac veins and channels draining directly into the cardiac chambers, particularly the right atrium and the right ventricle.

The coronary sinus

This large vessel drains the great and middle cardiac veins, the posterior left ventricular vein and other smaller tributaries. Opening into the right atrium posteriorly immediately above the triscupid valve, it accounts for most of the venous drainage of the left ventricle.

The anterior cardiac veins

These are a series of parallel veins running across the anterior surface of the right ventricle and drain separately into the right atrium.

Direct channels

These include the Thebesian, the arteriosinusoidal and the arterioluminal vessels. The Thebesian vessels are venous channels which pass directly from the venous end of capillaries or from deep coronary veins to the cardiac chambers. The arteriosinusoidal and arterioluminal vessels, on the other hand, arise from small arteries or arterioles. Wearn and his colleagues (1933) showed that these channels communicate with the capillaries of the coronary microcirculation and run directly into the cardiac chambers as illustrated in Fig. 2.1.

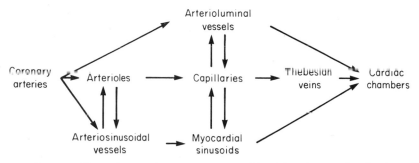

Fig. 2.1   Channels returning coronary venous blood directly to cardiac chambers. This diagram illustrates the communication of the arterioluminal vessels, the arteriosinusoidal vessels and the Thebesian veins with the coronary microcirculation (Wearn et al., 1933).

The capillary bed and collaterals

During their course on the epicardial surface, the coronary arteries send off branches which penetrate the full thickness of the myocardium. These branches divide repeatedly and terminate in a rich network of metarterioles, precapillaries and true capillaries whose patency is controlled by precapillary muscular sphincters richly innervated by autonomic nerve endings (Provenza and Scherlis, 1959). These capillaries run in parallel to, and between, myocardial fibres. According to Honig and Bourdeau-Martini (1974), there are approximately 4500 capillaries per square millimetre in the left ventricle — a capillary to each muscle fibre and a minimum intercapillary distance of 11 μm. Under basal metabolic conditions only 20–25 per cent of these capillaries are open (Myers and Honig, 1964).

The coronary arteries are end arteries — that is, each branch supplies the capillary bed of a strictly limited territory. However, anastomotic channels between coronary arteries are easily identifiable. Baroldi, Mantero and Scomazzoni (1956) described both homocoronary collaterals (between branches of the same coronary artery) and intercoronary collaterals (between branches of the right and left coronary arteries) in the human heart. These collaterals are only potential channels and are non-functional in healthy subjects (Goldstein et al., 1975). With the progressive development of stenosis in a coronary artery, the pressure gradient between the normally perfused and the ischaemic regions of the heart, as well as the release of vasodilators by ischaemic tissue, causes these channels to proliferate and to become functional. Thus the extent of ischaemia in the region supplied by the narrowed artery is reduced. Goldstein *et al.* (1974) found that it was possible for these collateral vessels to acquire a responsiveness to vaso-dilators in patients with ischaemic heart disease. This finding will partly explain the relief of angina pectoris by glyceryl trinitrate and other coronary vasodilators.

Coronary blood flow and its regulation

Blood flow in any regional circulation is directly related to the mean perfusion pressure and is inversely related to the resistance of its micro-circulation:

$$\text{Flow} = \frac{\text{Arteriovenous pressure gradient}}{\text{Resistance}}$$

In the absence of coronary artery stenosis, the mean aortic pressure can be regarded as the perfusion pressure of the coronary circulation. Mosher and his associates (1964) demonstrated that changes in the perfusion pressure of normal coronary arteries produce immediate changes in coronary blood flow in the same direction; but the flow always returns to its initial level within a few cardiac cycles, provided that the work of the heart remains constant. Conversely, when the perfusion pressure is maintained constant, a change in the work of the heart is accompanied by an equal change in coronary blood flow. This is a perfect example of autoregulation; that is, the heart is able to control its blood flow according to its metabolic needs. This control is independent of arterial perfusion pressure in the range of 8–24 kPa (60–180 mmHg).

Coronary vascular resistance

Since the phenomenon of autoregulation is independent of the perfusion pressure, its mechanism must lie with the ability of the coronary micro-circulation to change its resistance according to metabolic demand. Klocke *et al.* (1976) have described three functional components of coronary resistance in the normal heart:

Total coronary resistance	= Basal viscous resistance	+ Compressive resistance	+ Autoregulatory resistance

Basal viscous resistance

This is defined as the resistance of the fully dilated coronary microcirculation when the heart is in diastole. Its contribution to total coronary resistance is comparatively small in the normal heart. When stenotic lesions are present in major coronary arteries, the resistance across stenotic segments may be regarded as part of this basal viscous resistance, which can become the most important component of total coronary resistance.

Compressive resistance

During systole, pressure developed within the muscular wall of the heart leads to extravascular compression of the capillary bed. This compression in the left ventricular myocardium is so forceful that left coronary arterial flow is momentarily reversed during early systole. Hence most of the left coronary arterial flow occurs in diastole when extravascular compression is minimal. This extravascular component of coronary resistance is not uniform throughout the full thickness of the ventricular wall — an observation made by Johnson and DiPalma as early as 1939. Since it is highest at the subendocardial surface and lowest at the subepicardial surface, blood flow during systole is proportionately lower in the subendocardium than in the subepicardium. In the normal heart this ratio is reversed during diastole, and total regional subendocardial and subepicardial flows in each cardiac cycle are about equal.

Autoregulatory resistance

This refers to that portion of the coronary resistance which varies according to metabolic needs — that is, lowered resistance with increased metabolic rate, and *vice versa*. The autoregulatory resistance is normally high and is the most important component of total coronary resistance. When metabolic demand is high, maximum autoregulatory vasodilation can reduce resistance and increase flow fourfold (Klocke *et al.*, 1976). Since compressive resistance is higher in the subendocardium than in the subepicardium and yet flows in both regions are about equal, this must mean that autoregulatory resistance is lower in the subendocardium than in the subepicardium. This gradient in autoregulatory resistance across the superficial and deep layers of the ventricular myocardium has been confirmed by the findings of Myers and Honig (1964), which indicate that there are 30 per cent more open capillaries in the subendocardium than in the subepicardium.

The combination of a higher compressive resistance and a lower autoregulatory resistance in the subendocardium has important clinical implications. It means that the regional circulation of the subendocardium has less reserve capacity to meet demands of increased flow. This is confirmed by the clinical observation that the subendocardium is more vulnerable to ischaemic injury.

The mechanism of autoregulation

Despite intense efforts in many laboratories, the mechanism of coronary autoregulation remains controversial. Metabolic, neural and myogenic mechanisms have been proposed; but the role played by the last two must be regarded as secondary to that of the metabolic mediators.

Metabolic mechanism

Myocardial hypoxia is the most potent stimulus known to reduce coronary resistance. Rubio and Berne (1975) have found that many factors, including a lowering of oxygen content of coronary venous blood to below 5.5 ml/dl (5.5 ml/100 ml), an accumulation of hydrogen, potassium, lactate and phosphate ions, and an accumulation of carbon dioxide, adenosine and prostaglandin, can mediate the observed coronary vasodilation in response to an increase in myocaridal work. However, adenosine is recognized by most investigators as the metabolic regulator of coronary resistance (Rubio and Berne, 1969; Fox *et al.*, 1974). It is postulated that adenosine, a potent vasodilator and a product of dephosphorylation of cellular AMP, accumulates in the myocardial cell during cellular hypoxia, be it hypoxaemic or ischaemic in origin. Being able to cross myocardial cell membrane, it diffuses into the interstitial space to act on coronary resistance vessels. With myocardial flow increased, myocardial oxygenation is restored, and the rate of formation of this breakdown product is reduced as the concentration of intracellular AMP declines. As excess adenosine is washed away by the increase in coronary flow, the negative feedback loop of autoregulation is complete (Fig. 2.2).

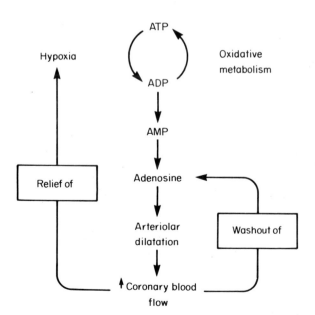

Fig. 2.2   The autoregulation of coronary blood flow. Adenosine plays a central role in ensuring that the oxygen cost of myocardial work is met by an adequate coronary blood flow.

Neural mechanism

The coronary microcirculation is richly supplied with autonomic nerve endings (Provenza and Scherlis, 1959). It has been demonstrated that alpha-adrenergic stimulation constricts coronary vessels, while beta-adrenergic and vagal stimulations reduce coronary resistance (Berne, DeGeest and Levy, 1965; Pitt, Elliot and Gregg, 1967; Feigl, 1969). However, the changes in myocardial work associated with sympathetic or parasympathetic stimulation have a more profound influence on coronary flow and over-ride the primary changes in coronary resistance associated with neural stimulation.

Myogenic mechanism

Bayliss described in 1902 his observation that arterial smooth muscle reacted to stretch by contraction and to a decrease in stretch by relaxation. More than half a century later, similar myogenic tone was demonstrated in coronary resistance vessels of rodents by Uchida and Bohr (1969). However, the magnitude of this tonic contraction and relaxation is small. Any role played by this intrinsic property of arterial smooth muscle in the auto-regulation of coronary blood flow in man can only be minor.

Coronary blood flow in the ischaemic heart

When coronary arteries are narrowed, a new component of coronary resistance, the stenotic resistance, is introduced. Although autoregulatory resistance is the major component of total resistance of the normal coronary circulation, the stenotic resistance across narrowed segments of coronary arteries predominates in the ischaemic heart. When obstruction is less than 90 per cent, an autoregulated compensatory dilatation of coronary resistance vessels will help to maintain total coronary resistance and resting coronary flow normal, but at the expense of a loss of reserve capacity to increase flow during stress (Klocke *et al.*, 1976). In the presence of a critical stenosis, this autoregulated compensatory mechanism is exhausted, the resistance vessels are fully dilated, and coronary flow becomes totally dependent on perfusion pressure proximal to the obstruction. Any decrease in perfusion pressure is accompanied by a drastic reduction in coronary flow to below normal values.

Since most of the myocardial blood flow occurs during diastole, diastolic blood pressure gives a better estimate of perfusion pressure. The exact lower limit of perfusion pressure required to maintain perfusion of ischaemic regions is unknown. It depends largely on the state of collateral flow. However, a *diastolic blood pressure* of 8 kPa (60 mmHg) is generally accepted as the absolute lower limit below which perfusion of ischaemic regions is likely to be compromised.

Perfusion of the myocardium is also more efficient when the diastolic phase of the cardiac cycle is longer than the systolic phase. This is particularly true in the subendocardium (Buckberg *et al.*, 1972). At a normal heart rate of 75 per minute, diastole occupies more than 60 per cent of the cardiac cycle. When the heart rate increases, systolic interval changes little while diastolic interval decreases. At a maximum heart rate of 180 per minute, diastole occupies only 40 per cent of the cardiac cycle (Folkow and Neil, 1971). The heart rate at which blood flow to ischaemic regions begins to fall is also not known, but many patients with ischaemic heart disease have angina when their heart rate approaches 100 per minute.

Energy metabolism of the myocardium

Cardiac metabolism has been the subject of several excellent reviews (Bing, 1965; Opie, 1968, 1969a, b; Neely and Morgan, 1974). Unlike skeletal muscle, the heart can use many substrates for energy metabolism. They include free fatty acids, glucose, lactate, pyruvate, acetate, ketone bodies and amino acids. Within limits, the uptake and utilization of a particular substrate is related to its arterial concentration and the availability of oxygen; but the utilization of substrates other than free fatty acids and glucose is usually limited.

The utilization of free fatty acids and glucose

Under normal aerobic conditions, free fatty acids are the substrate of choice in the postabsorptive state. They supply 60 per cent of the energy requirements of the heart by undergoing oxidative metabolism via the Krebs cycle to yield high energy phosphate bonds as illustrated in Fig. 2.3. Their uptake by myocardial cells is directly proportional to their arterial concentration, and they are not extracted by the myocardium when the arterial concentration is below 350 μmol/litre (Carlsten et al., 1963).

Under aerobic conditions, carbohydrate metabolism accounts for only 30–40 per cent of the energy requirements of the heart, but its role can be increased during periods of increased metabolic needs and hypoxia. Carbohydrate metabolism also can be increased when the arterial concentration of free fatty acids is low. Glucose uptake by myocardial cells is insulin dependent (Goodale, Olson and Hackel, 1959), and the threshold of uptake is an arterial concentration of 3.3 mmol/l (Goodale and Hackel, 1953). The metabolism of glucose is also summarized in Fig. 2.3. It is first broken down to pyruvate via the Embden–Meyerhof pathway (also known as anaerobic glycolysis) to release one-nineteenth of the energy extractable from a glucose molecule. Subsequently pyruvate is oxidized to carbon dioxide and water via the Krebs cycle (also known as the citric acid cycle or the tricarboxylic acid cycle) to yield the rest of the energy as ATP.

The metabolism of free fatty acids and that of glucose by the myocardium are intimately related, and they are interchangeable as sources of energy in the following manner (Neely and Morgan, 1974):

1. Free fatty acids and their oxidation inhibit glycogenolysis and glucose uptake by myocardial cells and inhibit anaerobic glycolysis and oxidation of pyruvate. The administration of insulin can improve glucose uptake, but inhibition of glucose metabolism remains.

2. When the serum concentration of free fatty acids is below the threshold of 350 μmol/litre, the myocardium can switch to the metabolism of glucose for energy.

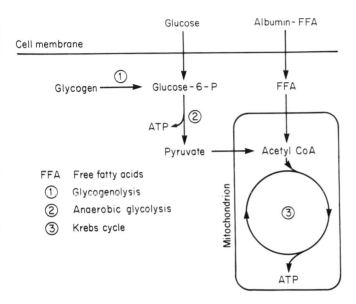

Fig. 2.3 Normal myocardial metabolism. Oxidative metabolism in the mitochondria supplies nearly all the energy requirements of the myocardial cell, energy provided by the anaerobic breakdown of glucose is normally of minor importance.

Although free fatty acids are the preferred substrate under normal aerobic conditions, they are less than optimal for the ischaemic myocardium because:

1. Free fatty acids cannot be metabolized anaerobically.
2. They increase oxygen consumption of the heart by an unknown mechanism so that their metabolism requires more oxygen per unit of energy production than glucose (Challoner and Steinberg, 1966). It may not be possible for the ischaemic myocardium to meet this increase in oxygen demand.
3. They have a depressant effect on myocardial function (Henderson *et al.*, 1970); a high serum concentration is associated with a higher incidence of ventricular arrhythmias and death after acute myocardial infarction (Oliver, Kurien and Greenwood, 1968).

Energy metabolism of the ischaemic heart

Since glucose can be metabolized partly by the anaerobic Embden–Meyerhof pathway, its metabolism by the hypoxaemic and the ischaemic heart is of interest to clinicians. Hypoxaemia implies a reduction of arterial oxygen content without interruption in coronary blood flow, and ischaemia is a condition of tissue hypoxia as the result of a reduction in coronary blood flow. When the heart is only hypoxaemic, oxidative metabolism of free fatty acids is not possible; but glucose uptake and glycogenolysis are stimulated, and anaerobic glycolysis becomes the only source of energy. It can supply as much as 10–15 per cent of the high energy ATP that is formed in the well oxygenated heart (Neely and Morgan, 1974). This rate of energy production is capable of sustaining the integrity of myocardial cells, but is not sufficient to maintain contractile function of the myocardium (Weissler *et al.*, 1968). With myocardial ischaemia not only is oxygen delivery restricted, but substrate availability and the washout of acid metabolites are also markedly reduced. When ischaemia is absolute, glycolytic flux involving consumption of the glycogen store is transiently accelerated, but soon falls to very low levels due to inhibition by lactic acidosis (Rovetto, Whitmer and Neely, 1973). However, except in the central necrotic zone of an infarct, ischaemia is seldom absolute. In areas where ischaemia is less severe, anaerobic glycolysis can increase and approach that seen in hypoxaemia alone (Opie, 1972).

Determinants of myocardial work

Other than maintaining basal metabolic needs of cardiac muscle, the energy released by the oxidation of free fatty acids and glucose is consumed by the heart to generate pressure and to maintain an adequate cardiac output. Most of the work is done by the left ventricle — right ventricular work being only one-sixth of that of the left ventricle. Since oxidative metabolism is the only source of energy to fuel myocardial work, myocardial oxygen demand is closely related to energy needs; and determinants of myocardial work are also determinants of myocardial oxygen consumption. Six such factors have been identified (Sonnenblick and Skelton, 1971):

1. Basal metabolism.
2. Activation energy.
3. External work.
4. Systolic wall tension.
5. Contractility.
6. Heart rate.

Of the six factors mentioned, the first three are classified as minor; and the last three, major.

Basal metabolism

The energy utilization of the heart at standstill is very high. It consumes approximately 2 ml of oxygen per 100 g of heart muscle per minute (McKeever, Gregg and Canney, 1958). This is six to seven times higher than that of skeletal muscle, and it represents 20 per cent of the total oxygen consumption of the normal beating heart. This basal consumption appears to be relatively constant.

Activation energy

The energy cost of activation includes two components: electrical depolarization and repolarization (Klocke, Braunwald and Ross, 1966), and the calcium flux associated with mechanical contraction and relaxation (Davies, 1963). The work of electrical activation is very small and represents less than 1 per cent of the total oxygen consumption of the beating heart (Klocke, Braunwald and Ross, 1966). But the energy expenditure of mechanical activation has not been fully quantified. Nevertheless, the total cost of activation appears to be small.

External work

The external work of the intact heart per beat is equal to the product of the stroke volume and the mean developed pressure:

Stroke work = Stroke volume × Mean aortic pressure

This external work accounts for approximately 17 per cent of the oxygen cost of myocardial work (Burns and Covell, 1972). As can be seen in the next section, the energy required to generate pressure — that is, pressure work — is much more costly than stroke work. Therefore an increase in stroke volume at constant aortic pressure can be achieved with a relatively small increase in myocardial oxygen consumption; but an increase in aortic pressure at constant stroke output can be accomplished only with a large increase in the oxygen cost of myocardial work.

Systolic wall tension

The high energy cost of generating pressure by the mammalian heart was observed first by Evans and Matsuoka (1914–1915). It is now recognized that systolic wall tension rather than pressure is the most important factor in determining the amount of work done by the left ventricle (Robard *et al.*, 1964). It accounts for 30–40 per cent of the energy needs of the beating heart (Barash and Kopriva, 1980).

According to the law of LaPlace, systolic wall tension of a spherical ventricle ejecting its stroke output is directly proportional to the product of the ventricular systolic pressure and the left ventricular end-diastolic radius (wall thickness being ignored):

$$\text{Systolic wall tension} \propto \text{Ventricular systolic pressure} \times \text{Left ventricular radius}$$

In the absence of aortic stenosis, ventricular systolic pressure is equal to *arterial systolic blood pressure*. Provided that the compliance of the ventricle is constant, left ventricular end-diastolic radius is directly proportional to left ventricular filling pressure at the end of diastole. Therefore the equation for systolic wall tension can be rewritten as follows:

$$\begin{array}{ccc} \text{Systolic} & \text{Arterial} & \text{Left} \\ \text{wall} \quad \propto & \text{systolic} \quad \times & \text{ventricular} \\ \text{tension} & \text{blood} & \text{filling} \\ & \text{pressure} & \text{pressure} \end{array}$$

Systolic wall tension is also called afterload; and left ventricular filling pressure, preload. At the bedside, left ventricular filling pressure can be measured directly as left ventricular end-diastolic pressure and indirectly as mean left atrial pressure, mean pulmonary capillary wedge pressure or pulmonary diastolic pressure. The normal range of left ventricular filling pressure is 0.8–1.6 kPa (6–12 mmHg). The practical aspect of measuring left ventricular filling pressure is discussed under 'Invasive haemodynamic monitoring' in Chapter 6.

Since both arterial systolic blood pressure and left ventricular filling pressure influence systolic wall tension independently, these two haemodynamic variables are usually considered as individual factors determining myocardial work and oxygen demand. An increase in arterial systolic blood pressure or ventricular filling pressure beyond their normal range will increase myocardial energy needs, and *vice versa*.

Contractility

Normally, contractility accounts for 10–15 per cent of the oxygen cost of myocardial work (Barash and Kopriva, 1980). However, the effect of changes in contractility on myocardial work is complex and depends on the state of the myocardium before the inotropic stimulus is applied. When the heart is normal in size, an increase in contractility by a variety of stimuli is accompanied by an increase in work and oxygen demand (Sonnenblick *et al.*, 1965). This increase is related to an increase in the speed and the extent of shortening of myocardial fibres and is not the result of any significant change in basal metabolism (Klocke *et al.*, 1965). Conversely, a mild to moderate degree of myocardial depresson of the normal heart is associated with a fall in myocardial work. However, when depression of contractility is severe enough to cause ventricular failure, the ventricle dilates. Consequently the increase in myocardial work associated with the increase in wall tension (due to the increase in left ventricular radius) over-rides the reduced workload associated with the depressed contractility. Therefore oxygen consumption of the heart increases. For this reason, the improved contractility following digitalization will increase the work of the normal heart but decrease the work of the failing heart (Covell *et al.*, 1966).

It is difficult to measure myocardial contractility, be it in the laboratory or at the bedside. The clinical methods of estimating contractility are discussed under 'The measurement of contractility' in Chapter 6. In general, contractility is considered normal when stroke work index and left ventricular filling pressure are within normal limits.

Heart rate

Although the energy cost of each heart beat is determined by activation energy, external work, systolic wall tension and contractility, the major determinant of work done by the heart over one minute is heart rate:

| Myocardial work per minute | = | Myocardial work per beat | × | Heart rate |

Heart rate also has a minor effect on contractility — an increase in heart rate is accompanied by a minor increase in contractility (Boerth *et al.*, 1969). This phenomenon is known as the Bowditch effect. Thus heart rate increases myocardial work a little more than that predicted by the increase in frequency of contraction alone.

Heart rate and arterial systolic blood pressure can be linked by their product — the rate–pressure product — to make an excellent index of myocardial work. Patients with ischaemic heart disease usually develop angina at a relatively constant rate–pressure product (Robinson, 1967). It was pointed out in an earlier section that heart rate is also a determinant of myocardial blood flow (see 'Coronary blood flow in the ischaemic heart' in this chapter). In order to maintain adequate perfusion of ischaemic regions and to minimize an excess increase in myocardial work, heart rate should be kept below 90 beats per minute in these patients. Depending on the heart rate, arterial systolic blood pressure should be kept at a level below that dictated by the rate–pressure product at which a patient develops anginal symptoms (see 'Indices of myocardial ischaemia and myocardial work' in Chapter 6).

Conclusion

The heart is an aerobic organ relying almost entirely on the oxidation of free fatty acids and carbohydrates in the Krebs cycle for energy to do work. Normally, coronary blood flow is regulated according to metabolic needs so that blood flow always meets the energy requirements of the heart. This autoregulation of coronary blood flow is mediated chiefly by adenosine, a potent vasodilator, which is found in the interstitium of cardiac muscle during hypoxaemic and ischaemic hypoxia. The capillary bed of an ischaemic region of the myocardium is fully dilated in the presence of critical stenosis of a coronary artery. Since autoregulation to increase blood flow to meet increased metabolic needs in this region is no longer possible, blood flow to this region is dependent on perfusion pressure. In order to maintain adequate perfusion of the myocardium in patients with chronic myocardial ischaemia, their diastolic blood pressure should not be allowed to fall below 8 kPa (60 mmHg). Perfusion of the ischaemic myocardium is also more efficient at a slower heart rate.

There are three major determinants of myocardial work — namely, heart rate, systolic wall tension and contractility. Since systolic wall tension is affected by arterial systolic blood pressure and left ventricular filling pressure independently, the four haemodynamic variables which determine myocardial work are heart rate, arterial systolic blood pressure, left ventricular filling pressure and contractility. To avoid ischaemic injury of the myocardium in the presence of a fixed myocardial blood flow, it is necessary to maintain these haemodynamic variables within acceptable limits in patients with ischaemic heart disease. Heart rate should not be allowed to rise above 90 beats per minute. A slower heart rate also will benefit myocardial perfusion. Depending on the heart rate, arterial systolic blood pressure should be kept below that dictated by the rate–pressure product at which a patient develops signs of myocardial ischaemia. Usually, left ventricular filling pressure is measured indirectly as mean pulmonary capillary wedge pressure or pulmonary diastolic pressure. It should be kept within the normal limits of 0.8–1.6 kPa (6–12 mmHg.) It is difficult to measure myocardial contractility at the bedside. If ventricular pump function is not compromised, a mild to moderate depression of myocardial contractility is acceptable.

Glucose is a more suitable energy substrate for the ischaemic myocardium. Its metabolism requires less oxygen than free fatty acids for each unit of energy production, it does not depress myocardial contractility, it does not cause arrhythmias, and it can be broken down partly via anaerobic glycolysis to provide some energy during hypoxaemic and ischaemic hypoxia of the myocardium. The use of glucose as a source of energy by the heart can be increased by maintaining normoglycaemia in the presence of insulin and by suppressing the serum concentration of free fatty acids to below threshold value.

References

Anderson, J. E. (1978). *Grant's Atlas of Anatomy*, 7th edn. Williams & Wilkins: Baltimore.

Barash, P. G. and Kopriva, C. J. (1980). The rate–pressure product in clinical anesthesia: boon or bane? *Anesthesia and Analgesia . . . Current Researches* **59**, 229.

Baroldi, G., Mantero, O. and Scomazzoni, G. (1956). The collaterals of the coronary arteries in normal and pathologic hearts. *Circulation Research* **4**, 223.

Bayliss, W. M. (1902). On the local reactions of the arterial wall to changes of internal pressure. *Journal of Physiology* **28**, 220.

Berne, R. M., DeGeest, H. and Levy, M. N. (1965). Influence of the cardiac nerves on coronary resistance. *American Journal of Physiology* **208**, 763.

Bing, R. J. (1965). Cardiac metabolism. *Physiological Reviews* **45**, 171.

Boerth, R. C., Covell, J. W., Pool, P. E. and Ross, J. Jr (1969). Increased myocardial oxygen consumption and contractile state associated with increased heart rate in dogs. *Circulation Research* **24**, 725.

Buckberg, G. D., Fixler, D. E., Archie, J. P. and Hoffman, J. I. E. (1972). Experimental subendocardial ischemia in dogs with normal coronary arteries. *Circulation Research* **30**, 67.

Burns, J. W. and Covell, J. W. (1972). Myocardial oxygen consumption during isotonic and isovolumic contractions in the intact heart. *American Journal of Physiology* **223**, 1491.

Carlsten, A., Hallgren, B., Jagenburg, R., Svanborg, A. and Werko, L. (1963). Myocardial arteriovenous differences of individual free fatty acids in healthy human individuals. *Metabolism* **12**, 1063.

Challoner, D. R. and Steinberg, D. (1966). Effect of free fatty acid on the oxygen consumption of perfused rat heart. *American Journal of Physiology* **210**, 280.

Covell, J. W., Braunwald, E., Ross, J. Jr and Sonnenblick, E. H. (1966). Studies on digitalis. XVI. Effects on myocardial oxygen consumption. *Journal of Clinical Investigation* **45**, 1535.

Davies, R. E. (1963). A molecular theory of muscle contraction: calcium-dependent contractions with hydrogen bond formation plus ATP-dependent extensions of part of the myosin–actin cross bridges. *Nature* **199**, 1068.

Evans, C. L. and Matsuoka, Y. (1914–1915). The effect of various mechanical conditions on the gaseous metabolism and efficiency of the mammalian heart. *Journal of Physiology* **49**, 378.

Feigl, E. O. (1969). Parasympathetic control of coronary blood flow in dogs. *Circulation Research* **25**, 509.

Folkow, B. and Neil, E. (1971). *Circulation*. Oxford University Press: New York, London and Toronto.

Fox, A. C., Reed, G. E., Glassman, E., Kaltman, A. J. and Silk, B. B. (1974). Release of adenosine from human hearts during angina induced by rapid atrial pacing. *Journal of Clinical Investigation* **53**, 1447.

Goldstein, R. E., Stinson, E. B., Scherer, J. L., Seningen, R. P., Grehl, T. M. and Epstein, S. E. (1974). Intraoperative coronary collateral function in patients with coronary occlusive disease. *Circulation* **49**, 298.

Goldstein, R. E., Michaelis, L. L., Morrow, A. G. and Epstein, S. E. (1975). Coronary collateral function in patients without occlusive coronary artery disease. *Circulaton* **51**, 118.

Goodale, W. T. and Hackel, D. B. (1953). Myocardial carbohydrate metabolism in normal dogs, with effects of hyperglycemia and starvation. *Circulation Research* **1**, 509.

Goodale, W. T., Olson, R. E. and Hackel, D. B. (1959). The effects of fasting and diabetes mellitus on myocardial metabolism in man. *American Journal of Medicine* **27**, 212.

Henderson, A. H., Most, A. S., Parmley, W. W., Gorlin, R. and Sonnenblick, E. H. (1970). Depression of myocardial contractility in rates by free fatty acids during hypoxia. *Circulation Research* **26**, 439.

Honig, C. R. and Bourdeau-Martini, J. (1974). Extravascular component of oxygen transport in normal and hypertrophied hearts with special reference to oxygen therapy. *Circulation Research* **34** and **35**, Suppl. II, 11–97.

Johnson, J. R. and DiPalma, J. R. (1939). Intramyocardial pressure and its relation to aortic blood pressure. *American Journal of Physiology* **125**, 234.

Klocke, F. J., Braunwald, E. and Ross, J. Jr (1966). Oxygen cost of electrical activation of the heart. *Circulation Research* **18**, 357.

Klocke, F. J., Kaiser, G. A., Ross, J. Jr and Braunwald, E. (1965). Mechanism of increase of myocardial oxygen uptake produced by catecholamines. *American Journal of Physiology* **209**, 913.

Klocke, F. J., Mates, R. E., Copley, D. P. and Orlick, A. E. (1976). Physiology of the coronary circulation in health and coronary artery disease. In: *Progress in Cardiology*, Vol. 5, pp. 1–17. Ed. by P. N. Yu and J. F. Goodwin. Lea & Febiger: Philadelphia.

McKeever, W. P., Gregg, D. E. and Canney, P. C. (1958). Oxygen uptake of the nonworking left ventricle. *Circulation Research* **6**, 612.

Mosher, P., Ross, J. Jr, McFate, P. A. and Shaw, R. F. (1964). Control of coronary blood flow by an autoregulatory mechanism. *Circulation Research* **14**, 250.

Myers, W. W. and Honig, C. R. (1964). Number and distribution of capillaries as determinants of myocardial oxygen tension. *American Journal of Physiology* **207**, 653.

Neely, J. R. and Morgan, H. E. (1974). Relationship between carbohydrate and lipid metabolism and the energy balance of heart muscle. *Annual Review of Physiology* **36**, 413.

Oliver, M. F., Kurien, V. A. and Greenwood, T. W. (1968). Relation between serum free fatty acids and arrhythmias and death after acute myocardial infarction. *Lancet* **i**, 710.

Opie, L. H. (1968). Metabolism of the heart in health and disease. Part I. *American Heart Journal* **76**, 685.

Opie, L. H. (1969a). Metabolism of the heart in health and disease. Part II. *American Heart Journal* **77**, 100.

Opie, L. H. (1969b). Metabolism of the heart in health and disease. Part III. *American Heart Journal* **77**, 383.

Opie, L. H. (1972). Metabolic response during impending myocardial infarction. I. Relevance of studies of glucose and fatty acid metabolism in animals. *Circulation* **45**, 483.

Pitt, B., Elliot, E. C. and Gregg, D. E. (1967). Adrenergic receptor activity in the coronary arteries of the unanesthetized dog. *Circulation Research* **21**, 75.

Provenza, D. V. and Scherlis, S. (1959). Demonstration of muscle sphincters as a capillary component in the human heart. *Circulation* **20**, 35.

Robinson, B. F. (1967). Relation of heart rate and systolic blood pressure to the onset of pain in angina pectoris. *Circulation* **35**, 1073.

Rodbard, S., Williams, C. B., Rodbard, D. and Berglund, E. (1964). Myocardial tension and oxygen uptake. *Circulation Research* **14**, 139.

Rovetto, M. J., Whitmer, J. T. and Neely, J. R. (1973). Comparison of the effects of anoxia and whole heart ischemia on carbohydrate utilization in isolated working rat hearts. *Circulaton Research* **32**, 699.

Rubio, R. and Berne, R. M. (1969). Release of adenosine by the normal myocardium in dogs and its relationship to the regulation of coronary resistance. *Circulation Research* **25**, 407.

Rubio, R. and Berne, R. M. (1975). Regulaton of coronary blood flow. *Progress in Cardiovascular Diseases* **18**, 105.

Schlesinger, M. J. (1940). Relation of anatomic pattern to pathologic conditions of the coronary arteries. *Archives of Pathology* **30**, 403.

Sonnenblick, E. H. and Skelton, C. L. (1971). Oxygen consumption of the heart: physiological principles and clinical implications. *Modern Concepts of Cardiovascular Disease* **40**, 9.

Sonnenblick, E. H., Ross, J. Jr, Covell, J. W., Kaiser, G. A. and Braunwald, E. (1965). Velocity of contraction as a determinant of myocardial oxygen consumption. *American Journal of Physiology* **209**, 919.

Uchida, E. and Bohr, D. F. (1969). Myogenic tone in isolated perfused vessels: occurrence among vascular beds and along vascular trees. *Circulation Research* **25**, 549.

Wearn, J. T., Mettier, S. R., Klumpp, T. G. and Zschiesche, L. J. (1933). The nature of the vascular communications between the coronary arteries and the chambers of the heart. *American Heart Journal* **9**, 143.

Weissler, A. M., Kruger, F. A., Baba, N., Scarpelli, D. G., Leighton, R. F. and Gallimore, J. K. (1968). Role of anaerobic metabolism in the preservation of functional capacity and structure of anoxic myocardium. *Journal of Clinical Investigation* **47**, 403.

3

Protection of the ischaemic myocardium

Protection of the ischaemic myocardium was first put into practice during the last decade by cardiac physicians. They found that a large number of victims with acute myocardial infarction, who survived ventricular arrhythmias in the coronary care unit, later developed incapacitating ventricular failure. Their experience at the bedside suggests that the ischaemic injury around the necrotic centre of an infarct is reversible and that injured myocardium can be preserved. Patients will recover with more functional myocardium and a better prognosis, provided that measures aimed at improving the balance of myocardial energy supply and demand are instituted early in the course of acute myocardial infarction.

The surgical patient who also has ischaemic heart disease and the victim of acute myocardial infarction have many problems in common. During anaesthesia and major operations haemodynamic instability is not uncommon. Hypertension increases the work of the heart, hypotension reduces coronary perfusion, and tachycardia both increases metabolic demand and restricts diastolic coronary flow. These haemodynamic changes can be complicated further by a fall in oxygen content of arterial blood due to ventilation/perfusion inequalities following induction of anaesthesia and due to blood loss. The reported incidence of postoperative myocardial infarction varies. While Topkins and Artusio (1964) reported an incidence of only 0.66 per cent in a group of unselected patients in their retrospective study, Hunter and his colleagues (1968) reported an incidence of 2 per cent in their prospective study. However, in a group of selected patients who had preoperative electocardiographic signs of chronic myocardial ischaemia, Mauney, Ebert and Sabiston (1970) reported that 8 per cent had an acute myocardial infarction postoperatively, and another 10 per cent had electrocardiographic evidence of new or additional myocardial ischaemia.

It is obvious that many of these factors which can precipitate acute myocardial ischaemia during anaesthesia and operation are preventable, controllable and correctable. Since the myocardium of these surgical patients is not injured, the emphasis is on prevention of ischaemic injury. It is in this role that the anaesthetist can participate fully to protect the ischaemic myocardium. While the basic principles will be reviewed in this chapter, the practice of protection of the ischaemic myocardium will be discussed in Part III, on 'Anaesthesia in patients with ischaemic heart disease'.

Basic principles

While the determinant of myocardial energy supply is the adequacy of myocardial blood flow which governs the availability of oxygen and energy substrates, the major determinants of myocardial work and energy requirements are heart rate, systolic blood pressure, left ventricular filling pressure and contractility (see Chapter 2). The goal in protection of the ischaemic myocardium is to maintain a balance between myocardial energy supply and myocardial energy needs. Although blood flow to the ischaemic zone is relatively fixed, energy supply can be sustained by maintaining myocardial oxygenation in the face of a reduced coronary blood flow and by maintaining a continuous supply of the oxygen-sparing substrate, glucose. To maintain energy expenditure within the bounds of this limited supply would mean abolishing abnormal increases in the haemodynamic determinants of myocardial work. The means available to anaesthetists to manipulate these factors include the use of:

1. Oxygen therapy.
2. Glucose-insulin-potassium (G-I-K) solution.
3. Beta-adrenergic antagonists.
4. Vasodilators.
5. Inotropic agents.
6. Inhalational anaesthetics.

Oxygen therapy

The normal heart extracts 75 per cent of the 19 ml of oxygen carried by each 100 ml of coronary arterial blood. This degree of oxygen extraction is near maximum, and the ischaemic myocardium tolerates poorly any fall in the oxygen content of arterial blood. Since the amount of oxygen dissolved in plasma is small and can be ignored, the oxygen content of arterial blood is a function of its haemoglobin concentration and oxygen saturation:

$$O_2 \text{ content} = \text{Hb conc} \times O_2 \text{ saturation} \times 1.39$$

In order to maintain delivery of oxygen to the myocardium, both the haemoglobin concentration and the oxygen saturation of arterial blood should be kept within normal limits. Anaemia should be treated, and blood loss replaced. Due to the sigmoid configuration of the oxygen-haemoglobin dissociation curve, an arterial oxygen tension of 8 kPa (60 mmHg) is consistent with a saturation of 90 per cent. They should be kept above these limits.

In addition to maintaining a normal oxygen content of coronary arterial blood, it was found that the administration of 100 per cent oxygen to victims of acute myocardial infarction had a protective value (Madias, Madias and Hood, 1976). Saltzman (1975) has proposed that at least two mechanisms are at play to increase oxygen delivery to the ischaemic myocardium when inspired oxygen fraction is increased above normal:

1. Arterial oxygen tension rises to supranormal values when the inspired

oxygen fraction is increased. Although the rise in oxygen content of arterial blood can be only minor, the increase in oxygen tension provides a more favourable diffusion gradient for oxygen transport to the ischaemic tissue.

2. High arterial oxygen tension causes vasoconstriction in the normally perfused region of the heart and diverts blood flow to the ischaemic zone.

One hundred per cent oxygen is, of course, not suitable for long-term therapy due to pulmonary toxicity. However, animal experiments indicate that an inspired oxygen fraction of 0.4 is just as effective in protection of the ischaemic myocardium (Maroko *et al.*, 1975).

Glucose-insulin-potassium (G-I-K) solution

In the fasting state the role played by glucose in the energy metabolism of the normal heart is secondary to that of free fatty acids, but its role during hypoxaemic and ischaemic hypoxia of the myocardium can be increased (Neely and Morgan, 1974). Provided that coronary blood flow is not totally interrupted, there are advantages for the ischaemic myocardium to use glucose instead of free fatty acids as an energy substrate (see 'The utilization of free fatty acids and glucose' in Chapter 2). In summary, they are:

1. The metabolism of glucose for energy requires less oxygen per unit of energy produced.

2. In the event of tissue hypoxia, glucose can supply some of the energy requirements by anaerobic glycolysis.

3. Unlike free fatty acids, glucose neither enhances irritability nor depresses contractility of the ischaemic myocardium. In fact, the simultaneous movement of potassium ions with glucose intracellularly has an anti-arrhythmic effect and enhances contractility.

4. Glucose can be given intravenously, and insulin will reduce its threshold of myocardial uptake.

With these arguments in mind, many authors have promoted glucose as the energy substrate of choice for the ischaemic myocardium. By administering a glucose-insulin-potassium solution intravenously to victims of acute myocardial infarction, Rogers and his colleagues (1976) succeeded in reducing the serum concentration of free fatty acids to below the threshold of myocardial uptake, in decreasing the size of the infarct, and in lowering the incidence of arrhythmias among their patients. The glucose-insulin-potassium solution used by these authors contained 300 g of glucose, 50 units of regular insulin and 80 mmol (mEq) of potassium dissolved in 1 litre of water. It was given at a rate of 1.5 ml/kg per hour.

The acceptance of this method of myocardial protection is far from being universal. Due to the high potassium concentration, the high osmolarity and the low pH of the solution, it must be administered via a central vein but not directly into the pulmonary artery (Dye *et al.*, 1978). During its infusion, serial measurements of blood sugar and serum potassium concentration should be done, and fluid balance should be monitored. Close observation of the patient should be continued for at least 24 hours after cessation of therapy because rebound hyperkalaemia can occur. Being incapable of handling the large fluid and potassium loads administered, patients with renal insufficiency should be excluded. For obvious reasons this form of therapy is also contraindicated in diabetics.

Beta-adrenergic antagonists

These competitive antagonists include acebutolol, alprenolol, atenolol, metoprolol, oxprenolol, pindolol, practolol, propranolol, sotalol, timolol and tolamolol. Propranolol is not only the oldest member of the group, it is also the most popular. All these agents can be administered orally. Other than practolol, propranolol is the only member which is available as an intravenous preparation. According to Shand (1975) the effects of beta-adrenergic antagonists on the determinants of myocardial work are:

1. Heart rate, cardiac output and contractility are reduced, while systolic blood pressure falls slightly or is unchanged.
2. Due to their negative inotropic property, there is a tendency for the heart to dilate; but the increase in ventricular size is usually small.
3. Although the systolic ejection period is lengthened, it is now believed that this variable has no effect on myocardial work.

Despite ischaemia, the heart with relatively normal ventricular function can tolerate a mild to moderate degree of depression without a significant effect on ventricular volume. The sum total of the said effects on the determinants of myocardial work is a reduction in myocardial energy requirements.

When ventricular function is marginal, the negative inotropic effect of beta-adrenergic antagonists can precipitate congestive heart failure and dilation of the ventricle. If that is the case, the rise in filling pressure can over-ride reductions in the other determinants of myocardial work, and myocardial metabolic needs will increase (see 'Contractility' in Chapter 2). Therefore beta-adrenergic antagonists are contraindicated in patients with congestive failure. A reduced dose should be given with care if ventricular function is impaired.

The effectiveness of these agents in maintaining the balance of myocardial blood flow and myocardial energy requirements, which is most apparent during physical exertion, has made them popular in the treatment of angina pectoris. They are also major antihypertensive agents. Propranolol already has found a place in the treatment of acute myocardial infarction (Mueller *et al.*, 1974). Its intravenous administration should be equally effective in the control of tachycardia and hypertension during anaesthesia and operation (see 'The treatment of sinus tachycardia and hypertension' in Chapter 8).

Vasodilators

To understand the action of vasodilators on myocardial work, it is necessary to review briefly the heterometric mechanism of Frank–Starling and the homoeometric mechanism of Anrep, which govern the pump function of the heart.

The Frank–Starling principle

This law of the heart states, in simple terms, that the stroke volume or stroke work of a normal ventricle bears a curvilinear relationship to its filling pressure as illustrated in Fig. 3.1 (Starling, 1915). When ventricular function is impaired, this relationship becomes more horizontal and is shifted to the right. In the failing heart there is an upper limit to this relationship, beyond which there is no increase in stroke volume or stroke work accompanying an increase in filling pressure. Stroke volume or stroke work may even decrease, and pulmonary congestion follows.

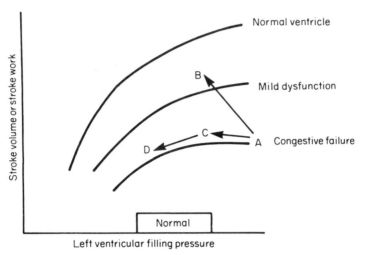

Fig 3.1 Frank–Starling ventricular function curves: In congestive failure the administration of a pure arterial vasodilator will reduce filling pressure and improve stroke volume. A pure venous vasodilator, on the other hand, will reduce congestion with little change in stroke output. But an excessive reduction in filling pressure can result in a drop in stroke volume.

The Anrep Effect

This homoeometric principle defines the ability of the normal heart to increase its contractility when systolic blood pressure is increased above normal. This enables the heart to maintain a constant stroke volume and a constant ventricular end-diastolic volume in the face of an increased aortic impedance (Sarnoff *et al.*, 1960; Sonnenblick and Downing, 1963). This intrinsic property of the heart can no longer be seen if cardiac function has been compromised by ischaemia or myocardial disease (Monroe *et al.*, 1972; Cohn, 1973a). This means that the failing heart will not be able to increase its contractility when blood pressure increases; therefore stroke volume will fall, and the heart will dilate. Conversely, if the blood pressure is lowered towards normal, the failing heart can eject its stroke volume more efficiently, and ventricular volume will fall. That is, changes in blood pressure lead to reciprocal changes in stroke volume of the impaired ventricle when blood pressure is above normal.

Vasodilators act by lowering elevated arterial pressure and ventricular filling pressure towards normal; this will reduce metabolic needs of the ischaemic heart and improve performance of the failing heart (Chatterjee *et al.*, 1973; Cohn, 1973b). As illustrated by the ventricular function curves in Fig. 3.1, the ischaemic ventricle working against an elevated arterial pressure will have a high filling pressure and can be described by point A on the lower ventricular function curve. The administration of a pure arterial vasodilator will reduce arterial blood pressure and aortic impedance, increase stroke volume, and reduce ventricular filling pressure. As systemic vascular resistance falls, the reduction in blood pressure is moderated by a rising cardiac output. The improved performance of the heart can be described now by point B. On the other hand, if a pure venous vasodilator is administered, cardiac performance will shift to point C, with a fall in left ventricular filling pressure and little change in stroke volume. However, if left ventricular filling pressure is allowed to fall to low normal values, stroke volume will deteriorate and shift to point D. Currently available vasodilators act with varying potency on both arterial resistance and venous capacitance vessels. With these agents, the actual improvement in ventricular function will lie somewhere between the theoretical changes described for pure arterial and pure venous vasodilators — that is, between points B and C.

It must be stressed that the goal of vasodilator therapy during anaesthesia and operation in patients with chronic myocardial ischaemia is not to practise controlled hypotension. Arterial hypotension will reduce myocardial blood flow, and left ventricular end-diastolic hypotension will reduce stroke volume. The cardiac output of patients with impaired ventricular function is optimal when left ventricular filling pressure is at the upper limit of normal. When glyceryl trinitrate was given to patients with acute myocardial infarction, Williams, Amsterdam and Mason (1975) found that a fall in their left ventricular filling pressure to low normal values would lead to a reduction of cardiac output and arterial hypotension. During the administration of nitroprusside to patients with ischaemic heart disease, Miller and his associates (1975) reported that the simultaneous infusion of dextran to restore left ventricular filling pressure to slightly above normal values would improve cardiac output. Therefore, the aim of vasodilator therapy during anaesthesia and operation in patients without myocardial injury should be limited to the control of acute hypertension — a common complication seen in these patients in the perioperative period. The incidence of inadvertent arterial hypotension can be minimized by maintaining left ventricular filling pressure at the upper limit of normal. Should filling pressure fall to low normal values, expansion of intravascular plasma volume is indicated.

Tachycardia, either reflex in nature or due to an intrinsic positive chronotropic action of some vasodilators, is another complication of vasodilator therapy. This elevation in heart rate is usually not severe, provided that the arterial pressure is kept normal and the ventricular filling pressure is kept at the upper limit of normal. Should it be a problem, the administration of propranolol intravenously should be considered (Wiener, Dwyer and Cox, 1969).

For the purpose of myocardial protection, a vasodilator must be safe for intravenous administration and evanescent in its action. Many vasodilators have been used in both medical and surgical patients for this purpose. They include sodium nitroprusside (Miller *et al.*, 1975; Lappas *et al.*, 1976), glyceryl trinitrate (Flaherty *et al.*, 1975; Kaplan, Dunbar and Jones, 1976), phentolamine (Kelly *et al.*, 1973; Henning, Shubin and Weil, 1977), trimetaphan (Shell and Sobel, 1974; Williams *et al.*, 1975) and chlorpromazine (Stinson *et al.*, 1975). The choice of vasodilators and their pharmacology will be discussed under 'The treatment of sinus tachycardia and hypertension' in Chapter 8.

Positive inotropic agents

The ability of a positive inotropic agent to reduce work of the failing heart illustrates the intricate relationship between all the determinants of myocardial work. In heart failure, left ventricular filling pressure is elevated and stroke output is reduced. Through sympathetic reflexes, tachycardia and systemic vasoconstriction are prominent features, and blood pressure may actually be above normal. All these factors contribute to impose an increased workload on the failing heart. Digitalization would improve myocardial contractility, ventricular performance and cardiac output. Following improvement in the peripheral circulation, heart rate, heart size and peripheral vascular resistance fall, and myocardial work is reduced despite an increase in contractility. In contrast, the size of a heart with normal ventricular function does not change following digitalization. The increase in contractility in this instance serves only to increase myocardial work without any benefit to the circulation. This interaction between contractility and heart size was demonstrated in dogs convincingly by Covell and his colleagues (1966). Therefore cardiac glycosides are contraindicated in the non-failing heart, except in the control of arrhythmias.

In the failing heart, catecholamines will have similar effects on myocardial work as digitalis. Although the marked positive chronotropic action of adrenaline and isoprenaline will negate any gain from the fall in filling pressure, dopamine and dobutamine are less likely to affect heart rate and would be more useful. In general, digitalis should be reserved for patients with congestive heart failure, and the catecholamines for patients who are hypotensive and in cardiogenic shock (see 'The treatment of hypotension' in Chapter 8).

Volatile anaesthetics

Volatile agents are myocardial depressants. The beneficial effect of a mild to moderate depression of contractility of the ischaemic heart with normal ventricular function is seen with beta-adrenergic antagonists. During anaesthesia and operation, similar myocardial depression of the non-failing heart with volatile anaesthetics should improve the balance of myocardial work and myocardial blood flow. Bland and Lowenstein (1976) found that the administration of halothane in dogs reduced the severity of myocardial ischaemia during acute coronary arterial occlusion; and Verrier *et al.* (1980) observed that dogs anaesthetized with halothane had a greater coronary vascular reserve to cope with ischaemic insults. Neither of these findings has been confirmed in patients with ischaemic heart disease, nor have similar actions of other volatile agents been demonstrated. But the administration of a potent inhalational agent to patients with ischaemic heart disease, by providing an adequate level of anaesthesia, will abolish the pressor response to noxious stimuli. Pressor response is a common complication seen in patients anaesthetized with narcotics alone (see 'Narcotic analgesics' in Chapter 4). Tachycardia and hypertension increase myocardial work; they must be prevented.

What is said about volatile anaesthetics applies only to patients with normal ventricular function as reflected by a normal left ventricular filling pressure. Volatile agents are contraindicated in patients already in congestive heart failure because the negative inotropic action of these agents will cause further ventricular dilation and deterioration in ventricular function. In patients with compensated heart failure and marginal cardiac function, caution is advised.

Conclusion

Injured myocardium in victims of acute myocardial infarction can be preserved. The myocardium of surgical patients who also have chronic myocardial ischaemia is not injured. Therefore the goal of management in these patients should be directed to the prevention of ischaemic injury. The principles of prevention of ischaemic injury and of preservation of injured myocardium are the same: factors increasing myocardial work should be controlled, and factors leading to anaemic, hypoxaemic and ischaemic tissue hypoxia should be corrected. The search for newer treatments and the assessment of their efficacy will remain a challenge to cardiac physicians and anaesthetists alike for the rest of the decade.

References

Bland, J. H. L. and Lowenstein, E. (1976). Halothane-induced decrease in experimental myocardial ischemia in the non-failing canine heart. *Anesthesiology* **45**, 287.

Chatterjee, K., Parmley, W. W., Ganz, W., Forrester, J., Walinsky, P., Crexells, C. and Swan, H. J. C. (1973). Hemodynamic and metabolic responses to vasodilator therapy in acute myocardial infarction. *Circulation* **48**, 1183.

Cohn, J. N. (1973a). Blood pressure and cardiac performance. *American Journal of Medicine* **55**, 351.

Cohn, J. N. (1973b). Vasodilator therapy for heart failure: the influence of impedance on left ventricular performance. *Circulation* **48**, 5.

Covell, J. W., Braunwald, E., Ross, J. Jr and Sonnenblick, E. H. (1966). Studies on digitalis. XVI. Effects on myocardial oxygen consumption. *Journal of Clinical Investigation* **45**, 1535.

Dye, L. E., Shin, M. S., Witten, D. M., Russell, R. O. Jr, Rackley, C. E. and Hogg, D. E. (1978). Pulmonary consolidation associated with infusion of a glucose–insulin–potassium solution in acute myocardial infarction. *Chest* **73**, 179.

Flaherty, J. T., Reid, P. R., Kelly, D. T., Taylor, D. R., Weisfeldt, M. L. and Pitt, B. (1975). Intravenous nitroglycerin in acute myocardial infarction. *Circulation* **51**, 132.

Henning, R J., Shubin, H. and Weil, M. H. (1977). Afterload reduction with phentolamine in patients with acute pulmonary edema. *American Journal of Medicine* **63**, 568.

Hunter, P. R., Endrey-Walder, P., Bauer, G. E. and Stephens, F. O. (1968). Myocardial infarction following surgical operations. *British Medical Journal* **4**, 725.

Kaplan, J. A., Dunbar, R. W. and Jones, E. L. (1976). Nitroglycerin infusion during coronary-artery surgery. *Anesthesiology* **45**, 14.

Kelly, D. T., Delgado, C. E., Taylor, D. R., Pitt, B. and Ross, R. S. (1973). Use of phentolamine in acute myocardial infarction associated with hypertension and left ventricular failure. *Circulation* **47**, 729.

Lappas, D. G., Lowenstein, E., Waller, J., Fahmy, N. R, and Daggett, W. M. (1976). Hemodynamic effects of nitroprusside infusion during coronary artery operation in man. *Circulation* **54**, Suppl. 3, III–4.

Madias, J. E., Madias, N. E. and Hood, W. B. Jr (1976). Precordial ST-segment mapping. 2. Effects of oxygen inhalation on ischemic injury in patients with acute myocardial infarction. *Circulation* **53**, 411.

Maroko, P. R., Radvany, P., Braunwald, E. and Hale, S. L. (1975). Reduction of infarct size by oxygen inhalation following acute coronary occlusion. *Circulation* **52**, 360.

Mauney, F. M., Ebert, P. A. and Sabiston, D. C. (1970). Postoperative myocardial infarction: a study of predisposing factors, diagnosis and mortality in a high risk group of surgical patients. *Annals of Surgery* **172**, 497.

Miller, R. R., Vismara, L. A., Zelis, R., Amsterdam, E. A. and Mason, D. T. (1975). Clinical use of sodium nitroprusside in chronic ischemic heart disease. *Circulation* **51**, 328.

Monroe, R. G., Gamble, W. J., LaFarge, C. G., Kumar, A. E., Stark, J., Sanders, G. L., Phornphutkul, C. and Davis, M. (1972). The Anrep effect reconsidered. *Journal of Clinical Investigation* **51**, 2573.

Mueller, H. S., Ayres, S. M., Religa, A. and Evans, R. G. (1974). Propranolol in the treatment of acute myocardial infarction. *Circulation* **49**, 1078.

Neely, J. R. and Morgan, H. E. (1974). Relationship between carbohydrate and lipid metabolism and the energy balance of heart muscle. *Annual Review of Physiology* **36**, 413.

Rogers, W. J., Stanley, A. W., Breinig, J. B., Prather, J. W., McDaniel, H. G., Moraski, R. E., Mantle, J. A., Russell, R. O. Jr and Rackley, C. E. (1976). Reduction of hospital mortality rate of acute myocardial infarction with glucose–insulin–potassium infusion. *American Heart Journal* **92**, 441.

Saltzman, H. A. (1975). Efficacy of oxygen enriched gas mixtures in the treatment of acute myocardial infarction. *Circulation* **52**, 357.

Sarnoff, S. J., Mitchell, J. H., Gilmore, J. P. and Remensnyder, J. P. (1960). Homeometric autoregulation in the heart. *Circulation Research* **8**, 1077.

Shand, D. G. (1975). Propranolol. *New England Journal of Medicine* **293**, 280.

Shell, W. E. and Sobel, B. E. (1974). Protection of jeopardized ischemic myocardium by reduction of ventricular afterload. *New England Journal of Medicine* **291**, 481.

Sonnenblick, E. H. and Downing, S. E. (1963). Afterload as a primary determinant of ventricular performance. *American Journal of Physiology* **204**, 604.

Starling, E. H. (1915). The Law of the Heart. The Linacre Lecture, Cambridge.

Stinson, E. B., Holloway, E. L., Derby, G., Oyer, P. E., Hollingsworth, J., Griepp, R. B. and Harrison, D. C. (1975). Comparative hemodynamic responses to chlorpromazine, nitroprusside, nitroglycerin, and trimethaphan immediately after open-heart operations. *Circulation* **51** and **52**, Suppl. I, I–26.

Topkins, M. J. and Artusio, J. F. Jr (1964). Myocardial infarction and surgery. A five year study. *Anesthesia and Analgesia . . . Current Researches* **43**, 716.

Verrier, E. D., Edelist, G., Consigny, P. M., Robinson, S. and Hoffman, J. I. E. (1980). Greater coronary vascular reserve in dogs anesthetized with halothane. *Anesthesiology* **53**, 445.

Wiener, L., Dwyer, E. M. Jr and Cox, J. W. (1969). Hemodynamic effects of nitroglycerin, propranolol, and their combination in coronary heart disease. *Circulation* **39**, 623.

Williams, D. O., Amsterdam, E. A. and Mason, D. T. (1975). Hemodynamic effects of nitroglycerin in acute myocardial infarction. *Circulation* **51**, 421.

Williams, D. O., Hilliard, G. K., Merwin, R., Maddox, D., Miller, R. and Mason, D. T. (1975). Impedance reduction with trimethaphan (Arfonad) for pump failure complicating coronary heart disease. *Clinical Research* **23**, 215A.

4

The circulatory effects of anaesthetic agents

Advances in laboratory techniques and monitoring in the operating theatre have led to a greater understanding of the circulatory actions of anaesthetic drugs. The amount of literature accumulated on the subject is voluminous. A discussion on the anaesthetic management of patients with ischaemic heart disease would be incomplete without a review of these findings. However, the direct extrapolation of this knowledge to patients at the bedside is complicated by several factors:

1. Circulatory reflexes are diverse and complex; the interaction between cardiac function and the peripheral circulation is intricate. Differentiation between primary and secondary circulatory effects of anaesthetic agents is sometimes difficult.

2. Experimental conditions in studies involving human subjects are difficult to control. For example, respiratory acidosis following the administration of an anaesthetic drug is often left uncorrected, and the effects of surgical stimulation on the circulation are ignored. It is known that the circulation can adapt to the depressant action of some inhalational anaesthetics during prolonged anaesthesia, but the possibility of similar adaptation has not been explored with other agents.

3. Differences in drug response among laboratory animals have always been a problem. Physiological function in health and pathological function in disease also vary. The circulatory effects of drugs observed in healthy volunteers, and even those observed in patients with valvular heart disease, may not be applicable to patients with ischaemic heart disease.

4. The dose–effect relationship of a drug varies considerably among individual patients, and statistical significance is not synonymous with clinical importance. Compared with healthy individuals, the dose–effect relationship of an anaesthetic drug on the circulation of a patient with compromised cardiac reserve is shifted to the left — that is, a smaller dose will have a more potent action. The dose of anaesthetic agents should be adjusted accordingly in patients with ischaemic heart disease.

Despite the said limitations, research efforts of the last decade have been rewarded. The circulatory actions of many anaesthetic drugs have been documented both in healthy volunteers and in patients with heart disease. This knowledge has allowed the anaesthetist to choose his agents wisely, so that special requirements of patients with ischaemic heart disease can be met. Many of the laboratory techniques are also made available in the operating theatre, so that the haemodynamic variables of these patients can be monitored and the dose of these drugs can be titrated against their circulatory effects.

All anaesthetic drugs act on both the systemic and the regional circulations, but a discussion of their effects on all regional circulations is outside the scope of this monograph. In this chapter the actions of anaesthetic drugs on the heart, the coronary circulation and the systemic circulation will be reviewed, and findings relevant to patients with myocardial ischaemia stressed.

Inhalational anaesthetics

Nitrous oxide

Nearly one and a half centuries after its introduction into surgical anaesthesia, nitrous oxide is still the most widely used and most useful agent to date. For many years its cardiovascular effects have been overlooked. Not only does it have measurable haemodynamic effects, but also, curiously, it can interact with other agents to produce either circulatory stimulation or circulatory depression.

Circulatory effects

Nitrous oxide has a mild negative chronotropic and a mild negative inotropic effect on the heart (Eisele and Smith, 1972). Under nitrous oxide anaesthesia cardiac output will fall, but systemic vascular resistance will increase to the same extent, and blood pressure will remain constant. Similar depression has been observed in patients with ischaemic heart disease by Eisele et al. (1976), who reported a mild decrease in blood pressure and a moderate elevation of left ventricular filling pressure in these patients under the influence of 40% nitrous oxide.

Interaction with volatile anaesthetics

Nitrous oxide was found to have an alpha-adrenergic-like activity on the peripheral circulation when it was given to healthy patients under halothane anaesthesia (N.T. Smith et al., 1970). A similar, but milder, alpha-like activity of nitrous oxide was seen in patients with valvular heart disease during halothane anaesthesia in the study of Stoelting, Reis and Longnecker (1972). This stimulatory activity of nitrous oxide also was observed when it was administered to patients under ether (N. T. Smith, Eger, Gregory et al., 1972), fluroxene (Smith, Eger, Cullen et al., 1972) and isoflurane (Dolan et al., 1974) anaesthesia. On the contrary, Smith and his colleagues (1978) did not observe any circulatory stimulation when nitrous oxide was added to the anaesthetic mixture of patients under enflurane anaesthesia.

Interaction with narcotic analgesics

When nitrous oxide is added to the inspired gas of cardiac patients who have received large doses of morphine for anaesthesia, the combination has all the stigmata of a moderately potent cardiovascular depressant. Stoelting and Gibbs (1973) observed a mild to moderate reduction in blood pressure, heart rate, stroke volume and cardiac output in cardiac patients under the combined effects of morphine and nitrous oxide. Lappas *et al.* (1975) reported a fall in myocardial contractility and a rise in left ventricular filling pressure in patients with ischaemic heart disease under similar conditions. This circulatory depressant action of nitrous oxide during morphine anaesthesia is related to the inspired concentration of nitrous oxide (McDermott and Stanley, 1974). A similar circulatory depression was reported with the combination of nitrous oxide and fentanyl, with or without droperidol (Stoelting *et al.*, 1975).

Halothane

Despite the availability of newer agents, halothane remains a popular volatile anaesthetic in both Europe and North America. It is also the most widely studied agent of its class. Other than very infrequent reports of postoperative jaundice associated with repeated exposure, it is a safe agent.

Circulatory effects

Halothane has a dose-dependent depressant action on blood pressure, stroke volume and cardiac output, and a variable effect on systemic vascular resistance in man (Deutsch *et al.*, 1962; Eger *et al.*, 1970; Prys-Roberts *et al.*, 1974). In contrast to clinical experience, no change in heart rate following the administration of halothane was reported in these studies. The magnitude of circulatory depression in common anaesthetic concentrations is usually mild and is not a cause for alarm. Deutsch and his associates (1962) as well as Eger and others (1970) observed that there was an unexplained tendency for stroke volume and cardiac output of volunteers under halothane anaesthesia to recover with time, and for heart rate to rise above pre-anaesthetic values while arterial pressure remained depressed. This recovery was gradual in onset, was observable for many hours at different levels of halothane anaesthesia (Eger *et al.*, 1971), and was blocked by beta-adrenergic blockade (Price *et al.*, 1970). These findings suggest that beta-adrenergic activation is the underlying mechanism. The cause of this adrenergic stimulation is still unclear.

The mode of action of halothane in producing circulatory depression is complex. Price and Price (1966) proposed that it is due to a combination of depression of the vasomotor centre, ganglionic blockade and inhibition of the peripheral actions of catecholamines. Biscoe and Millar (1964) found evidence in cats that sensitization of the baroreceptor reflex may be a contributing cause. (When the baroreceptor reflex is sensitized, afferent impulses from baroreceptors are increased at a given blood pressure; the vasomotor centre then responds to this increase in afferent impulses by reducing sympathetic outflow and increasing vagal outflow.)

Effects on contractility

At common anaesthetic concentrations halothane is a moderately potent myocardial depressant in man (Price *et al.*, 1970; Rathod *et al.*, 1978; Sonntag *et al.*, 1978). Like stroke volume and heart rate, this depression of contractility also recovers with time and is blocked by beta-adrenergic blockade (Price *et al.*, 1970). There are reports indicating that the depression of contractility by halothane can be linked to a depression of cardiac actomyosin ATPase activity (Merin, Kumazawa and Honig, 1974), and that both the depression of contractility and the depression of ATPase activity are reversible by calcium (Merin, Kumazawa and Honig, 1974; Price, 1974; Denlinger *et al.*, 1975). These findings suggest that halothane depresses contractility by limiting the calcium flux during electromechanical coupling and by suppression of the rate of actin–myosin interaction during contraction.

Effects on myocardial energy metabolism

In two separate studies, Merin and colleagues (Merin, Kumazawa and Luka, 1976a; Merin, Verdouw and deJong, 1977) reported that the dose-dependent negative inotropic action of halothane on the hearts of laboratory animals was accompanied by a reduction in myocardial work. This reduction in myocardial work was equal to or greater than a concurrent reduction in coronary blood flow. Although there was no sign of anaerobic metabolism in these halothane-depressed hearts, other evidence suggests that substrate utilization for energy metabolism by myocardial cells is less than optimal when they are under the influence of halothane.

1. In a series of experiments Merin (1969, 1970a, b) observed that the myocardial threshold of glucose uptake was elevated from a normal of 3.3 mmol/litre (60 mg/100 ml) to 5.6 mmol/litre (100 mg/100 ml) in the halothane-depressed canine heart. The administration of glucose alone did not improve myocardial contractility, but the administration of insulin increased both glucose uptake and myocardial performance.

2. In a different series (Ko and Paradise, 1969, 1970, 1971; Paradise and Ko, 1970), Ko and Paradise found that anaerobic glycolysis was inhibited by halothane in both human and rodent cardiac tissue.

3. Stong, Hartzell and McCarl (1975) showed that halothane decreased the turnover of ATP by tissue culture of rodent cardiac cells and suggested that halothane could be interfering with electron transport and oxidative phosphorylation.

4. A decrease in the myocardial uptake of free fatty acids and pyruvate by the halothane-depressed canine hearts was also reported by Merin (1969).

There are speculations that the depression of myocardial contractility by halothane may be related to its adverse effects on myocardial energy metabolism, but this cause–effect relationship has not been proven.

Effects on the coronary circulation

Although there is agreement that both coronary blood flow and oxygen consumption are reduced in proportion to the reduction of myocardial work in the halothane-depressed heart, the effect of halothane on coronary vascular resistance remains controversial: an increase (Wolff *et al.*, 1972; G. Smith *et al.*, 1974), no change (Weaver, Bailey and Preston, 1970) and a decrease (Domenech *et al.*, 1977) — all have been reported. It is important to remember that vasodilation of healthy coronary vessels without improvement of collateral flow only encourages a 'coronary steal' of much needed flow away from ischaemic regions. Therefore, what is more relevant for patients with myocardial ischaemia is not whether halothane dilates the healthy coronary vascular bed, but whether halothane improves collateral flow to the ischaemic zone. Such data are not available. Bland and Lowenstein (1976) reported that 0.75% halothane would reduce myocardial ischaemia during acute coronary artery occlusion in dogs. G. Smith, Rogers and Thornburn (1980) observed that the ratio of oxygen availability to consumption in ischaemic areas following ligation of a branch of the left coronary artery in dogs was improved by the administration of 1% halothane. But there was no evidence of improved blood flow to the ischaemic zone in either study. The protective effects of halothane in these instances are likely the result of reductions in haemodynamic variables influencing myocardial work.

Effects on cardiac rhythm

In clinical anaesthesia, halothane is associated with a high incidence of nodal bradycardia. The administration of intravenous atropine in these cases often results in a faster nodal rate and not reversion to sinus rhythm. These observations are consistent with the laboratory findings that halothane can slow the rhythm of the primary pacemaker by reducing the rate of spontaneous depolarization (phase 4) of sinoatrial fibres and by increasing the threshold potential of these fibres (Hauswirth and Schaer, 1967; Reynolds, Chiz and Pasquet, 1970). These effects are not reversed by atropine.

Ventricular premature beats is another common arrhythmia associated with halothane anaesthesia during spontaneous respiration. Surgical stimulation and hypercarbia are important contributing factors (Robertson, Clement and Knill, 1981). Reynolds, Chiz and Pasquet (1970) observed that halothane reduced the rate of spontaneous depolarization, increased the threshold potential, and slowed the adrenaline-augmented rate of spontaneous depolarization of canine Purkinje tissue. Logic and Morrow (1972) found that halothane consistently depressed vagal escape pacemaker activity of canine ventricles and suppressed ventricular automaticity of dogs given a toxic dose of ouabain. These observations directly contradict the notion that the cause of halothane-related ventricular arrhythmias is an increased irritability of the ventricles. Atlee and Alexander (1977) reported that halothane increased the conduction times of the heart from the sinus node to the His bundle (the A–H interval) and from the His bundle to the ventricle (the H–V interval); but they drew no conclusion on the effect of halothane on the functional refractory period of conducting tissue. Furthermore, they observed that this depressed state of atrioventricular conduction was not reversed by atropine, lignocaine or phenytoin (Atlee and Rusy, 1972; Atlee, Homer and Tobey, 1975). These findings have prompted many authors, including Atlee, to suggest that the genesis of ventricular arrhythmias during halothane anaesthesia is a re-entry phenomenon (Hashimoto *et al.*, 1975; Zink, Sasyniuk and Dresel, 1975; Atlee *et al.*, 1978).

Interaction with cardiac drugs

The sensitization of the myocardium to the arrhythmogenic effect of adrenaline by halothane was first reported in man by Millar, Gilbert and Brindle (1958). Subsequently Katz, Matteo and Papper (1962) demonstrated that it is safe to allow local infiltration of the surgical field with adrenaline in patients under halothane anaesthesia, provided that the dose does not exceed 10 ml of 1:100 000 concentration in 10 minutes or 30 ml of the same concentration in 1 hour. In patients with ischaemic heart disease, the safety of adrenaline during halothane anaesthesia has not been evaluated specifically. In view of the lower arrhythmic threshold of the ischaemic myocardium and the adverse effect of catecholamines on myocardial work, the subcutaneous infiltration of adrenaline in these patients should be avoided altogether.

The combined cardiac depressant effect of halothane and beta-adrenergic antagonists is another cause for concern. In dogs the interaction of halothane and the beta antagonist, propranolol, has been characterized as additive and predictable (Roberts *et al.*, 1976). Earlier reports of adverse interactions in man were poorly documented (Ayscue, 1972; Viljoen, Estafanous and Kellner, 1972). As experience with these agents grows, many of the fears of interaction are alleviated (see Chapter 10).

Despite the fact that both halothane and cardiac glycosides prolong atrioventricular conduction, there has been no report of adverse interaction between halothane and digitalis. In fact, it has been reported that halothane increases the tolerance of the heart to digitalis-induced ventricular arrhythmias (Morrow and Townley, 1964).

Enflurane

Enflurane, a halogenated ether, resembles halothane both in physical properties and in pharmacological actions; but it produces more profound muscular relaxation, and has been reported to have epileptogenic properties (Linde *et al.*, 1970). Although enflurane is metabolized to a lesser degree than halothane and methoxyflurane, reports of nephrotoxicity in patients with pre-existing renal disease justify caution in these patients (Loehning and Mazze, 1974; Eichhorn *et al.*, 1976).

Circulatory effects

During controlled ventilation, enflurane has a dose-dependent depressant action on blood pressure, stroke volume and cardiac output, but variable effects on heart rate and systemic vascular resistance (Graves and Downs, 1974; Calverley, Smith, Prys-Roberts *et al.*, 1978). During spontaneous respiration this circulatory depression is partly obscured by the circulatory stimulating effects of a higher arterial carbon dioxide tension (Calverley, Smith, Jones *et al.*, 1978). The phenomenon of circulatory adaptation during prolonged enflurane anaesthesia is qualitatively similar to that during halothane anaesthesia (Calverley, Smith, Prys-Roberts *et al.*, 1978). At least one study found enflurane a more potent circulatory depressant than halothane (Calverley, Smith, Prys-Roberts *et al.*, 1978). The mechanism of circulatory depression is multifactorial. Skovsted and Price (1972) as well as Hagenau, Pietsch and Arndt (1976) found that enflurane, like halothane, sensitized the baroreceptor reflex and reduced cervical sympathetic outflow in animal models. Göthert, Kennerknecht and Thielecke (1976) found that the release of noradrenaline at sympathetic nerve endings in the heart of rabbits was suppressed.

Effects on contractility

All authors agreed that enflurane is a myocardial depressant, but they differed in their estimates of its relative potency. While Horan, Prys-Roberts, Hamilton *et al.* (1977) found its depressant action more potent than that of halothane in dogs, Kaplan, Miller and Bailey (1976) reported that its action was less than that of halothane in man.

Effects on the coronary circulation

Like halothane, enflurane has been shown to reduce both myocardial work and coronary blood flow (Theye and Michenfelder, 1975; Merin, Kumazawa and Luka, 1976b). A vasodilating action on healthy coronary vessels has been suggested by Tarnow *et al.* (1977), but this has yet to be confirmed.

Effects on cardiac rhythm

Atlee and Rusy (1977) observed that enflurane prolonged the A–H interval of the His-bundle electrocardiogram of dogs but was without effect on the H–V interval. This can explain the clinical experience that ventricular arrhythmias are less common during enflurane than during halothane anaesthesia.

Interaction with cardiac drugs

Enflurane was found more compatible with infiltration of the surgical field with adrenaline than halothane (Konchigeri, Shaker and Winnie, 1974; Lippmann and Reisner, 1974). Due to the gently sloping dose/response curve of enflurane–adrenaline interaction illustrated in Fig. 4.1 (Johnston, Eger and Wilson, 1976), a comparison of the compatibility of enflurane and adrenaline and that of halothane and adrenaline is not possible. There is no doubt that enflurane is the safer of the two agents, but ventricular arrhythmias have been reported with low doses of adrenaline during enflurane anaesthesia. Extra precaution is necessary in patients with chronic myocardial ischaemia.

Horan, Prys-Roberts, Hamilton *et al.* (1977) have reported that the combined depressant effect of enflurane and propranolol was tolerated poorly by healthy dogs. This finding is consistent with the more potent circulatory depressant action of enflurane. Like halothane, enflurane has been shown to abolish ventricular tachycardias precipitated by a continuous infusion of ouabain in dogs and to increase the dose of ouabain necessary to induce ventricular arrhythmias and death (Ivankovich *et al.*, 1976).

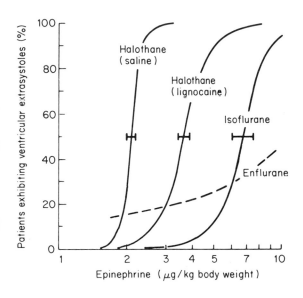

Fig. 4.1   The dose/response curve of adrenaline-induced ventricular arrhythmias in patients under halothane, enflurane and isoflurane anaesthesia (Johnston, Eger and Wilson, 1976). The ED_{50} of adrenaline in patients under isoflurane anaesthesia is three times that in patients under halothane anaesthesia. The ED_{50} in patients under enflurane anaesthesia cannot be determined, but even low doses of adrenaline can precipitate ventricular extrasystoles in approximately 20 per cent of the patients. (Reproduced with permission of the authors and the publisher.)

Isoflurane

Isoflurane is an isomer of enflurane. Its introduction into clinical anaesthesia was stopped short in 1975 by the study of Corbett (1976), which suggested that it might be a hepatocarcinogen in mice. Unfortunately the mice in Corbett's study were contaminated by polybrominated biphenyls — a known carcinogen. Subsequently a joint study by Eger and others (1978), including Corbett, confirmed the safety of isoflurane, and this agent will be available soon for general clinical use.

Circulatory effects

Clinical experience with this agent is still limited. During controlled ventilation, the observed circulatory effects of isoflurane in young healthy volunteers were a fall in blood pressure, a rise in heart rate and a constant cardiac output. The cardiac output was maintained by the increase in heart rate at the expense of a fall in stroke volume (Stevens *et al.*, 1971). In another study by the same authors (Cromwell *et al.*, 1971), both heart rate and cardiac output increased even further when the arterial carbon dioxide tension was allowed to rise during spontaneous ventilation. In older patients and in patients with ischaemic heart disease, Linde *et al.* (1975) and Mallow *et al.* (1976) reported that the depression of haemodynamic variables by isoflurane was quite similar to that by halothane.

Effects on contractility

Stevens *et al.* (1971) found that isoflurane had little depressant effect on the healthy myocardium. In this respect it is the least potent of all the halogenated volatile agents in clinical use (Tarnow *et al.*, 1977).

Effects on the coronary circulation

The action of isoflurane on the healthy canine coronary circulation is unique. Tarnow *et al.* (1977) reported that isoflurane reduced myocardial work and coronary vascular resistance without decreasing coronary blood flow — hence flow was in excess of demand, and coronary venous oxygen saturation rose. However, the influence of isoflurane on collateral flows to ischaemic regions of the myocardium remains unclear.

Effects on cardiac rhythm

Blitt *et al.* (1979) observed that isoflurane had no effect on atrioventricular conduction in dogs. This may explain the absence of ventricular arrhythmias observed with this agent (Pauca and Dripps, 1973).

Interaction with cardiac drugs

Johnston, Eger and Wilson (1976) found that the adrenaline-induced arrhythmic threshold in patients anaesthetized with isoflurane was three times that in those anaesthetized with halothane. This makes isoflurane even superior to enflurane when infiltration of the surgical field with adrenaline is necessary. With regard to its interaction with beta antagonists, Philbin and Lowenstein (1976) as well as Horan, Prys-Roberts, Roberts *et al.* (1977) found isoflurane at least as safe as, if not safer than, halothane. Like the other halogenated agents, isoflurane increased the tolerance of dogs to the arrhythmogenic action of ouabain (Ivankovich *et al.*, 1976).

Methoxyflurane

The use of methoxyflurane has largely been abandoned due to renal toxicity (Mazze, Shue and Jackson, 1971). However, subanaesthetic concentrations still are being used by some anaesthetists to supplement nitrous oxide anaesthesia. Under methoxyflurane anaesthesia blood pressure, stroke volume and systemic vascular resistance will fall (Walker, Eggers and Allan, 1962). Although heart rate may increase slightly, it will not be enough to compensate for the decrease in stroke volume. Consequently, cardiac output also will fall. The circulatory adaptation observed during prolonged anaesthesia is not as marked as that observed with halothane (Libonati, Cooperman and Price, 1971). Merin and Borgstedt (1971) found that coronary blood flow decreased together with the decline in myocardial work in dogs anaesthetized with methoxyflurane, but myocardial oxygenation remained adequate.

It is believed that methoxyflurane is safe with infiltration of the surgical field with adrenaline, and it has been advocated as the volatile agent of choice in patients with phaeochromocytomas (Bain and Spoerel, 1963). It also increased the tolerance of dogs to ouabain (Ivankovich *et al.*, 1976). However, the combined depressant action of methoxyflurane and beta blockade on the circulation has been described as dangerous (Saner *et al.*, 1975).

Intravenous anaesthetics

Thiopentone

Thiopentone was introduced for clinical use in 1934. Neary five decades later, it remains the most popular intravenous induction agent. With experience, anaesthetists have learned to use it safely by adjusting its dose according to the condition of the patient.

Circulatory effects

According to Etsten and Li (1955), Fieldman, Ridley and Wood (1955) and Flickinger *et al.* (1961), a bolus injection of thiopentone will produce falls in arterial pressure, stroke volume and cardiac output together with an increase in systemic vascular resistance. A decline in peripheral venous tone has been reported by Eckstein, Hamilton and McCammond (1961). The effect on heart rate is variable: a rise (Etsten and Li, 1955), no change (Flickinger *et al.*, 1961) and no consistent change (Fieldman, Ridley and Wood, 1955) have been reported. The reduction in systemic arterial pressure can be profound. It is due to reductions in venous return, stroke volume and cardiac output as a result of the transfer of blood from the central pool to the periphery. These circulatory effects are particularly severe in the old and the sick, but can be minimized by a rate of injection no faster than 50 mg per minute (Fieldman, Ridley and Wood, 1955).

Effects on contractility

Thiopentone usually is regarded as a potent myocardial depressant because of the consistent fall in blood pressure following its administration. Indeed, a decrease in myocardial function attributed to thiopentone has been reported in heart–lung preparations by Price and Helrich (1955), and a decrease in myocardial contractile force has been observed in dogs by Bendixen and Laver (1962). However, the interpretation of these results must remain open. In the study of Price and Helrich (1955), a continuous infusion of adrenaline was necessary to maintain the viability of the heart–lung preparations. In the study of Bendixen and Laver (1962), the cumulative dose of thiopentone each dog received was 20–30 mg/kg within a period of approximately 1 hour. The myocardial depressant effect of thiopentone observed in these studies may have been exaggerated by the methods used.

In a more recent study, minimal depression of sensitive indices of myocardial contractility was observed by Chamberlain, Seed and Chung (1977) at arterial concentrations sufficient to ensure surgical anaesthesia when thiopentone was injected directly into the left coronary artery of dogs. Depression was obvious only at concentrations likely to occur transiently following a large bolus injection. These observations have been confirmed by data obtained in man (Becker and Tonnesen, 1978). It can be concluded that plasma levels of thiopentone sufficient to obtain surgical anaesthesia produce insignificant and unimportant depression of myocardial contractility in man.

Effects on the coronary circulation

It was reported by Sonntag *et al.* (1975) that myocardial oxygen consumption increased following induction of anaesthesia with thiopentone in a group of healthy patients because of an increase in heart rate. This increase in demand was matched by an increase in coronary blood flow and a fall in coronary vascular resistance. These findings indicate that myocardial blood flow will change according to metabolic needs after the induction of anaesthesia with thiopentone. There is no reason to believe that thiopentone has a direct action on the healthy coronary circulation.

Diazepam

Oral diazepam is gaining popularity among anaesthetists in providing pre-anaesthetic sedation for surgical patients. It is also given intravenously by cardiac physicians in the coronary care unit and in the cardiac catheterization laboratory to alleviate anxiety of cardiac patients. At higher doses diazepam is an anaesthetic. Its use as an intravenous agent has been encouraged by reports of cardiovascular stability following induction of anaesthesia. It becomes cloudy when it is mixed with intravenous solutions; but there is no apparent loss of potency. For this and other reasons it has never been popular as an induction agent, except to supplement morphine anaesthesia in cardiac operations.

Circulatory effects

Following a tranquillizing dose of 10 mg or less, given intravenously to patients with ischaemic or other heart disease, diazepam will cause a mild decline in arterial pressure and either no change or only a mild increase in heart rate (Dalen *et al.*, 1969; Côté, Guéret and Bourassa, 1974; Markiewicz *et al.*, 1976). Contractility, cardiac output and systemic vascular resistance usually remain unchanged, but left ventricular filling pressure often falls.

Following the intravenous administration of up to 0.5 mg/kg for induction of anaesthesia, most authors observed a tachycardia and hypotension of a magnitude comparable to that of thiopentone (Fox, Wynands and Bhambhami, 1968; Wyant and Studney, 1970). But Knapp and Dubow (1970) reported a lower incidence of these complications in patients with cardiopulmonary disease.

Effects on the coronary circulation

Studies on the effect of diazepam on the coronary circulation have yielded conflicting results. Ikram, Rubin and Jewkes (1973) reported a dramatic increase, but Côté, Guéret and Bourassa (1974) reported no significant change in coronary blood flow after a tranquillizing dose was given to healthy patients or patients with chronic myocardial ischaemia. An increase in the overall coronary blood flow is not necessarily beneficial to the ischaemic myocardium. The effect on collateral flow is more important, and such data are lacking.

Effects on cardiac rhythm

Both anti-arrhythmic and arrhythmogenic properties of diazepam have been observed in patients (Van Loon, 1968; Barrett and Hey, 1970). These clinical reports are anecdotal in nature.

Droperidol

Droperidol is a butyrophenone with pharmacological properties similar to the phenothiazines. It is used in combination with fentanyl to produce neurolept-analgesia, and with fentanyl, nitrous oxide and a muscle relaxant to produce neurolept-anaesthesia. Remarkable cardiovascular stability has been reported in both instances (Zauder *et al.*, 1965; Corssen, 1966).

Circulatory effects

As much as 0.3 mg/kg of droperidol is required for the induction of neurolept-anaesthesia. Following induction of anaesthesia, blood pressure and systemic vascular resistance will fall, and cardiac output will increase (Zauder *et al.*, 1965; Ferrari *et al.*, 1974). With the exception of systemic vascular resistance, these changes are usually small in magnitude and transient in duration. The underlying mechanism of the decline in systemic vascular resistance has been attributed to alpha-adrenergic blockade (Whitwam and Russell, 1971), a non-specific vasodilatory effect (Puddy, 1971) and a fall in blood viscosity (Aronson, Magora and London, 1970). Despite these observations, extreme hypertension following the administration of droperidol in patients with phaeochromocytomas has been reported (Sumikawa and Amakata, 1977; Bittar, 1979). This paradox may be due to the ability of droperidol to facilitate the release of noradrenaline from presynaptic storage vesicles (Hyatt, Muldoon and Rorie, 1980).

Effects on cardiac rhythm

Droperidol has an anti-arrhythmic action capable of increasing the adrenaline-induced arrhythmic threshold in man (Long, Dripps and Price, 1967). This anti-arrhythmic property of droperidol is supported by evidence that it is capable of converting ventricular tachycardia induced by ouabain to sinus rhythm in dogs (Ivankovich *et al.*, 1975).

Ketamine

Ketamine is a phencyclidine derivative. Its ability to cause circulatory stimulation is unique among intravenous anaesthetics. It has profound analgesic properties, but causes little or no respiratory depression. However, indications for its use remain limited because of a high incidence of emergence delirium.

Circulatory effects

Unlike other intravenous anaesthetics, ketamine 1–2 mg/kg given intravenously for induction will cause a dramatic increase in arterial blood pressure, heart rate and cardiac output, but no change in stroke volume and inconsistent change in systemic vascular resistance (Virtue *et al.*, 1967; Wilson, Traber and McCoy, 1968; Tweed, Minuck and Mymin, 1972). A 20–40 per cent rise in heart rate and systolic blood pressure is not uncommon. In animal models, ketamine was observed to have an indirect stimulatory action on the heart, but a direct depressant effect on myocardial function (Traber, Wilson and Priano, 1968; Goldberg, Keane and Phear, 1970; Valicenti *et al.*, 1973).

Effects on the coronary circulation

Kettler and Sonntag (1974) reported that the pressor response following the administration of ketamine was associated with an increase in myocardial work and an equal increase in coronary blood flow in healthy dogs. However, in another study, Folts, Afonso and Rowe (1975) observed a fall in coronary venous oxygen content despite an increase in coronary blood flow. These results indicate that the increase in coronary blood flow following the administration of ketamine may not be adequate to meet the increase in myocardial work and metabolic needs imposed by the pressor response.

Therefore the use of ketamine in patients with ischaemic heart disease is contraindicated.

Effects on cardiac rhythm

Following the administration of ketamine, sinus tachycardia is the rule. There is no agreement on the effect of ketamine on adrenaline-induced ventricular arrhythmias. Dowdy and Kaya (1968) reported an anti-arrhythmic effect; but Koehntop, Liao and Van Bergen (1977) reported an enhancement of the arrhythmogenic action of adrenaline. In yet another study, ketamine was found to be capable of converting ouabain-induced ventricular tachycardia to sinus rhythm in dogs (Ivankovich et al., 1975).

The mechanism of pressor response

Considerable efforts were made in search of the underlying mechanism of this unique pressor effect of ketamine. Some authors observed that the pressor response following the administration of ketamine was abolished by general anaesthesia in man (Stanley, 1973), and by muscarinic blockade in a patient who had transection of the spinal cord at C7-8 (Chodoff, 1972). Others found in dogs that this pressor effect was blocked by epidural anaesthesia (Traber and Wilson, 1969), ganglionic blockade (Traber, Wilson and Priano, 1970a), and a combination of muscarinic and alpha-adrenergic blockade (Traber, Wilson and Priano, 1971), but not by beta-adrenergic blockade alone (Traber, Wilson and Priano, 1970b). Still others reported that the activity of ketamine was cocaine-like (Miletich et al., 1973). The inhibition of the baroreceptor reflex by ketamine was another possibility suggested (Dowdy and Kaya, 1968). Despite intensive efforts, the mechanism of this pressor effect remains elusive. Central activation of the vasomotor centre and peripheral actions via the sympathoadrenal axis seem likely. This hypothesis is supported by a report of similar pressor response to small doses of ketamine administered via an artery supplying the cerebral hemisphere in goats (Ivankovich et al., 1974) and by another report of elevated plasma catecholamine levels following ketamine anaesthesia in man (Baraka, Harrison and Kachachi, 1973).

Althesin

Althesin is a mixture of two steroids, alphaxalone and alphadolone acetate, dissolved in 20% polyoxyethylated castor oil (Cremophor EL). The safety of this agent is overshadowed by reports of a high incidence of adverse reactions related to histamine release (Clarke et al., 1975; Evans and Keogh, 1977).

Circulatory effects

Althesin is a myocardial depressant (Foëx and Prys-Roberts, 1972) with circulatory effects comparable to those of thiopentone (Lyons and Clarke,

1972; Savege *et al.*, 1972). Normally 0.05–0.1 ml/kg of Althesin is given for the induction of anaesthesia. With the loss of consciousness both blood pressure and stroke volume will decline (Campbell *et al.*, 1971; Coleman *et al.*, 1972). Since heart rate is invariably elevated, cardiac output is maintained at or above pre-induction levels. Miller, Bradford and Campbell (1972) reported similar haemodynamic changes in elderly patients following the induction of anaesthesia with Althesin, but they recommended that a less than normal dose be given slowly.

Muscle relaxants

Suxamethonium

This is an acetylcholine analogue. Circulatory changes following the administration of suxamethonium are directly related to its effects on heart rate and cardiac rhythm.

Effects on cardiac rhythm

The effects of suxamethonium on heart rate and cardiac rhythm are not simply vagomimetic in nature. They are modified by the age of the patient, the mode of administration, interaction with other drugs, underlying heart disease and other systemic illness:

1. After a single dose of suxamethonium suitable for intubation, slowing of the heart rate is common in children but is unusual in adults. In adults a small and transient increase in heart rate and blood pressure is normal (Williams *et al.*, 1961; Stoelting and Peterson, 1975a, b).

2. Bradycardia and asystole have been reported in adults following the administration of a second or a third dose of suxamethonium given within 3–5 minutes after the first dose (Bullough, 1959; Foster, 1961). Stoelting and Peterson (1975b) observed that intramuscular atropine failed to prevent a relative slowing of the heart rate following the administration of a second dose of suxamethonium, although an absolute slowing of the heart rate did not occur. These same authors and others reported that the incidence of bradycardia following a second dose of suxamethonium was reduced or prevented by pretreatment of the patient with a small dose of tubocurarine (Stoelting and Peterson, 1975a), pancuronium (Mathias, Evans-Prosser and Churchill-Davidson, 1970) or gallamine (Stoelting, 1977a).

3. List (1971) reported that the incidence of unifocal, bigeminal and multifocal ventricular arrhythmias was increased in cardiac patients after the second dose of suxamethonium.

4. Cardiovascular collapse following the administration of suxamethonium has been reported in patients suffering from severe burns (Tolmie, Joyce and Mitchell, 1967), massive trauma (Mazze, Escue and Houston, 1969) and a variety of neurosurgical disorders (Thomas, 1969; Cooperman,

Strobel and Kennell, 1970; Stone, Beach and Hamelberg, 1970). The common factor in these reports is a large increase in serum potassium concentration following the administration of suxamethonium. Similar large increases in serum potassium concentration have been reported in patients suffering from uraemia (Powell, 1970), encephalitis (Cowgill, Mostello and Shapiro, 1974), Parkinson's disease (Gravlee, 1980), peripheral vascular disease complicated by muscle wasting (Rao and Shanmugam, 1979) and ruptured cerebral aneurysms (Iwatsuki *et al.*, 1980). Weintraub, Heisterkamp and Cooperman (1969) found that the pretreatment of injured patients with 0.1 mg/kg of tubocurarine would reduce by one-half the elevation in serum potassium caused by suxamethonium. Therefore precurarization offers only partial protection of these susceptible patients.

Interaction with cardiac drugs

No adverse interaction between suxamethonium and beta-adrenergic antagonists has been reported. A mild increase or no change in heart rate following the admnistration of suxamethonium can be expected even in patients on propranolol (unpublished observation). On the contrary, ventricular arrhythmias induced by suxamethonium in digitalized patients have been reported in the past (Dowdy and Fabian, 1963) but have not been heard of in recent years.

Tubocurarine

Circulatory effects

The most prominent haemodynamic effect of tubocurarine is in its hypotensive action. This fall in blood pressure is related to the dose of tubocurarine, the alveolar concentration of halothane and the depth of anaesthesia (Chatas, Gottlieb and Sweet, 1963; Munger, Miller and Stevens, 1974). Hypotension can be particularly severe in patients over 60 years of age and in patients who are hypertensive (Chatas, Gottlieb and Sweet, 1963). In addition to the fall in blood pressure, tubocurarine can cause a mild increase in heart rate, a decline in cardiac output and a reduction in systemic vascular resistance (Stoelting, 1972). The cause of hypotension is multifactorial. Ganglionic blockade (Hughes and Chapple, 1976), reduction in spontaneous postganglionic sympathetic activity (McCullough *et al.*, 1970) and histamine release (Comroe and Dripps, 1946) are important contributing factors.

Effects on contractility

Commercial preparations of tubocurarine manufactured in the United States and Japan have been shown by Carrier and Murphy (1970) as well as Dowdy *et al.* (1971) to have a minor but detectable negative inotropic action due to the presence of anti-bacterial preservatives such as *p*-chloro-*m*-cresol, benzyl alcohol or chlorobutol (chlorobutanol). In the United Kingdom, Tubarine (Stabalized) has only half the concentration of benzyl alcohol found in its American counterparts, and Tubarine (Miscible) has no preservatives. No negative inotropic property has been reported with these two preparations. Despite these differences, Stoelting (1971) found that all tubocurarine preparations, with or without preservatives, could cause hypotension in man. The negative inotropic property of anti-bacterial preservatives is not a cause of the hypotensive action of tubocurarine.

Effects on cardiac rhythm

Dowdy and Fabian (1963) reported an anti-arrhythmic action of tubocurarine in man. This observation is supported by evidence from animal studies demonstrating the ability of tubocurarine to abolish ventricular arrhythmias induced by digitalis and adrenaline (Dowdy, Duggar and Fabian, 1965; Tucker and Munson, 1975).

Dimethyl tubocurarine

This member of the curare family is more potent than tubocurarine and has a longer duration of action (Hughes, Ingram and Payne, 1976). It has been shown to have little effect on ganglionic transmission and on the release of histamine (McCullough *et al.*, 1972). Stoelting (1974) reported that the incidence of hypotension after its administration, even in the presence of halothane, was lower than that with tubocurarine. However, hypotension as low as that seen after tubocurarine can occur as a result of a fall in systemic vascular resistance (Heinonen and Yrjölä, 1980).

Pancuronium

Circulatory effects

Pancuronium administered intravenously can cause a marked elevation of heart rate together with a smaller but significant increase in blood pressure and cardiac output, but no significant change in stroke volume and systemic vascular resistance (Kelman and Kennedy, 1971; Stoelting, 1972). The pressor response is not affected by the simultaneous administration of halothane (Miller *et al.*, 1975). After a bolus dose of 0.1 mg/kg, a heart rate exceeding 100 beats per minute is not uncommon. The increase in blood pressure often occurs later than the tachycardia and can clearly be related to provocative acts such as tracheal intubation (Barnes and Brindle-Smith, 1981).

The mechanism of pressor response

Pancuronium was found to have no effect at sympathetic ganglia (Hughes and Chapple, 1976) and no effect on the release of histamine (Dobkin, Arandia and Levy, 1973). Despite a direct positive inotropic action demonstrated by Seed and Chamberlain (1977) in dogs, the pressor response following the administration of pancuronium is most likely the result of inhibition of noradrenaline re-uptake and of cardiac vagal blockade. Findings in support of this hypothesis are:

1. The uptake of noradrenaline into neuronal sites of the rodent heart was inhibited by pancuronium at concentrations which produce tachycardia (Conway, Salt and Barnes, 1979).

2. Pancuronium did not produce further circulatory changes in man after tachycardia was induced by atropine (Miller *et al.*, 1975).

3. Vagal slowing of the heart induced by an acute elevation of blood pressure via the baroreceptor reflex was partially inhibited by pancuronium in man (Duke, Mittler and Wade, 1974).

4. A postganglionic vagolytic action of pancuronium was demonstrated in laboratory animals (Hughes and Chapple, 1976; Son and Waud, 1977; Son and Waud, 1978) and in the isolated heart preparation (Goat and Feldman, 1972).

Other effects

There are conflicting reports on the effect of pancuronium on the sympatho-adrenal axis. Nana, Cardan and Domokos (1973) reported a rise, but Zsigmond *et al.* (1974) reported no change in the plasma levels of catecholamines following the administration of pancuronium. An increase in the incidence of arrhythmias related to the use of pancuronium has been reported by some authors (Miller *et al.*, 1975; Basta and Lichtiger, 1977). Geha *et al.* (1977) observed that pancuronium was capable of returning the prolonged atrioventricular conduction time of dogs anaesthetized with halothane to normal. The significance of these reports is not clear.

Gallamine

Gallamine always causes tachycardia in man in doses which block neuro-muscular function (N. T. Smith and Whitcher, 1967; Kennedy and Farman, 1968; Stoelting, 1973). Following an injection of gallamine, changes in stroke volume are usually variable, but cardiac output is always elevated due to an increase in heart rate. Although Brown and Crout (1970) observed a positive inotropic action of gallamine in guinea-pigs and cats, it is not a consistent feature in man (Longnecker, Stoelting and Morrow, 1973). The pressor effect of gallamine is produced principally by cardiac vagal blockade (Hughes and Chapple, 1976; Son and Waud, 1977; Son and Waud, 1978).

Narcotic analgesics

The use of a narcotic analgesic to supplement anaesthesia has been in practice for decades. Observations of cardiovascular stability following the administration of large doses of morphine to patients requiring mechanical ventilation in the intensive care unit prompted Lowenstein and his group (1969) to use large doses of intravenous morphine (0.5–3 mg/kg) as the sole anaesthetic in patients requiring cardiac operations. Since 1969, morphine and other narcotic analgesics have become popular as the main agent in providing anaesthesia for cardiac and critically ill patients.

Morphine

Circulatory effects

Morphine is a potent relaxant of vascular smooth muscle. It can act on the arterial and the venous side of the circulation alike to lower systemic vascular resistance and to increase venous capacitance (Ward, McGrath and Weil, 1972; Hsu, Hickey and Forbes, 1979). The circulatory response to a large dose of intravenous morphine varies according to the physiological status of the patient and the underlying heart disease. It has been shown:

1. To have a minimal effect on the circulatory dynamics of supine healthy adults (Drew, Dripps and Comroe, 1946).
2. To cause no change or only a slight fall in blood pressure, no change in heart rate, a mild to moderate elevation in stroke volume and cardiac output, a fall in systemic vascular resistance and a rise in central venous pressure of patients with disease of the aortic or mitral valve (Lowenstein *et al.*, 1969; Stoelting and Gibbs, 1973).
3. To cause a short-lived and small reduction in blood pressure and heart rate but no significant change in stroke volume or cardiac output of patients with ischaemic heart disease (Stoelting and Gibbs, 1973).
4. To cause hypotension in many patients suffering from acute myocardial infarction, although this was highly variable and not always predictable (Thomas *et al.*, 1965).

Effects on contractility

Animal data on this subject are contradictory (Vasko *et al.*, 1966; Goldberg and Padget, 1969; Sullivan and Wong, 1973). The effect of anaesthetic doses of morphine on myocardial contractility can be regarded as insignificant in man (Wong *et al.*, 1973).

Morphine–oxygen anaesthesia would seem ideal for patients with ischaemic heart disease; but there are practical disadvantages. Two years after the publication of his original article, Lowenstein (1971) put the issue of morphine anaesthesia into perspective and advised discretion. The disadvantages of morphine anaesthesia are:

1. Hypotension, sometimes alarming, is not uncommon following large doses of intravenous morphine. Although it is known that hypovolaemia, a head-up tilt and a fast rate of injection (faster than 5 mg per minute) will

accentuate this problem, there are other unpredictable factors, including individual sensitivity.

2. Morphine is an analgesic. Its ability to provide amnesia and hypnosis is not consistent. Morphine, 3 mg/kg, usually fails to induce unconsciousness in patients undergoing coronary artery bypass operations.

3. Hypertension and tachycardia related to direct laryngoscopy and surgical stimulation are common during morphine anaesthesia. The ischaemic heart will not be able to cope with the increase in myocardial work.

4. Both motor disturbances and psychosis after large doses of morphine have been reported (Arens et al., 1972; Berryhill, Benumof and Janowsky, 1979).

5. Morphine is a potent antidiuretic (Papper and Papper, 1964). Its renal and other metabolic effects are poorly understood.

6. Morphine anaesthesia is practical only with patients in whom controlled ventilation is planned after the operation.

In order to improve on morphine anaesthesia, some authors (Arens et al., 1972; Stanley et al., 1973) tried even larger doses of morphine (as much as 11 mg/kg). Anaesthesia was still inadequate with these very large doses; and complications of large fluid requirement, oliguria and metabolic acidosis were observed.

Other authors have tried using other agents to supplement morphine–oxygen anaesthesia. They found that the haemodynamic response of patients to morphine was dramatically modified by these adjuvant agents:

1. McDermott and Stanley (1974) observed depressions of blood pressure, heart rate, stroke volume and cardiac output in a dose-related fashion when nitrous oxide was added to patients anaesthetized with morphine and oxygen. Lappas et al. (1975) reported a fall in indices of myocardial contractility and a rise in the left ventricular filling pressure under similar conditions. These depressions were seen in healthy volunteers (Wong et al., 1973), in patients with valvular heart disease and in those with ischaemic heart disease (Stoelting and Gibbs, 1973).

2. Similar circulatory depression was seen when low concentrations of halothane (less than 0.5%) were added to patients with chronic myocardial ischaemia anaesthetized with large doses of morphine (Stoelting et al., 1974).

3. Milder, but similar, circulatory depression was seen with the addition of 5–10 mg of diazepam, but not with the addition of 2.5–5 mg of droperidol (Stanley et al., 1976).

4. Stoelting (1977b) reported that patients responded to the subsequent infusion of a large dose of morphine with a mild to moderate fall in blood pressure, stroke volume and cardiac index if they had received a thio-barbiturate for the induction of anaesthesia.

These circulatory changes following the addition of adjuvants to patients under the effect of large doses of morphine are usually related to the dose of the adjuvant. The said observations should not discourage the use of these adjuvants to supplement morphine–oxygen anaesthesia, except in patients who cannot tolerate any degree of circulatory depression. While the optimum dose of morphine remains to be defined, there is little indication to go beyond 2 mg/kg (Lowenstein, 1971).

Fentanyl

Fentanyl, a synthetic agent, is approximately 100 times more potent than morphine in analgesic action, but it has a shorter duration of action. It can be given alone or combined with droperidol in a 1 : 50 ratio as Thalamonal (Innovar). Following the administration of a small dose of fentanyl (up to 10 μg/kg), with or without droperidol, minimal circulatory changes were observed in healthy volunteers (Tammisto, Takki and Toikka, 1970) and in patients with heart disease (Tarhan et al., 1971). The observed circulatory effects following the administration of a moderate dose (10–20 μg/kg) are qualitatively similar to those observed after the infusion of morphine (Stoelting et al., 1975). In a series of studies, Stanley and his associates found that large doses of fentanyl (20–50 μg/kg) had minimal effects on haemodynamic variables (Stanley and Webster, 1978; Lunn et al., 1979; Stanley, Philbin and Coggins, 1979). However, they found that the combination of fentanyl and nitrous oxide as well as that of fentanyl and diazepam had depressant effects similar to those of morphine and the respective adjuvants. The advantage of this agent lies in its analgesic potency.

Pethidine

Pethidine has only one-tenth the analgesic potency of morphine. A 15 per cent rise in heart rate was the only prominent feature observed in conscious volunteers given a moderately large dose of pethidine (5 mg/kg in five divided doses) (Tammisto, Takki and Toikka, 1970). On the contrary, hypotension together with a large fall in cardiac output (Stanley and Liu, 1977) and a sustained rise in central venous pressure (Stephen, Davie and Scott, 1970) were observed when pethidine was given to patients anaesthetized with nitrous oxide. There has never been any serious contemplation to use large doses of pethidine in place of morphine for anaesthesia.

References

Arens, J. F., Benbow, B. P., Ochsner, J. L. and Theard, R. (1972). Morphine anesthesia for aortocoronary bypass procedures. *Anesthesia and Analgesia . . . Current Researches* **51,** 901.

Aronson, H. B., Magora, F. and London, M. (1970). The influence of droperidol on blood viscosity in man. *British Journal of Anaesthesia* **42,** 1089.

Atlee, J. L. III and Alexander, S. C. (1977). Halothane effects on conductivity of the AV node and His–Purkinje system in the dog. *Anesthesia and Analgesia . . . Current Researches* **56,** 378.

Atlee, J. L. III and Rusy, B. F. (1972). Halothane depression of A-V conduction studied by electrograms of the bundle of His in dogs. *Anesthesiology* **36,** 112.

Atlee, J. L. III and Rusy, B. F. (1977). Atrioventricular conduction times and atrioventricular nodal conductivity during enflurane anesthesia in dogs. *Anesthesiology* **47,** 498.

Atlee, J. L. III, Homer, L. D. and Tobey, R. E. (1975). Diphenylhydantoin and lidocaine modification of A-V conduction in halothane-anesthetized dogs. *Anesthesiology* **43,** 49.

Atlee, J. L. III, Rusy, B. F., Kreul, J.F. and Eby, T. (1978). Supraventricular excitability in dogs during anesthesia with halothane and enflurane. *Anesthesiology* **49,** 407.

Ayscue, Q. A. (1972). The experts opine. *Survey of Anesthesiology* **16,** 484.

Bain, J. A. and Spoerel, W. E. (1963). Methoxyflurane for the management of phaeochromocytoma. *Canadian Anaesthetists' Society Journal* **10,** 481.

Baraka, A., Harrison, T. and Kachachi, T. (1973). Catecholamine levels after ketamine anesthesia in man. *Anesthesia and Analgesia . . . Current Researches* **52,** 198.

Barnes, P. K. and Brindle-Smith, G. (1981). Comparison of the effects on heart rate and arterial pressure of pancuronium and ORG NC45 in Anaesthetized Man. *British Journal of Anaesthesia* **53,** 666P.

Barrett, J. S. and Hey, E. B. Jr (1970). Ventricular arrhythmias associated with the use of diazepam for cardioversion. *Journal of the American Medical Association* **214,** 1323.

Basta, J. W. and Lichtiger, M. (1977). Comparison of metocurine and pancuronium — Myocardial tension-time index during endotracheal intubation. *Anesthesiology* **46,** 366.

Becker, K. E. Jr and Tonnesen, A. S. (1978). Cardiovascular effects of plasma levels of thiopental necessary for anesthesia. *Anesthesiology* **49,** 197.

Bendixen, H. H. and Laver, M. B. (1962). Thiopental sodium in dogs. *Anesthesia and Analgesia . . . Current Researches* **41,** 674.

Berryhill, R. E., Benumof, J. L. and Janowsky, D. S. (1979). Morphine-induced hyperexcitability in man. *Anesthesiology* **50,** 65.

Biscoe, T. J. and Millar, R. A. (1964). The effect of halothane on carotid sinus baroreceptor activity. *Journal of Physiology* **173,** 24.

Bittar, D. A. (1979). Innovar-induced hypertensive crises in patients with pheochromocytoma. *Anesthesiology* **50,** 366.

Bland, J. H. L. and Lowenstein, E. (1976). Halothane-induced decrease in experimental myocardial ischemia in the non-failing canine heart. *Anesthesiology* **45,** 287.

Blitt, C. D., Raessler, K. L., Wightman, M. A., Groves, B. M., Wall, C. L. and Geha, D. G. (1979). Atrioventricular conduction in dogs during anesthesia with isoflurane. *Anesthesiology* **50,** 210.

Brown, B. R. Jr and Crout, J. R. (1970). The sympathomimetic effect of gallamine on the heart. *Journal of Pharmacology and Experimental Therapeutics* **172,** 266.

Bullough, J. (1959). Intermittent suxamethonium injections. *British Medical*

Journal **1**, 786.

Calverley, R. K., Smith, N. T., Jones, C. W., Prys-Roberts, C. and Eger, E. I. II (1978). Ventilatory and cardiovascular effects of enflurane anesthesia during spontaneous vetilation in man. *Anesthesia and Analgesia . . . Current Researches* **57**, 610.

Calverley, R. K., Smith, N. T., Prys-Roberts, C., Eger, E. I. II and Jones, W. C. (1978). Cardiovascular effects of enflurane anesthesia during controlled ventilation in man. *Anesthesia and Analgesia . . . Current Researches* **57**, 619.

Campbell, D., Forrester, A. C., Miller, D. C., Hutton, I., Kennedy, J. A., Lawrie, T. D. V., Lorimer, A. R. and McCall, D. (1971). A preliminary clinical study of CT1341—A steroid anaesthetic agent. *British Journal of Anaesthesia* **43**, 14.

Carrier, O. Jr and Murphy, J. C. (1970). The effects of *d*-tubocurarine and its commercial vehicles on cardiac function. *Anesthesiology* **33**, 627.

Chamberlain, J. H., Seed, R. G. F. L. and Chung, D. C. W. (1977). Effect of thiopentone on myocardial function. *British Journal of Anaesthesia* **49**, 865.

Chatas, G. J., Gottlieb, J. D. and Sweet, R. B. (1963). Cardiovascular effects of *d*-tubocurarine during fluothane anesthesia. *Anesthesia and analgesia . . . Current Researches* **42**, 65.

Chodoff, P. (1972). Evidence for central adrenergic action of ketamine: report of a case. *Anesthesia and Analgesia . . . Current Researches* **51**, 247.

Clarke, R. S. J., Dundee, J. W., Garrett, R. T., McArdle, G. K. and Sutton, J. A. (1975). Adverse reactions to intravenous anaesthetics. *British Journal of Anaesthesia* **47**, 575.

Coleman, A. J., Downing, J. W., Leary, W. P., Moyes, D. G. and Styles, M. (1972). The immediate cardiovascular effects of Althesin (Glaxo CT 1341), a steroid induction agent, and thiopentone in man. *Anaesthesia* **27**, 373.

Comroe, J. H. Jr and Dripps, R. D. (1946). The histamine-like action of curare and tubocurarine injected intracutaneously and intra-arterially in man. *Anesthesiology* **7**, 260.

Conway, C. M., Salt, P. J. and Barnes, P. K. (1979). Inhibition of neuronal uptake of noradrenaline by pancuronium in the isolated perfused rat heart. *British Journal of Anaesthesia* **51**, 44P.

Cooperman, L. H., Strobel, G. E. Jr and Kennell, E. M. (1970). Massive hyperkalemia after administration of succinylcholine. *Anesthesiology* **32**, 161.

Corbett, T. H. (1976). Cancer and congenital anomalies associated with anesthetics. *Annals of the New York Academy of Sciences* **271**, 58.

Corssen, G. (1966). Neuroleptanalgesia and anesthesia: Its usefulness in poor-risk surgical cases. *Southern Medical Journal* **59**, 801.

Côté, P., Guéret, P. and Bourassa, M. G. (1974). Systemic and coronary hemodynamic effects of diazepam in patients with normal and diseased coronary arteries. *Circulation* **50**, 1210.

Cowgill, D. B., Mostello, L. A. and Shapiro, H. M. (1974). Encephalitis and a hyperkalemic response to succinylcholine. *Anesthesiology* **40**, 409.

Cromwell, T. H., Stevens, W. C., Eger, E. I. II, Shakespeare, T. F., Halsey, M. J., Bahlman, S. H. and Fourcade, H. E. (1971). The cardiovascular effects of compound 469 (Forane*) during spontaneous ventilation and CO_2 challenge in man. *Anesthesiology* **35**, 17.

Dalen, J. E., Evans, G. L., Banas, J. S. Jr, Brooks, H. L., Paraskos, J. A. and Dexter, L. (1969). The hemodynamic and respiratory effects of diazepam (Valium). *Anesthesiology* **30**, 259.

Denlinger, J. K., Kaplan, J. A., Lecky, J. H. and Wollman, H. (1975). Cardiovascular responses to calcium administered intravenously to man during halothane anesthesia. *Anesthesiology* **42**, 390.

Deutsch, S., Linde, H. W., Dripps, R. D. and Price, H. L. (1962). Circulatory and respiratory actions of halothane in normal man. *Anesthesiology* **23**, 631.

Dobkin, A. B., Arandia, H. Y. and Levy, A. A. (1973). Effect of pancuronium bromide on plasma histamine levels in man. *Anesthesia and Analgesia . . . Current Researches* **52**, 772.

Dolan, W. M., Stevens, W. C., Eger, E. I. II, Cromwell, T. H., Halsey, M. J., Shakespeare, T. F. and Miller, R. D. (1974). The cardiovascular and respiratory effects of isoflurane–nitrous oxide anaesthesia. *Canadian Anaesthetists' Society Journal* **21**, 557.

Domenech, R. J., Macho, P., Valdes, J. and Penna, M. (1977). Coronary vascular resistance during halothane anesthesia. *Anesthesiology* **46**, 236.

Dowdy, E. G. and Fabian, L. W. (1963). Ventricular arrhythmias induced by succinylcholine in digitalized patients: a preliminary report. *Anesthesia and Analgesia . . . Current Researches* **42**, 501.

Dowdy, E. G. and Kaya, K. (1968). Studies of the mechanism of cardiovascular responses to CI-581. *Anesthesiology* **29**, 931.

Dowdy, E. G., Duggar, P. N. and Fabian, L. W. (1965). Effect of neuromuscular blocking agents on isolated digitalized mammalian hearts. *Anesthesia and Analgesia . . . Current Researches* **44**, 608.

Dowdy, E. G., Holland, W. C., Yamanaka, I. and Kaya, K. (1971). Cardioactive properties of *d*-tubocurarine with and without preservatives. *Anesthesiology* **34**, 256.

Drew, J. H., Dripps, R. D. and Comroe, J. H. Jr (1946). Clinical studies on morphine. II. The effect of morphine upon the circulation of man and upon the circulatory and respiratory response to tilting. *Anesthesiology* **7**, 44.

Duke, P. C., Mittler, G. and Wade, J. G. (1974). The effect of pancuronium on reflex regulation of heart rate in man. *Canadian Anaesthetists' Society Journal* **21**, 139.

Eckstein, J. W., Hamilton, W. K. and McCammond, J. M. (1961). The effect of thiopental on peripheral venous tone. *Anesthesiology* **22**, 525.

Eger, E. I. II, Smith, N. T., Stoelting, R. K., Cullen, D. J., Kadis, L. B. and Whitcher, C. E. (1970). Cardiovascular effects of halothane in man. *Anesthesiology* **32**, 396.

Eger, E. I. II, Smith, N. T., Cullen, D. J., Cullen, B. F. and Gregory, G. A. (1971). A comparison of the cardiovascular effects of halothane, fluroxene, ether and cyclopropane in man: a resume. *Anesthesiology* **34**, 25.

Eger, E. I. II, White, A. E., Brown, C. L., Biava, C. G., Corbett, T. H. and Stevens, W. C. (1978). A test of the carcinogenicity of enflurane, isoflurane, halothane, methoxyflurane, and nitrous oxide in mice. *Anesthesia and Analgesia . . . Current Researches* **57**, 678.

Eichhorn, J. H., Hedley-Whyte, J., Steinman, T. I., Kaufmann, J. M. and Laasberg, L. H. (1976). Renal failure following enflurane anesthesia. *Anesthesiology* **45**, 557.

Eisele, J. H. and Smith, N. T. (1972). Cardiovascular effects of 40 percent nitrous oxide in man. *Anesthesia and Analgesia . . . Current Researches* **51**, 956.

Eisele, J. H., Reitan, J. A., Massumi, R. A., Zelis, R. F. and Miller, R. R. (1976). Myocardial performance and N_2O analgesia in coronary-artery disease. *Anesthesiology* **44**, 46.

Etsten, B. and Li, T. H. (1955). Hemodynamic changes during thiopental anesthesia in humans: cardiac output, stroke volume, total peripheral resistance, and intrathoracic blood volume. *Journal of Clinical Investigation* **34**, 500.

Evans, J. M. and Keogh, J. A. M. (1977). Adverse reactions to intravenous anaesthetic induction agents. *British Medical Journal* **2**, 735.

Ferrari, H. A., Gorten, R. J., Talton, I. H., Canent, R. and Goodrich, J. K. (1974). The action of droperidol and fentanyl on cardiac output and related hemodynamic parameters. *Southern Medical Journal* **67**, 49.

Fieldman, E. J., Ridley, R. W. and Wood, E. H. (1955). Hemodynamic studies during thiopental sodium and nitrous oxide anesthesia in humans. *Anesthesiology* **16**, 473.

Flickinger, H., Fraimow, W., Cathcart, R. T. and Nealon, T. F. Jr (1961). Effect of thiopental induction on cardiac output in man. *Anesthesia and Analgesia . . . Current Researches* **40**, 693.

Foëx, P. and Prys-Roberts, C. (1972). Pulmonary haemodynamics and myocardial effects of Althesin (CT 1341) in the goat. *Postgraduate Medical Journal* **48**, Suppl. II, 24.

Folts, J. D., Afonso, S. and Rowe, G. G. (1975). Systemic and coronary haemodynamic effects of ketamine in intact anaesthetized and unanaesthetized dogs. *British Journal of Anaesthesia* **47**, 686.

Foster, B. (1961). Suxamethonium and cardiac rhythm. *British Medical Journal* **1**, 129.

Fox, G. S., Wynands, J. E. and Bhambhami, M. (1968). A clinical comparison of diazepam and thiopentone as induction agents to general anaesthesia. *Canadian Anaesthetists' Society Journal* **15**, 281.

Geha, D. G., Rozelle, B. C., Raessler, K. L., Groves, B. M., Wightman, M. A. and Blitt, C. D. (1977). Pancuronium bromide enhances atrioventricular conduction in halothane-anesthetized dogs. *Anesthesiology* **46**, 342.

Goat, V. A. and Feldman, S. A. (1972). The effect on non-depolarizing muscle relaxants on the cholinergic mechanisms in the isolated rabbit heart. *Anaesthesia* **27**, 143.

Goldberg, A. H. and Padget, C. H. (1969). Comparative effects of morphine and fentanyl on isolated heart muscle. *Anesthesia and Analgesia . . . Current Researches* **48,** 978.

Goldberg, A. H., Keane, P. W. and Phear, W. P. C. (1970). Effects of ketamine on contractile performance and excitability of isolated heart muscle. *Journal of Pharmacology and Experimental Therapeutics* **175,** 388.

Göthert, M., Kennerknecht, E. and Thielecke, G. (1976). Inhibition of receptor-mediated noradrenaline release from the sympathetic nerves of the isolated rabbit heart by anaesthetics and alcohols in proportion to their hydrophobic property. *Naunyn-Schmiedeberg's Archives of Pharmacology* **292,** 145.

Graves, C. L. and Downs, N. H. (1974). Cardiovascular and renal effects of enflurane in surgical patients. *Anesthesia and Analgesia . . . Current Researches* **53,** 898.

Gravlee, G. P. (1980). Succinylcholine-induced hyperkalemia in a patient with Parkinson's disease. *Anesthesia and Analgesia . . . Current Researches* **59,** 444.

Hagenau, W., Pietsch, D. and Arndt, J. O. (1976). Der Effekt von Halothan und Enflurane sowie von Propanidid und Ketamin auf die Aktivitat der Barorezeptoren des Aortenbogens decerebrierter Katzen. *Anaesthetist* **25,** 331.

Hashimoto, K., Endoh, M., Kimura, T. and Hashimoto, K. (1975). Effects of halothane on automaticity and contractile force of isolated blood-perfused canine ventricular tissue. *Anesthesiology* **42,** 15.

Hauswirth, O. and Schaer, H. (1967). Effects of halothane on the sino-atrial node. *Journal of Pharmacology and Experimental Therapeutics* **158,** 36.

Heinonen, J. and Yrjölä, H. (1980). Comparison of haemodynamic effects of metocurine and pancuronium in patients with coronary artery disease. *British Journal of Anaesthesia* **52,** 931.

Horan, B. F., Prys-Roberts, C., Hamilton, W. K. and Roberts, J. G. (1977). Haemodynamic responses to enflurane anaesthesia and hypovolaemia in the dog, and their modification by propranolol. *British Journal of Anaesthesia* **49,** 1189.

Horan, B. F., Prys-Roberts, C., Roberts J. G., Bennett, M. J. and Foëx, P. (1977). Haemodynamic responses to isoflurane anaesthesia and hypovolaemia in the dog, and their modification by propranolol. *British Journal of Anaesthesia* **49,** 1179.

Hsu, H. O., Hickey, R. F. and Forbes, A. R. (1979). Morphine decreases peripheral vascular resistance and increases capacitance in man. *Anesthesiology* **50,** 98.

Hughes, R. and Chapple, D. J. (1976). Effects of non-depolarizing neuromuscular blocking agents on peripheral autonomic mechanisms in cats. *British Journal of Anaesthesia* **48,** 59.

Hughes, R., Ingram, G. S. and Payne, J. P. (1976). Studies on dimethyl tubocurarine in anesthetized man. *British Journal of Anaesthesia* **48,** 969.

Hyatt, M., Muldoon, S. M. and Rorie, D. K. (1980). Droperidol, a selective antagonist of postsynaptic α-adrenoceptors in the canine saphenous vein.

Anesthesiology **53**, 281.

Ikram, H., Rubin, A. P. and Jewkes, R. F. (1973). Effect of diazepam on myocardial blood flow of patients with and without coronary artery disease. *British Heart Journal* **35**, 626.

Ivankovich, A. D., El-Etr, A. A., Janeczko, G. F. and Maronic, J. P. (1975). The effects of ketamine and of Innovar anesthesia on digitalis tolerance in dogs. *Anesthesia and Analgesia . . . Current Researches* **54**, 106.

Ivankovich, A. D., Miletich, D. J., Reimann, C., Albrecht, R. F. and Zahed, B. (1974). Cardiovascular effects of centrally administered ketamine in goats. *Anesthesia and Analgesia . . . Current Researches* **53**, 924.

Ivankovich, A. D., Miletich, D. J., Grossman, R. K., Albrecht, R. F., El-Etr, A. A. and Cairoli, V. J. (1976). The effect of enflurane, isoflurane, fluroxene, methoxyflurane and diethyl ether anesthesia on ouabain tolerance in the dog. *Anesthesia and Analgesia . . . Current Researches* **55**, 360.

Iwatsuki, N., Kuroda, N., Amaha, K. and Iwatsuki, K. (1980). Succinyl-choline-induced hyperkalemia in patients with ruptured cerebral aneurysms. *Anesthesiology* **53**, 64.

Johnston, R. R., Eger, E. I. II and Wilson, C. (1976). A comparative interaction of epinephrine with enflurane, isoflurane, and halothane in man. *Anesthesia and Analgesia . . . Current Researches* **55**, 709.

Kaplan, J. A., Miller, E. D. and Bailey, D. R. (1976). A comparative study of enflurane and halothane using systolic time intervals. *Anesthesia and Analgesia . . . Current Researches* **55**, 263.

Katz, R. L., Matteo, R. S. and Papper, E. M. (1962). The injection of epinephrine during general anesthesia: with halogenated hydrocarbons and cyclopropane in man. *Anesthesiology* **23**, 597.

Kelman, G. R. and Kennedy, B. R. (1971). Cardiovascular effects of pancuronium in man. *British Journal of Anaesthesia* **43**, 335.

Kennedy, B. R. and Farman, J. V. (1968). Cardiovascular effects of gallamine triethiodide in man. *British Journal of Anaesthesia* **40**, 773.

Kettler, D. and Sonntag, H. (1974). Intravenous anesthetics: coronary blood flow and myocardial oxygen consumption (with special reference to Althesine). *Acta Anaesthesiologica Belgica* **25**, 384.

Knapp, R. B. and Dubow, H. (1970). Comparison of diazepam with thiopental as an induction agent in cardiopulmonary disease. *Anesthesia and Analgesia . . . Current Researches* **49**, 722.

Ko, K. C. and Paradise, R. R. (1969). The effects of substrates on con-tractility of rat atria depressed with halothane. *Anesthesiology* **31**, 532.

Ko, K. C. and Paradise, R. R. (1970). The effects of substrates on halothane-depressed isolated human atria. *Anesthesiology* **33**, 508.

Ko, K. C. and Paradise, R. R. (1971). Contractile depression of rat atria by halothane in the absence of glucose. *Anesthesiology* **34**, 152.

Koehntop, D. E., Liao, J. C. and Van Bergen, F. H. (1977). Effects of pharmacologic alterations of adrenergic mechanisms by cocaine, tropo-lone, aminophylline, and ketamine on epinephrine-induced arrhythmias during halothane–nitrous oxide anesthesia. *Anesthesiology* **46,** 83.

Konchigeri, H. N., Shaker, M. H. and Winnie, A. P. (1974). Effect of epinephrine during enflurane anesthesia. *Anesthesia and Analgesia . . . Current Researches* **53,** 894.

Lappas, D. G., Buckley, M. J., Laver, M. B., Daggett, W. M. and Lowenstein, E. (1975). Left ventricular performance and pulmonary circulation following addition of nitrous oxide to morphine during coronary-artery surgery. *Anesthesiology* **43,** 61.

Libonati, M., Cooperman, L. H. and Price, H. L. (1971). Time-dependent circulatory effects of methoxyflurane in man. *Anesthesiology* **34,** 439.

Linde, H. W., Lamb, V. E., Quimby, C. W. Jr, Homi, J. and Eckenhoff, J. E. (1970). The search for better anesthetic agents: clinical investigation of Ethrane. *Anesthesiology* **32,** 555.

Linde, H. W., Oh, S. O., Homi, J. and Joshi, C. (1975). Cardiovascular effects of isoflurane and halothane during controlled ventilation in older patients. *Anesthesia and Analgesia . . . Current Researches* **54,** 701.

Lippmann, M. and Reisner, L. S. (1974). Epinephrine injection with enflurane anesthesia: incidence of cardiac arrhythmias. *Anesthesia and Analgesia . . . Current Researches* **53,** 886.

List, W. F. M. (1971). Succinylcholine-induced cardiac arrhythmias. *Anesthesia and Analgesia . . . Current Researches* **50,** 361.

Loehning, R. W. and Mazze, R. I. (1974). Possible nephrotoxicity from enflurane in a patient with severe renal disease. *Anesthesiology* **40,** 203.

Logic, J. R. and Morrow, D. H. (1972). The effect of halothane on ventricular automacity. *Anesthesiology* **36,** 107.

Long, G., Dripps, R. D. and Price, H. L. (1967). Measurement of anti-arrhythmic potency of drugs in man: effects of dehydrobenzperidol. *Anesthesiology* **28,** 318.

Longnecker, D. E., Stoelting, R. K. and Morrow, A. G. (1973). Cardiac and peripheral vascular effects of gallamine in man. *Anesthesia and Analgesia . . . Current Researches* **52,** 931.

Lowenstein, E. (1971). Morphine 'anesthesia' — a perspective. *Anesthiology* **35,** 563.

Lowenstein, E., Hallowell, P., Levine, F. H., Daggett, W. M., Austen, W. G. and Laver, M. B. (1969). Cardiovascular response to large doses of intravenous morphine in man. *New England Journal of Medicine* **281,** 1389.

Lunn, J. K., Stanley, T. H., Eisele, J., Webster, L. and Woodward, A. (1979). High dose fentanyl anesthesia for coronary artery surgery: plasma fentanyl concentrations and influence of nitrous oxide on cardiovascular responses. *Anesthesia and Analgesia . . . Current Researches* **58,** 390.

Lyons, S. M. and Clarke, R. S. J. (1972). A comparison of different drugs for anaesthesia in cardiac surgical patients. *British Journal of Anaesthesia* **44,** 575.

McCullough, L. S., Reier, C. E., Delaunois, A. L., Gardier, R. W. and Hamelberg, W. (1970). The effects of *d*-tubocurarine on spontaneous postganglionic sympathetic activity and histamine release. *Anesthesiology* **33,** 328.

McCullough, L. S., Stone, W. A., Delaunois, A. L., Reier, C. E. and Hamelberg, W. (1972). The effect of dimethyl tubocurarine iodide on cardiovascular parameters, postganglionic sympathetic activity, and histamine release. *Anesthesia and Analgesia . . . Current Researches* **51**, 554.

McDermott, R. W. and Stanley, T. H. (1974). The cardiovascular effects of low concentrations of nitrous oxide during morphine anesthesia. *Anesthesiology* **41**, 89.

Mallow, J. E., White, R. D., Cucchiara, R. F. and Tarhan, S. (1976). Hemodynamic effects of isoflurane and halothane in patients with coronary artery disease. *Anesthesia and Analgesia . . . Current Researches* **55**, 135.

Markiewicz, W., Hunt, S., Harrison, D. C. and Alderman, E. L. (1976). Circulatory effects of diazepam in heart disease. *Journal of Clinical Pharmacology* **16**, 637.

Mathias, J. A., Evans-Prosser, C. D. G. and Churchill-Davidson, H. C. (1970). The role of the non-depolarizing drugs in the prevention of suxamethonium bradycardia. *British Journal of Anaesthesia* **42**, 609.

Mazze, R. I., Escue, H. M. and Houston, J. B. (1969). Hyperkalemia and cardiovascular collapse following administration of succinylcholine to the traumatized patient. *Anesthesiology* **31**, 540.

Mazze, R. I., Shue, G. L. and Jackson, S. H. (1971). Renal dysfunction associated with methoxyflurane anesthesia: a randomized, prospective clinical evaluation. *Journal of the American Medical Association* **216**, 278.

Merin, R. G. (1969). Myocardial metabolism in the halothane-depressed canine heart. *Anesthesiology* **31**, 20.

Merin, R. G. (1970a). The relationship between myocardial function and glucose metabolism in the halothane-depressed heart. I. The effect of hyperglycemia. *Anesthesiology* **33**, 391.

Merin, R. G. (1970b). The relationship between myocardial function and glucose metabolism in the halothane-depressed heart. II. The effect of insulin. *Anesthesiology* **33**, 396.

Merin, R. G. and Borgstedt, H. H. (1971). Myocardial function and metabolism in the methoxyflurane-depressed canine heart. *Anesthesiology* **34**, 562.

Merin, R. G., Kumazawa, T. and Honig, C. R. (1974). Reversible interaction between halothane and Ca^{++} on cardiac actomyosin adenosine triphosphatase: mechanism and significance. *Journal of Pharmacology and Experimental Therapeutics* **190**, 1.

Merin, R. G., Kumazawa, T. and Luka, N. L. (1976a). Myocardial function and metabolism in the conscious dog and during halothane anesthesia. *Anesthesiology* **44**, 402.

Merin, R. G., Kumazawa, T. and Luka, N. L. (1976b) Enflurane depresses myocardial function, perfusion, and metabolism in the dog. *Anesthesiology* **45**, 501.

Merin, R. G., Verdouw, P. D. and deJong, J. W. (1977). Dose-dependent depression of cardiac function and metabolism by halothane in swine (*Sus scrofa). Anethesiology* **46,** 417.

Miletich, D. J., Ivankovic, A. D., Albrecht, R. F., Zahed, B. and Ilahi, A. A. (1973). The effect of ketamine on catecholamine metabolism in the isolated perfused rat heart. *Anesthesiology* **39,** 271.

Millar, R. A., Gilbert, R. G. B. and Brindle, G. F. (1958). Ventricular tachycardia during halothane anaesthesia. *Anaesthesia* **13,** 164.

Miller, D. C., Bradford, E. M. and Campbell, D. (1972). Haemodynamic effects of Althesin in poor-risk patients. *Postgraduate Medical Journal* **48,** Suppl. II, 133.

Miller, R. D., Eger, E. I. II, Stevens, W. C. and Gibbons, R. (1975). Pancuronium-induced tachycardia in relation to alveolar halothane, dose of pancuronium, and prior atropine. *Anesthesiology* **42,** 352.

Morrow, D. H. and Townley, N. T. (1964). Anesthesia and digitalis toxicity: an experimental study. *Anesthesia and Analgesia . . . Current Researches* **43,** 510.

Munger, W. L., Miller, R. D. and Stevens, W. C. (1974). The dependence of *d*-tubocurarine-induced hypotension on alveolar concentration of halothane, dose of *d*-tubocurarine, and nitrous oxide. *Anesthesiology* **40,** 442.

Nana, A., Cardan, E. and Domokos, M. (1973). Blood catecholamine changes after pancuronium. *Acta Anaesthesiologica Scandinavica* **17,** 83.

Papper, S. and Papper, E. M. (1964). The effects of preanesthetic, anesthetic, and postoperative drugs on renal function. *Clinical Pharmacology and Therapeutics* **5,** 205.

Paradise, R. R. and Ko, K. C. (1970). The effect of fructose on halothane-depressed rat atria. *Anesthesiology* **32,** 124.

Pauca, A. L. and Dripps, R. D. (1973). Clinical experience with isoflurane (Forane*). *British Journal of Anaesthesia* **45,** 697.

Philbin, D. M. and Lowenstein, E. (1976). Lack of beta-adrenergic activity of isoflurane in the dog: a comparison of circulatory effects of halothane and isoflurane after propranolol administration. *British Journal of Anaesthesia* **48,** 1165.

Powell, J. N. (1970). Suxamethonium-induced hyperkalaemia in a uraemic patient. *British Journal of Anaesthesia* **42,** 806.

Price, H. L. (1974). Calcium reverses myocardial depression caused by halothane: site of action. *Anesthesiology* **41,** 576.

Price, H. L. and Helrich, M. (1955). The effect of cyclopropane, diethyl ether, nitrous oxide, thiopental and hydrogen ion concentration on the myocardial function of the dog heart–lung preparation. *Journal of Pharmacology and Experimental Therapeutics* **115,** 206.

Price, H. L. and Price, M. L. (1966). Has halothane a predominant circulatory action? *Anesthesiology* **27,** 764.

Price, H. L., Skovsted, P., Pauca, A. L. and Cooperman, L. H. (1970). Evidence for β-receptor activation produced by halothane in normal man. *Anesthesiology* **32,** 389.

Prys-Roberts, C., Lloyd, J. W., Fisher, A., Kerr, J. H. and Patterson, T. J. S. (1974). Deliberate profound hypotension induced with halothane: studies of haemodynamics and pulmonary gas exchange. *British Journal of Anaesthesia* **46**, 105.

Puddy, B. R. (1971). Effects of droperidol on the vasoconstriction produced by noradrenaline, histamine, sympathetic nerve stimulation and potassium ions in the isolated rabbit auricular artery. *British Journal of Anaesthesia* **43**, 441.

Rao, T. L. K. and Shanmugam, M. (1979). Succinylcholine administration — another contraindication? *Anesthesia and Analgesia . . . Current Researches* **58**, 61.

Rathod, R., Jacobs, H. K., Kramer, N. E., Rao, T. L. K., Salem, M. R. and Towne, W. D. (1978). Echocardiographic assessment of ventricular performance following induction with two anesthetics. *Anesthesiology* **49**, 86.

Reynolds, A. K., Chiz, J. F. and Pasquet, A. F. (1970). Halothane and methoxyflurane — a comparison of their effects on cardiac pacemaker fibers. *Anesthesiology* **33**, 602.

Roberts, J. G., Foëx, P., Clarke, T. N. S. and Bennett, M. J. (1976). Haemodynamic interactions of high-dose propranolol pretreatment and anaesthesia in the dog. I: Halothane dose-response studies. *British Journal of Anaesthesia* **48**, 315.

Robertson, B. J., Clement, J. L. and Knill, R. L. (1981). Enhancement of the arrhythmogenic effect of hypercarbia by surgical stimulation during halothane anaesthesia in man. *Canadia Anaesthetists' Society Journal* **28**, 342.

Saner, C. A., Foëx, P., Roberts, J. G. and Bennett, M. J. (1975). Methoxyflurane and practolol: a dangerous combination? *British Journal of Anaesthesia* **47**, 1025.

Savege, T. M., Foley, E. I., Ross, L. and Maxwell, M. P. (1972). A comparison of the cardiorespiratory effects during induction of anaesthesia of Althesin with thiopentone and methohexitone. *Postgraduate Medical Journal* **48**, Suppl. II, 66.

Seed, R. F. and Chamberlain, J. H. (1977). Myocardial stimulation by pancuronium bromide. *British Journal of Anaesthesia* **49**, 401.

Skovsted, P. and Price, H. L. (1972). The effects of Ethrane on arterial pressure, preganglionic sympathetic activity, and barostatic reflexes. *Anesthesiology* **36**, 257.

Smith, G., Rogers, K. and Thorburn, J. (1980). Halothane improves the balance of oxygen supply to demand in acute experimental myocardial ischaemia. *British Journal of Anaesthesia* **52**, 577.

Smith, G., Vance, J. P., Brown, D. M. and McMillan, J. C. (1974). Changes in canine myocardial blood flow and oxygen consumption in response to halothane. *British Journal of Anaesthesia* **46**, 821.

Smith, N. T., Calverley, R. K., Prys-Roberts, C., Eger, E. I. II and Jones, C. W. (1978). Impact of nitrous oxide on the circulation during enflurane anesthesia in man. *Anesthesiology* **48**, 345.

Smith, N. T., Eger, E. I. II, Cullen, B. F. Sawyer, D. C. and Gregory, G. A. (1972). The cardiovascular responses to the addition of nitrous oxide to fluroxene in man. *British Journal of Anaesthesia* **44**, 142.

Smith, N. T., Eger, E. I. II, Gregory, G. A., Cullen, B. F. and Cullen, D. J.

(1972). The cardiovascular responses to the addition of nitrous oxide to diethyl ether in man. *Canadian Anaesthetists' Society Journal* **19**, 42.

Smith, N. T., Eger, E. I. II, Stoelting, R. K., Whayne, T. F., Cullen, D. and Kadis, L. B. (1970). The cardiovascular and sympathomimetic responses to the addition of nitrous oxide to halothane in man. *Anesthesiology* **32**, 410.

Smith, N. T. and Whitcher, C. E. (1967). Hemodynamic effects of gallamine and tubocurarine administered during halothane anesthesia. *Journal of the American Medical Association* **199**, 114.

Son, S. L. and Waud, B. E. (1977). Potencies of neuromuscular blocking agents at the receptors of the atrial pacemaker and the motor endplate of the guinea pig. *Anesthesiology* **47**, 34.

Son, S. L. and Waud, D. R. (1978). A vagolytic action of neuromuscular blocking agents at the pacemaker of the isolated guinea pig atrium. *Anesthesiology* **48**, 191.

Sonntag, H., Donath, U., Hillebrand, W., Merin, R. G. and Radke, J. (1978). Left ventricular function in conscious man and during halothane anesthesia. *Anesthesiology* **48**, 320.

Sonntag, H., Hellberg, K., Schenk, H. D., Donath, U., Regensburger, D., Kettler, D., Duchanova, H. and Larsen, R. (1975). Effects of thiopental (Trapanal) on coronary blood flow and myocardial metabolism in man. *Acta Anaesthesiologica Scandinavica* **19**, 69.

Stanley, T. H. (1973). Blood-pressure and pulse-rate responses to ketamine during general anesthesia. *Anesthesiology* **39**, 648.

Stanley, T. H. and Liu, W. S. (1977). Cardiovascular effects of meperidine–N_2O anesthesia before and after pancuronium. *Anesthesia and Analgesia . . . Current Researches* **59**, 669.

Stanley, T. H. and Webster, L. R. (1978). Anesthetic requirements and cardiovascular effects of fentanyl–oxygen and fentanyl–diazepam–oxygen anesthesia in man. *Anesthesia and Analgesia . . . Current Researches* **57**, 411.

Stanley, T. H., Bennett, G. M., Loeser, E. A., Kawamura, R. and Sentker, C. R. (1976). Cardiovascular effects of diazepam and droperidol during morphine anesthesia. *Anesthesiology* **44**, 255.

Stanley, T. H., Gray, N. H., Stanford, W. and Armstrong, R. (1973). The effects of high-dose morphine on fluid and blood requirements in open-heart operations. *Anesthesiology* **38**, 536.

Stanley, T. H., Philbin, D. M. and Coggins, C. H. (1979). Fentanyl–oxygen anaesthesia for coronary artery surgery: cardiovascular and antidiuretic hormone responses. *Canadian Anaesthetists' Society Journal* **26**, 168.

Stephen, G. W., Davie, I. and Scott, D. B. (1970). Circulatory effects of pentazocine and pethidine during general anaesthesia with nitrous oxide, oxygen and halothane. *British Journal of Anaesthesia* **42**, 311.

Stevens, W. C., Cromwell, T. H., Halsey, M. J., Eger, E. I. II, Shakespeare, T. F. and Bahlman, S. H. (1971). The cardiovascular effects of a new inhalation anesthetic, Forane, in human volunteers at constant arterial carbon dioxide tension. *Anesthesiology* **35**, 8.

Stoelting, R. K. (1971). Blood-pressure responses to *d*-tubocurarine and its preservatives in anesthetized patients. *Anesthesiology* **35**, 315.

Stoelting, R. K. (1972). The hemodynamic effects of pancuronium and *d*-tubocurarine in anesthetized patients. *Anesthesiology* **36**, 612.

Stoelting, R. K. (1973). Hemodynamic effects of gallamine during halothane–nitrous oxide anesthesia. *Anesthesiology* **39**, 645.

Stoelting, R. K. (1974). Hemodynamic effects of dimethyltubocurarine during nitrous oxide–halothane anesthesia. *Anesthesia and Analgesia . . . Current Researches* **53**, 513.

Stoelting, R. K. (1977a). Comparison of gallamine and atropine as pretreatment before anesthetic induction and succinylcholine administration. *Anesthesia and Analgesia . . . Current Researches* **56**, 493.

Stoelting, R. K. (1977b). Influence of barbiturate anesthetic induction on circulatory responses to morphine. *Anesthesia and Analgesia . . . Current Researches* **56**, 615.

Stoelting, R. K. and Gibbs, P. S. (1973). Hemodynamic effects of morphine and morphine–nitrous oxide in valvular heart disease and coronary-artery disease. *Anesthesiology* **38**, 45.

Stoelting, R. K. and Peterson, C. (1975a). Adverse effects of increased succinylcholine dose following *d*-tubocurarine pretreatment. *Anesthesia and Analgesia . . . Current Researches* **54**, 282.

Stoelting, R. K. and Peterson, C. (1975b). Heart-rate slowing and junctional rhythm following intravenous succinylcholine with and without intramuscular atropine preanesthetic medication. *Anesthesia and Analgesia . . . Current Researches* **54**, 705.

Stoelting, R. K., Reis, R. R. and Longnecker, D. E. (1972). Hemodynamic responses to nitrous oxide–halothane and halothane in patients with valvular heart disease. *Anesthesiology* **37**, 430.

Stoelting, R. K., Creasser, C. W., Gibbs, P. S. and Peterson, C. (1974). Circulatory effects of halothane added to morphine anesthesia in patients with coronary-artery disease. *Anesthesia and Analgesia . . . Current Researches* **53**, 449.

Stoelting, R. K., Gibbs, P. S., Creasser, C. W. and Peterson, C. (1975). Hemodynamic and ventilatory responses to fentanyl, fentanyl–droperidol, and nitrous oxide in patients with acquired valvular heart disease. *Anesthesiology* **42**, 319.

Stone, W. A., Beach, T. P. and Hamelberg, W. (1970). Succinylcholine–danger in the spinal-cord-injured patient. *Anesthesiology* **32**, 168.

Stong, L. J., Hartzell, C. R. and McCarl, R. L. (1975). Halothane and the beating response and ATP turnover rate of heart cells in tissue culture. *Anesthesiology* **42**, 123.

Sullivan, D. L. and Wong, K. C. (1973). The effects of morphine on the isolated heart during normothermia and hypothermia. *Anesthesiology* **38**, 550.

Sumikawa, K. and Amakata, Y. (1977). The pressor effect of droperidol on a patient with pheochromocytoma. *Anesthesiology* **46**, 359.

Tammisto, T., Takki, S. and Toikka, P. (1970). A comparison of the circulatory effects in man of the analgesics fentanyl, pentazocine and pethidine. *British Journal of Anaesthesia* **42**, 317.

Tarhan, S., Moffitt, E. A., Lundborg, R. O. and Frye, R. L. (1971). Hemodynamic and blood-gas effects of Innovar in patients with acquired heart disease. *Anesthesiology* **34**, 250.

Tarnow, J., Eberlein, H. J., Oser, G., Patschke, D., Schneider, E., Schweichel, E. and Wilde, J. (1977). Hamodynamik, Myokardkontraktilitat, Ventrikelvolumina und Sauerstoffversorgung des Herzens unter verschiedenen Inhalationsanaesthetika. *Anaesthesist* **26**, 220.

Theye, R. A. and Michenfelder, J. D. (1975). Whole-body and organ V_{O_2} changes in enflurane, isoflurane, and halothane *British Journal of Anaesthesia* **47**, 813.

Thomas, E. T. (1969). Circulatory collapse following succinylcholine: report of a case. *Anesthesia and Analgesia . . . Current Researches* **48**, 333.

Thomas, M., Malmcrona, R., Fillmore, S. and Shillingford, J. (1965). Haemodynamic effects of morphine in patients with acute myocardial infarction. *British Heart Journal* **27**, 863.

Tolmie, J. D., Joyce, T. H. and Mitchell, G. D. (1967). Succinylcholine danger in the burned patient. *Anesthesiology* **28**, 467.

Traber, D. L. and Wilson, R. D. (1969). Involvement of the sympathetic nervous system in the pressor response to ketamine. *Anesthesia and Analgesia . . . Current Researches* **48**, 248.

Traber, D. L., Wilson, R. D. and Priano, L. L. (1968). Differentiation of the cardiovascular effects of CI-581. *Anesthesia and Analgesia . . . Current Researches* **47**, 769.

Traber, D. L., Wilson, R. D. and Priano, L. L. (1970a). Blockade of the hypertensive response to ketamine. *Anesthesia and Analgesia . . . Current Researches* **49**, 420.

Traber, D. L., Wilson, R. D. and Priano, L. L. (1970b). The effect of beta-adrenergic blockade on the cardiopulmonary response to ketamine. *Anesthesia and Analgesia . . . Current Researches* **49**, 604.

Traber, D. L., Wilson, R. D. and Priano, L. L. (1971). The effect of alpha-adrenergic blockade on the cardiopulmonary response to ketamine. *Anesthesia and Analgesia . . . Current Researches* **50**, 737.

Tucker, W. K. and Munson, E. S. (1975). Effects of succinylcholine and d-tubocurarine on epinephrine-induced arrhythmias during halothane anesthesia in dogs. *Anesthesiology* **42**, 41.

Tweed, W. A., Minuck, M. and Mymin, D. (1972). Circulatory responses to ketamine anesthesia. *Anesthesiology* **37**, 613.

Valicenti, J. F., Newman, W. H., Bagwell, E. E., Pruett, J. K. and Robie, N. W. (1973). Myocardial contractility during induction and steady-state ketamine anesthesia. *Anesthesia and Analgesia . . . Current Researches* **52**, 190.

Van Loon, G. R. (1968). Ventricular arrhythmias treated by diazepam. *Canadian Medical Association Journal* **98**, 785.

Vasko, J. S., Henney, R. P., Brawley, R. K., Oldham, H. N. and Morrow, A. G. (1966). Effects of morphine on ventricular function and myocardial contractile force. *American Journal of Physiology* **210**, 329.

Viljoen, J. F., Estafanous, F. G. and Kellner, G. A. (1972). Propranolol and cardiac surgery. *Journal of Thoracic and Cardiovascular Surgery* **64**, 826.

Virtue, R. W., Alanis, J. M., Mori, M., Lafargue, R. T., Vogel, J. H. K. and Metcalf, D. R. (1967). An anesthetic agent: 2-orthochlorophenyl, 2-methylamino cyclohexanone HCl (CI-581). *Anesthesiology* **28**, 823.

Walker, J. A., Eggers, G. W. N. Jr and Allen, C. R. (1962). Cardiovascular effects of methoxyflurane anesthesia in man. *Anesthesiology* **23**, 639.

Ward, J. M., McGrath, R. L. and Weil, J. V. (1972). Effects of morphine on the peripheral vascular response to sympathetic stimulation. *American Journal of Cardiology* **29**, 659.

Weaver, P. C., Bailey, J. S. and Preston, T. D. (1970). Coronary artery blood flow in the halothane-depressed canine heart. *British Journal of Anaesthesia* **42**, 678.

Weintraub, H. D., Heisterkamp, D. V. and Cooperman, L. H. (1969). Changes in plasma potassium concentration after depolarizing blockers in anaesthetized man. *British Journal of Anaesthesia* **41**, 1048.

Whitwam, J. G. and Russell, W. J. (1971). The acute cardiovascular changes in adrenergic blockade by droperidol in man. *British Journal of Anaesthesia* **43**, 581.

Williams, C. H., Deutsch, S., Linde, H. W., Bullough, W. and Dripps. R. D. (1961). Effects of intravenously administered succinyldicholine on cardiac rate, rhythm, and arterial blood pressure in anesthetized man. *Anesthesiology* **22**, 947.

Wilson, R. D., Traber, D. L. and McCoy, N. R. (1968). Cardiopulmonary effects of CI-581 — the new dissociative anesthetic. *Southern Medical Journal* **61**, 692.

Wolff, G., Claudi, B., Rist, M., Wardak, M. R., Niederer, W. and Graedel, E. (1972). Regulation of coronary blood flow during ether and halothane anaesthesia. *British Journal of Anaesthesia* **44**, 1139.

Wong, K. C., Martin, W. E., Hornbein, T. F., Freund, F. G. and Everett, J. (1973). The cardiovascular effects of morphine sulfate with oxygen and with nitrous oxide in man. *Anesthesiology* **38**, 542.

Wyant, G. M. and Studney, L. J. (1970). A study of diazepam (Valium) for induction of anaesthesia. *Canadian Anaesthetists' Society Journal* **17**, 166.

Zauder, H. L., DelGuercio, L. R. M., Feins, N., Barton, N. and Wollman, S. (1965). Hemodynamics during neurolept analgesia. *Anesthesiology* **26**, 266.

Zink, J., Sasyniuk, B. I. and Dresel, P. E. (1975). Halothane–epinephrine-induced cardiac arrhythmias and the role of heart rate. *Anesthesiology* **43**, 548.

Zsigmond, E. K., Matsuki, A., Kothary, S. P. and Kelsch, R. C. (1974). The effect of pancuronium bromide on plasma norepinephrine and cortisol concentrations during thiamylal induction. *Canadian Anaesthetists' Society Journal* **21**, 147.

5

Assessment and preparation of the patient

Ischaemic heart disease, like degenerative or neoplastic disease, strikes at victims in their mature years. As many as 5 per cent of the adult population in Western Europe and North America have ischaemic heart disease. Therefore it can be expected that a significant number of surgical patients are also suffering from chronic myocardial ischaemia.

The aetiology of ischaemic heart disease is still unknown, but there are certain genetic, metabolic and environmental factors as well as personality traits identifiable in individuals suffering from the disease (Blackburn, 1974; Gertler and White, 1976). Age over 40 years and the male sex are the most important risk factors. Other major factors include arterial hypertension, hypercholesterolaemia and heavy cigarette smoking. The risk is also increased in diabetics, in patients with a strong family history, and in subjects who are obese and physically inactive. An increased prevalence in ambitious and driving individuals (type A personality) (Hartman, 1978) and in patients with hyperuricaemia (Persky *et al.*, 1979) is also reported. There is also higher mortality from ischaemic heart disease among females using oral contraceptives (Beral and Kay, 1977; Vessey, McPherson and Johnson, 1977). This risk is compounded if the user is also a smoker. Moderate coffee and alcohol consumptions are not risk factors (Yano, Rhoads and Kagan, 1977).

During the preoperative visit, the anaesthetist can identify the patient prone to ischaemic heart disease by the presence of major risk factors in the patient's history. All males over 40 years of age and females over 50 years must be considered possible victims of ischaemic heart disease.

The diagnosis of myocardial ischaemia

The most acute manifestation of myocardial ischaemia is *myocardial infarcation.* Although pain is not the only sympton of myocardial ischaemia, *angina pectoris* is a common complaint. *Stable angina* is chest pain related to exertion and relieved by rest or glyceryl trinitrate. Severe angina may suddenly develop without relief, or stable anginal symptoms may change in character, severity, extent of radiation and duration; the pain may become crescendo in nature or may even occur at rest without increased enzyme titre or serial electrocardiographic changes to suggest acute myocardial infarction. This is *unstable angina.* It is synonymous with impending myocardial infarction, pre-infarction angina, coronary insufficiency or intermediate coronary syndrome. Unstable angina implies a precarious blood flow to the affected myocardium and should be managed as acute myocardial infarction. A clinical history of typical angina pectoris alone is a sensitive and specific indicator of severe ischaemic heart disease (Piessens *et al.*, 1974), and a documented history of previous infarction makes the diagnosis unequivocal.

It is important to remember that a patient can have chest pain due to other aetiology such as hiatus hernia, gall bladder disease or chest wall pain. In those situations where the cause of chest pain is in doubt, a documentation of transient S_3 and S_4 gallop rhythms, mitral regurgitant murmur due to papillary muscle dysfunction, or electrocardiographic changes during an attack of pain will identify its cardiac origin. On the other hand, absence of anginal symptoms does not rule out myocardial ischaemia. Many patients with ischaemic heart disease develop ischaemic myopathy, rate and rhythm disturbances or die suddenly without a history of angina.

When angina is atypical, definitive diagnosis is more difficult. Vigorous investigation is necessary.

Laboratory methods

Electrocardiography

Electrocardiography is a useful diagnostic aid, especially when a previous electrocardiogram is available for comparison. Special attention should be paid to signs of myocardial ischaemia (ST segment depression), myocardial injury (ST segment elevation) and myocardial death (pathological Q wave). Disturbances of rate and rhythm are sometimes the only signs of ischaemic myopathy. As many as 50–83 per cent of patients with ischaemic heart disease have a normal electrocardiogram at rest (Master and Geller, 1969).

Exercise electrocardiography

The use of exercise to increase myocardial work and to induce myocardial ischaemia in susceptible patients forms the basis of the exercise stress test (Kappagoda, 1980). It is a useful non-invasive diagnostic test for patients with atypical angina, but it is contraindicated when the patient's resting electrocardiogram is unstable and when acute myocardial infarction or unstable angina is suspected.

The stress test was first made popular by the Master's 'two-step' exercise test (Master, Friedman and Dack, 1942) during which the number of steps taken by a patient is predetermined by his age and weight. With the motorized treadmill or the bicycle ergometer, exercise can now be graded and increased until angina develops or until a given percentage of the maximum heart rate, adjusted for the patient's age, is achieved. A horizontal or down-sloping ST segment depression of 1 mm or more on the electrocardiogram during or immediately after exercise is the usually accepted criterion of myocardial ischaemia (Piessens et al., 1974). This simple approach lacks sensitivity and specificity (Redwood and Epstein, 1972). Refinement in the interpretation of the stress test is being introduced to grade the response of the patient according to the presence of pre-test risk factors, the degree of ST segment depression, the duration of ischaemic changes, and the development of arrhythmias, hypotension or other clinical symptoms and signs consistent with myocardial ischaemia during and after exercise (Rifkin and Hood, 1977; Berman, Wynne and Cohn, 1978; Selzer, Cohn and Goldschlager, 1978; Cohn et al., 1979).

Radionuclide myocardial scintigraphy

After the intravenous administration of a radionuclide (potassium-43, caesium-129, rubidium-81 or thallium-201), the regional myocardial distribution of the radioactive isotope can be detected externally by a scintillation camera. Since it is distributed to the entire myocardium in proportion to the magnitude of the regional myocardial blood flow (Zaret, 1977), both ischaemic and infarcted myocardium will appear as a 'cold spot'. Thallium-201 is the most popular indicator used in clinical laboratories. It is a simple and safe non-invasive laboratory investigation. The sensitivity of this method may be increased by comparing myocardial perfusion scintigrams obtained with the patient at rest and after exercise.

Some other radionuclides (^{99m}Tc-tetracycline and ^{99m}Tc-pyrophosphate) are selectively concentrated in newly infarcted myocardium (hours to days old) (Wynne, Holman and Lesch, 1978). The infarcted region will show up as a 'hot spot' in these infarct-avid myocardial scintigrams.

Scintigraphy can also be performed after intracoronary injection of the radioactive isotopes of potassium and its analogues, and radioactive-labelled macro-aggregated albumin or microspheres (Strauss and Pitt, 1976). Regional myocardial uptake and washout of xenon-133 can also be determined after intracoronary injection (Cannon, Weiss and Sciacca, 1977). These invasive techniques are used only during coronary angiography.

Coronary angiography

Diagnostic coronary angiography is an invasive technique and should not be abused (Phibbs, 1979). It gives definitive information on the state of the coronary arteries, the location of diseased segments and the presence or absence of perfusion from collaterals (Abrams and Adams, 1969a, b). It is helpful when chest pain is atypical and other laboratory methods fail to establish a diagnosis. More commonly it is performed to assess the patient for coronary artery bypass operations.

Biochemical assays

The laboratory assay of serum activities of the enzymes lactate dehydrogenase (LD) and aspartate transaminase (AST) is an established practice in the diagnosis of acute myocardial infarction (Wilkinson, 1976). (Aspartate transaminase was named glutamate-oxaloacetate transaminase in the past.) Serum lactate dehydrogenase activity begins to rise 12 hours after the onset of myocardial necrosis, reaches a peak at 24–48 hours, and remains elevated for 7–10 days. Serum aspartate transaminase activity begins to rise as early as 6 hours after acute myocardial infarction, reaches a peak in 24–36 hours, and gradually returns to normal by the fifth day. However, changes in the serum activities of these enzymes are not specific for myocardial injury.

More recently it has been found that lactate dehydrogenase can be separated by electrophoresis and other techniques into five isoenzymes. Myocardial cells are more abundant in LD_1; a smaller quantity of LD_2 is also present. Activity of LD_1 rises and falls with lactate dehydrogenase activity after acute myocardial infarction (Wilkinson, 1976). This isoenzyme is also present in erythrocytes. Its activity is also elevated in certain haematological disorders and in muscular dystrophy.

Creatine kinase (CK), formerly called creatine phosphokinase, is abundant in myocardium, skeletal muscle and brain; but its isoenzyme, MB-CK (also known as CK_2), is a specific myocardial enzyme (Roberts *et al.*, 1975). The activity of the MB isoenzyme is elevated soon after acute myocardial infarction and returns to normal in 1–2 days. The rate of rise and fall in the serum activity of this isoenzyme, when obtained by serial determinations, is also a good index of the degree of myocardial damage (Shell and Sobel, 1976).

Myoglobinaemia occurs 6–12 hours after acute myocardial infarction. Serum myoglobin concentration can now be determined by very sensitive radioimmunoassay (Stone *et al.*, 1975). It is also elevated in skeletal muscle disorders.

Assessment of the cardiac status and preparation of the patient

Accurate preoperative assessment is essential so that patients can be brought to an optimum condition before operation. In a prospective study involving 1000 patients, Goldman and his colleagues (1977) found nine specific factors which they used successfully to predict the risk of postoperative life-threatening or fatal cardiac complications. Seven of the nine factors pertain to the cardiac status and general health of the patient; the other two, the type of surgical operation. These factors are:

1. S_3 gallop or jugular venous distension during the preoperative physical examination   (11 points).
2. Cardiac rhythms other than sinus or premature atrial contractions on

the preoperative electrocardiogram   (7 points).

3. More than 5 premature ventricular beats per minute documented at any time before the operation   (7 points).

4. A previous myocardial infarction within 6 months before the scheduled operation   (10 points).

5. Aortic stenosis   (3 points).

6. Age over 70 years   (5 points).

7. Poor general medical condition: arterial oxygen tension < 8 kPa (60 mmHg), arterial carbon dioxide tension > 6.7 kPa (50 mmHg), serum potassium < 3 mmol/l (3 mEq/l), serum bicarbonate < 20 mmol/l (20 mEq/l), serum urea > 18 mmol/l (blood urea nitrogen > 50 mg/100 ml), serum creatinine > 265 μmol/l (3 mg/100 ml), elevated transaminase, signs of chronic liver disease or patient bed-ridden from any non-cardiac cause   (3 points).

8. Intraperitoneal, intrathoracic or aortic operations   (3 points).

9. Emergency operations   (4 points).

Points (shown in parenthesis) were assigned to each factor in this study of Goldman et al. (1977), and a cardiac risk index for each patient was calculated by obtaining the sum of all the points the patient had accumulated. Four categories of patients (Class I to IV) were recognized (Table 5.1). Three-quarters of the class IV patients (score ≥ 26) had life-threatening cardiac complications postoperatively and half of them died as a consequence. This index is particularly applicable to patients with ischaemic heart disease. Of the nine factors, factor 1 (signs of heart failure), factors 2 and 3 (abnormal cardiac rhythms) and factor 7 (poor general medical condition) are potentially correctable, and factor 4 (operation within 6 months after an acute myocardial infarction) and factor 9 (emergency operations) are possibly avoidable. The prognostic significance of ventricular dysfunction, arrhythmias and a history of previous myocardial infarction is obvious.

Table 5.1   Cardiac risk index (Goldman et al., 1977)

Class	Score
I	0–5
II	6–12
III	13–25
IV	≥26

The assessment and treatment of ventricular dysfunction

The degree of left ventricular impairment is a major factor influencing the prognosis of patients with ischaemic heart disease (Burggraf and Parker, 1975). Similarly, congestive heart failure is a major factor in predicting postoperative cardiac complications (Goldman et al., 1977). The importance of maintaining optimum ventricular function in the patient with ischaemic heart disease cannot be emphasized too strongly.

The direct consequence of left ventricular impairment is pulmonary venous congestion. The clinical signs of left heart failure are pulsus alternans, rales, gallop rhythm and an accentuated pulmonic second sound. The patient complains of exertional dyspnoea, orthopnoea or paroxysmal nocturnal dyspnoea. In more severe cases the patient is dyspnoeic at rest and pulmonary oedema is imminent. Systemic complaints related to impaired cardiac output are anorexia, general malaise and easy fatigability. When more than 40 per cent of the ventricular muscle mass is lost, cardiogenic shock follows. Right heart impairment is accompanied by systemic venous congestion. The signs of right heart failure are dependent oedema, hepatomegaly, jugular venous distension and hepatojugular reflux. Although the left ventricle may fail alone, combined left and right failure (congestive heart failure) is usual. When heart failure develops in a previously stable patient, a precipitating cause can often be identified. The common causes are severe infections, myocardial infarction, arrhythmias, anaemia and mismanagement of fluid therapy.

Many patients have milder forms of ventricular dysfunction. The functional capacity of such a patient can be assessed by obtaining a detailed history of his exercise tolerance, which should include questions in the following areas:

1. Changes in physical activity.
2. Current exercise tolerance in terms of daily activities.
3. A comparison of current activities with those of peers.
4. Specific factors limiting physical activity.

The degree of incapacity can be classified according to the criteria of the New York Heart Association.

Class I: No limitation of ordinary physical activities.

Class II: Exertion from ordinary daily physical activities will result in fatigue, palpitation or dyspnoea.

Class III: Exertion from less than ordinary daily physical activities will result in fatigue, palpitation or dyspnoea.

Class IV: Patient is symptomatic at rest.

Attention to details in history taking is important. Vague answers can be misleading. For example:

1. There are other factors — such as intermittent claudication, respiratory disease, anaemia and arthritis — which can limit a patient's physical activity.

2. Due to the insidious onset, the patient may not be able to recall any change in exercise tolerance or may attribute its decline to advancing age.

3. The patient may be pacing himself according to his physical incapacity and can walk 'for miles without stopping' at his own pace.

4. The patient's peers may be worse cardiac invalids.

It may be necessary to pace the patient down the hospital corridor to determine his true disability. When exercising within his functional reserve, his blood pressure, pulse rate and respiratory rate should return to resting values within 2 minutes after cessation of exercise (Master, 1934–35).

In the assessment of ventricular function, electrocardiography, chest x-ray and other laboratory methods are also helpful.

Electrocardiography

Ventricular dysfunction is often, but not always, associated with asynergy of an ischaemic region or with ventricular aneurysm. The electrocardiographic signs of ventricular asynergy and ventricular aneurysm are pathological Q waves with or without persistent ST segment elevation (Bodenheimer, Banka and Helfant, 1975). A normal resting 12-lead electrocardiogram (defined by the absence of pathological Q waves, hypertrophy patterns, conduction abnormalities and abnormalities of repolarization as reflected by ST–T wave changes) is a reliable sign that ventricular asynergy and ventricular aneurysm are absent; but when other abnormalities are present, the absence of Q waves or ST segment changes alone does not rule out the absence of asynergy or aneurysm (Swartz et al., 1977).

Chest radiography

Cardiac enlargement or abnormal configuration of the cardiac silhouette, pulmonary venous and lymphatic congestion, and hydrothorax are radiological signs of ventricular failure. As with the electrocardiogram, the chest x-ray should be compared to old films of the patient when possible.

Other methods

Other laboratory methods of assessing ventricular function, which are available in specialized units, include the estimation of left ventricular ejection fraction, left ventricular wall motion and velocity of contraction by angiography (Dodge, 1977), echocardiography (Popp, 1977) and radionuclide imaging techniques (Pitt and Strauss, 1977).

If cardiac performance is compromised, treatment before anaesthesia and operation is mandatory. This will not be a problem when operation is not urgent. Treatment should include rest, oxygen therapy (when respiratory distress is present), the removal of precipitating causes, and the administration of a cardiac glycoside, a diuretic and a vasodilator. Improved ventricular function is accompanied by diuresis, a fall in resting heart rate, the clearing of symptons and signs related to systemic and pulmonary venous congestion, and improvement of exercise tolerance. When operation is urgent, rapidly acting intravenous medication should be used to bring the patient to an optimum condition in the time available. A short time well spent before operation will save endless anxiety afterwards.

Arrhythmias and their control

Disturbances of rate, rhythm and impulse conduction appear in many forms.

They can occur with or without angina or ventricular impairment. The causes may be ischaemic dysfunction of excitable and conducting tissues, fibrosis of the conducting system, electrolyte imbalance, or secondary to an overdose of digitalis or beta-blocking agents. Arrhythmias and conduction disturbances should be suspected if there is a history of palpitation or syncope, or if the patient's resting heart rate is below 60 per minute, is above 100 per minute, or is irregular. Diagnosis is by electrocardiography.

Arrhythmias and conduction disorders represent electrical instability of the heart. During operation and in the postoperative period haemodynamic instability, fluid and electrolyte shifts, acid–base disturbances and increased reflex irritability of the heart may enhance this instability. The incidence of arrhythmias in cardiac patients during anaesthesia and operation is high (Bertrand *et al.*, 1971). Before subjecting these patients to the stress of anaesthesia and operation, pre-existing arrhythmias should be controlled. The implantation of a pacemaker should be considered when there is doubt about the stability of cardiac impulse generation or conduction.

Atrial fibrillation and flutter

These are common supraventricular arrhythmias. When the ventricular response is fast, ventricular filling is impaired and ventricular output is reduced. Digitalis is the drug of choice in both situations. The objective is to slow the ventricular rate to 70–80 per minute. In the absence of heart failure, small doses of propranolol orally or intravenously, given in small increments to slow the ventricular rate, may be useful when digitalis alone fails. Direct-current countershock after the induction of general anaesthesia to convert atrial flutter and atrial fibrillation to sinus rhythm is the treatment of choice in selected cases. Conversion to sinus rhythm with quinidine is a potentially hazardous procedure and is best left in the hands of an experienced physician.

Sinus bradycardia

A heart rate of 50 per minute is tolerated by most patients. When it is slower, cardiac output is impaired. Bradycardia may be induced by digitalis or by beta antagonists. If so, the treatment is withdrawal of the causative agent. When bradycardia is inappropriate, sick sinus syndrome should be suspected.

Sick sinus syndrome

This syndrome has many names and appears in many types of heart disease, including ischaemic heart disease (Rubenstein *et al.*, 1972). It is characterized by inappropriate sinus bradycardia or sinus arrest and sinoatrial block with Stokes–Adams syncope (Ferrer, 1973). In conjunction with sinus brady-cardia, paroxysmal atrial tachyarrhythmias may occur: hence the name 'tachycardia–bradycardia syndrome' (Kaplan *et al.*, 1973). It may also present as atrial fibrillation with a slow ventricular rate which is unrelated to digitalis. When this syndrome is diagnosed, the implantation of a demand pacemaker is indicated.

Ventricular premature beats

After acute myocardial infarction, ventricular ectopic activity is a harbinger of ventricular fibrillation. The significance of ventricular premature beats in patients with chronic myocardial ischaemia is only emerging (Lesch, 1977). The prevalence of ventricular arrhythmias in patients with acute or chronic myocardial ischaemia, the association of these arrhythmias with sudden death, and the proper management of these arrhythmias have been reviewed in detail by Bigger and his associates (1977). Patients who have ventricular premature beats together with documented ischaemic heart disease, as well as those who have ventricular premature beats and major risk factors associated with ischaemic heart disease, do have an increased risk of sudden death.

Frequent ventricular premature beats (more than 5 per minute on ECG monitoring or more than 10 per hour on Holter monitoring), those which fall on the preceding T waves (R on T), those which run together in two or more successive beats, bigeminal premature beats and multifocal premature beats are more serious than the occasional premature ventricular contractions. The incidence of sudden cardiac death is reduced with anti-arrhythmic therapy. If these malignant types are suspected, Holter monitoring is indicated. When confirmed, anti-arrhythmic treatment should be instituted before induction of anaesthesia.

Both phenytoin and beta antagonists are useful anti-arrhythmic drugs in long-term therapy (Bigger *et al.*, 1977). In order for phenytoin to be effective, a therapeutic blood level of 10 μg/ml or above has to be achieved (Vajda *et al.*, 1973), and an oral dose of 300-400 mg has to be administered each day. The therapeutic blood level of propranolol is 50–100 μg/ml (Shand, 1974). Due to individual pharmacokinetic factors, the oral dose of propranolol required to achieve this level varies between 80 and 320 mg per day.

Intravenous lignocaine (a bolus of 1 mg/kg or an infusion of 2–4 mg per minute) is the most widely used anti-arrhythmic agent in the hands of the anaesthetist. Although not suitable for long-term therapy, it is a most useful agent during operation and in the postoperative period.

Conduction disorders

Impulse conduction in certain atrioventricular and fascicular conduction abnormalities is unstable; total atrioventricular block can develop suddenly with ventricular standstill. *Traditionally*, transvenous pacing instituted before anaesthesia and operation *was* considered indicated in the following conduction abnormalities:

1. Second degree heart block (Mobitz type II).
2. Acquired third degree heart block with Stokes–Adams attack.
3. Right bundle branch block with left anterior hemiblock (the criterion

of left anterior hemiblock is left axis deviation of more than −30 degrees).

4. Right bundle branch block with left posterior hemiblock (the criterion of left posterior hemiblock is right axis deviation of more than +120 degrees).

5. Trifascicular disease (e.g. intermittent right and left bundle branch blocks or right bundle branch block with intermittent left anterior and left posterior hemiblocks), particularly in conjunction with episodes of documented myocardial ischaemia.

While the indication for transvenous pacing is well recognized in sick sinus syndrome, symptomatic second or third degree heart block and trifascicular disease, the indication in chronic bifascicular conduction disturbances is less convincing. Right bundle branch block with left anterior hemiblock together with symptomatic bradyarrhythmias and right bundle branch block with left posterior hemiblock imply more advanced disease of the conducting system (Narula and Samet, 1971; McAnulty et al., 1978). Transvenous pacing instituted before the induction of general anaesthesia is still recommended in these conditions. Most studies have shown that the prophylactic pre-operative implantation of a pacemaker in the asymptomatic patient with only right bundle branch block and left anterior hemiblock is not necessary (Berg and Kotler, 1971; Kunstadt et al., 1973; Venkataraman, Madias and Hood, 1975), even when the PR interval is prolonged (Pastore et al., 1978). Serious arrhythmias associated with the introduction of transvenous pacing electrodes have been reported (Pastore et al., 1978). The extent of the operation and its possible complications should be weighed against the potential benefit and hazard of pacemaker implantation.

Myocardial infarction and anaesthesia

All authors agreed that patients with a history of myocardial infarction in the past had an increased frequency of suffering another infarction in the postoperative period (Topkins and Artusio, 1964; Tarhan et al.,1972). The most quoted study was done by Tarhan and his colleagues (1972). Nearly 33 000 patients 30 years of age and over, who had non-cardiac operations, were included in this survey. The findings are summarized as follows.

1. The incidence of myocardial infarction within the first postoperative week was 0.13 per cent among patients *without a history* of previous infarction; it was 6.5 per cent among patients *with a positive history*. That is, there is a 50-fold difference in the postoperative infarction rate between these two groups of patients.

2. Of patients with a history of infarction within *3 months* before operation, 37 per cent had another infarction in the postoperative period. The rate was only 16 per cent if the previous infarction had occurred *4–6 months* before operation. The rate *stabilized* at 5 per cent if the previous infarction had occurred *7 or more months* before operation. The rate in this last group of patients is still 40 times that in patients without a history of previous infarction.

3. There was no relation between the type or duration of anaesthesia and the incidence of myocardial infarction in the postoperative period.

4. The incidence of a further myocardial infarction was three times greater after operations involving the thorax and the upper abdomen.

The survey also showed that the course of a myocardial infarction in these surgical patients was different from that in the general population:

1. The mortality of 54 per cent among these patients in the postoperative period was nearly twice that of non-surgical patients suffering from myocardial infarction in a general hospital and three times that of patients in a coronary care unit.
2. Eighty per cent of these deaths occurred within 48 hours after myocardial infarction.
3. One-fifth of the repeated infarctions were silent. Chest pain was not a reliable warning sign in these patients, probably due to the use of narcotic analgesics and sedatives for the relief of postoperative pain.

In a follow-up study 6 years later, Steen, Tinker and Tarhan (1978) found that the incidence of another infarction in the postoperative period in patients with a history of previous myocardial infarction had improved slightly, although the difference between the results of the two studies was statistically not significant. From these results it can be concluded that elective surgery should not be performed on patients with a history of myocardial infarction within the previous 6 months. If the operation is semi-urgent, a delay of 3 months is advisable. Only the life-threatening urgency of the patient's surgical illness justifies early intervention.

Complications arising from treatment of the disease

Not only will impairment of ventricular function, arrhythmias and a history of previous myocardial infarction complicate anaesthesia, the treatments received by these patients will give rise to other difficulties. Digitalis is a time-honoured drug in the treatment of heart failure, and propranolol or other beta-adrenergic antagonists are very popular in the management of myocardial ischaemia, arrhythmias and hypertension. Electrical pacing of the heart with an implanted artificial pacemaker is now routine in many disorders of cardiac impulse formation or conduction. These agents, old and new, have introduced special problems for the anaesthetist. The assessment and management of these complications are discussed separately in Chapters 10, 11 and 12.

Preoperative laboratory investigation

Preoperative laboratory investigation should be appropriate. The value of the electrocardiogram and the chest x-ray has already been discussed. They should be part of the examination of all male surgical patients over the age of 40 years and female patients over 50 years. Other more sophisticated methods of investigation of ischaemia, ventricular function and arrhythmias should be considered only when clinical assessment is a problem or when the patient is severely handicapped by the disease.

Preoperative laboratory investigation should also include determination of haemoglobin, serum electrolyte and blood sugar concentrations. Other tests to be considered when indicated are digitalis level, arterial blood gas tensions, pulmonary function studies, blood urea nitrogen, serum creatinine and liver function tests.

Haemoglobin concentration

The oxygen-carrying capacity of blood is determined by its haemoglobin concentration. Anaemia is a common cause of myocardial ischaemia and heart failure.

Serum electrolytes

Hypokalaemia is a common complication of diuretic therapy. It is an important cause of arrhythmias. Digitalis toxicity is enhanced by hypo-kalaemia, and the effect of non-depolarizing muscle relaxants is prolonged.

Blood sugar

Diabetes mellitus is an important risk factor. All patients with ischaemic heart disease should be screened for this common endocrine disorder. Determination of the fasting and the 2-hour postprandial blood glucose concentrations is recommended.

Serum digitalis concentration

Digitalis toxicity should be diagnosed on clinical grounds. As the therapeutic and toxic serum concentrations overlap, the best confirmation of toxicity is improvement following withdrawal of the cardiac glycoside. Assay of serum digoxin or digitoxin level is indicated when digitalis intoxication is suspected or when a drug history is unobtainable (see 'The use of serum concentration assay' in Chapter 11).

Arterial blood gas and pulmonary function studies

Arterial blood gas measurement gives useful information on overall respiratory function and acid–base disturbance. Hypoxaemia, hypercarbia and acidosis indicate a poor prognosis. Since cigarette smoking is a major risk factor, it is not uncommon to find that the patient who has ischaemic heart disease also has chronic obstructive lung disease. Pulmonary function tests can be helpful to define the reversible component of abnormal respiratory function and to guide therapy.

Tests of renal and hepatic functions

Low cardiac output and systemic venous congestion found in severe heart failure may disturb both renal and hepatic functions. Blood urea nitrogen, serum creatinine and bilirubin concentrations are useful indicators. They will return to normal with improvement of ventricular function.

General preparation of the patient

The general condition of the patient should be optimum before operation. Unnecessary 'emergency' surgery should be discouraged. Anaemia, electrolyte and acid–base abnormalities should be corrected. The diabetic should be treated, and the smoker should be persuaded to stop smoking. Respiratory disease should be treated with physiotherapy, bronchodilator therapy and antibiotics when indicated. Hypertensive patients are best left on their medications.

Pre-anaesthetic medication

Although it has been suggested that patients can arrive in the operating room co-operative and free from anxiety without the help of a sedative if the anaesthetist can impart confidence during his preoperative visit, patients with ischaemic heart disease are acutely aware of their chronic disability; they are more apprehensive than the general surgical population. They should be approached with sympathy and candour. The anaesthetist should be willing to discuss with his patients all aspects of general medical and anaesthetic management. Rapport and confidence should be established, but some pre-anaesthetic sedation is necessary.

Preoperative medication should include a suitable hypnotic given the night before operation. If the operation is scheduled late in the day, diazepam, 10 mg orally on rising, is indicated. The pre-anaesthetic sedative should be given 1–2 hours before the scheduled time of the operation. The aim is to produce mild sedation without undue respiratory depression. Any usual combination of a narcotic analgesic and a mood-modifying agent is acceptable. Anticholinergic drugs are not necessary; they cause a dry mouth and add to the distress of the patient.

References

Abrams, H. L. and Adams, D. F. (1969a). The coronary arteriogram (first of two parts): structural and functional aspects. *New England Journal of Medicine* **281**, 1276.

Abrams, H. L. and Adams, D. F. (1969b). The coronary arteriogram (second of two parts): structural and functional aspects. *New England Journal of Medicine* **281**, 1336.

Beral, V. and Kay, C. R. (1977). Mortality among oral-contraceptive users. *Lancet* **ii**, 727.

Berg, G. R. and Kotler, M. N. (1971). The significance of bilateral bundle branch block in the preoperative patient. *Chest* **59**, 62.

Berman, J. L., Wynne, J. and Cohn, P. F. (1978). A multivariate approach for interpreting treadmill exercise tests in coronary artery disease. *Circulation* **58**, 505.

Bertrand, C. A., Steiner, N. V., Jameson, A. G. and Lopez, M. (1971). Disturbances of cardiac rhythm during anesthesia and surgery. *Journal of the American Medical Association* **216**, 1615.

Bigger, J. T. Jr, Dresdale, R. J., Heissenbuttel, R. H., Weld, F. M. and Wit, A. L. (1977). Ventricular arrhythmias in ischemic heart disease: mechanism, prevalence, significance, and management. *Progress in Cardiovascular Diseases* **19**, 255.

Blackburn, H. (1974). Progress in the epidemiology and prevention of coronary heart disease. In: *Progress in Cardiology,* Vol. 3, pp. 1–35. Ed. by P. N. Yu and J. F. Goodwin. Lea & Febiger: Philadelphia.

Bodenheimer, M. M., Banka, V. S. and Helfant, R. H. (1975). Q waves and ventricular asynergy: predictive value and hemodynamic significance of anatomic localization. *American Journal of Cardiology* **35**, 615.

Burggraf, G. W. and Parker, J. O. (1975). Prognosis in coronary artery disease: angiographic, hemodynamic, and clinical factors. *Circulation* **51**, 146.

Cannon, P. J., Weiss, M. B. and Sciacca, R. R. (1977). Myocardial blood flow in coronary artery disease: studies at rest and during stress with inert gas washout techniques. *Progress in Cardiovascular Diseases* **20**, 95.

Cohn, K., Kamm, B., Feteih, N., Brand, R. and Goldschlager, N. (1979). Use of treadmill score to quantify ischemic response and predict extent of coronary disease. *Circulation* **59**, 286.

Dodge, H. T. (1977). Angiographic evaluation of ventricular function. *New England Journal of Medicine* **296**, 551.

Ferrer, M. I. (1973). Symposium: Cardiac arrhythmias (part 3). The sick sinus syndrome. *Circulation* **47**, 635.

Gertler, M. M. and White, P. D. (1976). *Coronary Heart Disease: A Twenty-Five Year Study in Retrospect.* Medical Economics Co., Book Division: Oradell, New Jersey.

Goldman, L., Caldera, D. L., Nussbaum, S. R., Southwick, F. S., Krogstad, D., Murray, B., Burke, D. S., O'Malley, T. A., Goroll, A. H., Caplan, C. H., Nolan, J., Carabello, B. and Slater, E. E. (1977). Multifactorial index of cardiac risk in noncardiac surgical procedures. *New England Journal of Medicine* **297**, 845.

Hartman, L. M. (1978). Behavioral prevention of ischemic heart disease. *Canadian Medical Association Journal* **119**, 599.

Kaplan, B. M., Langedorf, R., Lev. M. and Pick, A. (1973). Tachycardia–bradycardia syndrome (so-called 'sick sinus syndrome'). *American Journal of Cardiology* **31**, 497.

Kappagoda, C. T. (1980). Critical review of routine exercise testing. *Modern Medicine of Canada* **35**, 1187.

Kunstadt, D., Punja, M., Cagin, N., Fernandez, P., Levitt, B. and Yuceoglu, Y. Z. (1973). Bifascicular block: a clinical and electrophysiologic study. *American Heart Journal* **86**, 173.

Lesch, M. (1977). VPBs — the benign and the malignant. *New England Journal of Medicine* **297**, 782.

McAnulty, J. H., Rahimtoola, S. H., Murphy, E. S., Kauffman, S., Ritzmann, L. W., Kanarek, P. and DeMots, H. (1978). A prospective study of sudden death in 'high-risk' bundle-branch block. *New England Journal of Medicine* **299**, 209.

Master, A. M. (1934–35). The two-step test of myocardial function. *American Heart Journal* **10**, 495.

Master, A. M. and Geller, A. J. (1969). The extent of completely asymptomatic coronary artery disease. *American Journal of Cardiology* **23**, 173.

Master, A. M., Friedman, R. and Dack, S. (1942). The electrocardiogram after standard exercise as a functional test of the heart. *American Heart Journal* **24**, 777.

Narula, O. S. and Samet, P. (1971). Right bundle branch block with normal, left or right axis deviation: analysis by His bundle recordings. *American Journal of Medicine* **51**, 432.

Pastore, J. O., Yurchak, P. M., Janis, K. M., Murphy, J. D. and Zir, L. M. (1978). The risk of advanced heart block in surgical patients with right bundle branch block and left axis deviation. *Circulation* **57**, 677.

Persky, V. W., Dyer, A. R., Idris-Soven, E. Stamler, J., Shekelle, R. B., Schoenberger, J. A., Berkson, D. M. and Lindberg, H. A. (1979). Uric acid: a risk factor for coronary heart disease? *Circulaton* **59**, 969.

Phibbs, B. (1979). The abuse of coronary arteriography. *New England Journal of Medicine* **301**, 1394.

Piessens, J., Van Mieghem, W., Kesteloot, H. and De Geest, H. (1974). Diagnostic value of clinical history, exercise testing and atrial pacing in patients with chest pain. *American Journal of Cardiology* **33**, 351.

Pitt, B. and Strauss, H. W. (1977). Evaluation of ventricular function by radioisotopic technics. *New England Journal of Medicine* **296**, 1097.

Popp, R. L. (1977). Current concepts in cardiology: echocardiographic evaluation of left ventricular function. *New England Journal of Medicine* **296**, 856.

Redwood, D. R. and Epstein, S. E. (1972). Uses and limitations of stress testing in the evaluation of ischemc heart disease. *Circulation* **46**, 1115.

Rifkin, R. D. and Hood, W. B. Jr (1977). Bayesian analysis of electrocardiographic excrcise stress testing. *New England Journal of Medicine* **297**, 681.

Roberts, R., Gowda, K. S., Lundbrook, P. A. and Sobel, B. E. (1975). Specificity of elevated serum MB creatine phosphokinase activity in the diagnosis of acute myocardial infarction. *American Journal of Cardiology* **36**, 433.

Rubenstein, J. J., Schulman, C. L., Yurchak, P. M. and DeSanctis, R. W. (1972). Clinical spectrum of the sick sinus syndrome. *Circulation* **46**, 5.

Selzer, A., Cohn, K. and Goldschlager, N. (1978). On the interpretation of the exercise test. *Circulation* **58**, 193.

Shand, D. G. (1974). Individualization of propranolol therapy. *Medical Clinics of North America* **58**, 1063.

Shell, W. E. and Sobel, B. E. (1976). Biochemical markers of ischemic injury. *Circulation* **53**, Suppl. I, I-98.

Steen, P. A., Tinker, J. H. and Tarhan, S. (1978). Myocardial reinfarction after anesthesia and surgery. *Journal of the American Medical Association* **239**, 2566.

Stone, M. J., Willerson, J. T., Gomez-Sanchez, C. E. and Waterman, M. R. (1975). Radioimmunoassay of myoglobin in human serum: results in patients with acute myocardial infarction. *Journal of Clinical Investigation* **56**, 1334.

Strauss, H. W. and Pitt, B. (1976). Myocardial perfusion imaging in the evaluation of patients with coronary heart disease. In: *Progress in Cardiology*, Vol. 5, pp. 169–82. Ed. by P. N. Yu and J. F. Goodwin. Lea & Febiger: Philadelphia.

Swartz, M. H., Pichard, A. D., Meller, J., Teichholz, L. E. and Herman, M. V. (1977). The normal electrocardiogram as a predictor of left ventricular function in patients with coronary artery disease. *British Heart Journal* **39**, 208.

Tarhan, S., Moffitt, E. A., Taylor, W. F. and Giuliani, E. R. (1972). Myocardial infarction after general anesthesia. *Journal of the American Medical Association* **220**, 1451.

Topkins, M. J. and Artusio, J. F. (1964). Myocardial infarction and surgery: a five year study. *Anesthesia and Analgesia . . . Current Researches* **43**, 716.

Vajda, F. J. E., Prineas, R. J., Lovell, R. R. H. and Sloman, J. G. (1973). The possible effect of long-term high plasma levels of phenytoin on mortality after acute myocardial infarction. *European Journal of Clinical Pharmacology* **5**, 138.

Venkataraman, K., Madias, J. E. and Hood, W. B. Jr (1975). Indications for prophylactic preoperative insertion of pacemakers in patients with right bundle branch block and left anterior hemiblock. *Chest* **68**, 501.

Vessey, M. P., McPherson, K. and Johnson, B. (1977). Mortality among women participating in the Oxford/Family Planning Association Contraceptive Study. *Lancet* **ii**, 731.

Wilkinson, J. H. (1976). *The Principles and Practice of Diagnostic Enzymology*. Edward Arnold: London.

Wynne, J., Holman, B. L. and Lesch, M. (1978). Myocardial scintigraphy by infarct-avid radiotracers. *Progress in Cardiovascular Diseases* **20**, 243.

Yano, K., Rhoads, G. G. and Kagan, A. (1977). Coffee, alcohol and risk of coronary heart disease among Japanese men living in Hawaii. *New England Journal of Medicine* **297**, 405.

Zaret, B. L. (1977). Myocardial imaging with radioactive potassium and its analogs. *Progress in Cardiovascular Dieases* **20**, 81.

6

Monitoring

The continuous monitoring of physiological functions of the anaesthetized patient has directly contributed to the safety of modern anaesthesia. The monitoring of blood pressure, heart rate, cardiac rhythm, respiratory volumes and body temperature, etc. has become standard practice in the operating theatre. In the last decade clinical measurements in special areas have advanced rapidly. In patients with ischaemic heart disease, changes in the ST segment of the electrocardiogram is found useful as evidence of myocardial ischaemia; heart rate, systolic blood pressure and left ventricular filling pressure, either alone or in combination, are used as indirect indices of myocardial work. The introduction of the Swan–Ganz pulmonary arterial catheter has made simple the measurement of left ventricular filling pressure, cardiac output, systemic vascular resistance and pulmonary vascular resistance. The indices of myocardial ischaemia and myocardial work are helpful to guide therapy in protecting the ischaemic myocardium. Invasive haemodynamic monitoring can determine more accurately circulatory function. These invasive techniques are also necessary when potent vasoactive drugs are used to treat myocardial ischaemia. This chapter is dedicated to a discussion of the indications and the application of these special monitoring techniques in patients with ischaemic heart disease.

Indices of myocardial ischaemia and myocardial work

The electrocardiogram

Abnormalities of repolarization seen on the surface electrocardiogram as ST segment changes are some of the earliest signs of myocardial ischaemia. Therefore the electrocardiogram can be used for detecting myocardial ischaemia as well as for monitoring cardiac rate and rhythm. Mason *et al.* (1967) found that ischaemia of the anterior and lateral walls of the heart was more common during exercise electrocardiography in patients with angina pectoris. The precordial leads V_4, V_5 and V_6 were most often positive in this study. Since electrocardiographic monitoring with multiple leads is not practical during operation, the precordial lead V_5 (left anterior axillary line at the fifth interspace) should be used (Kaplan and King, 1976). If the electrocardioscope is designed for monitoring bipolar limb leads only, a modified V_5 should be used. The most popular modifications are the CM_5 (Foëx and Prys-Roberts, 1974) and the CS_5 (Blitt, 1980). In the CM_5

modification, the right arm electrode of lead I is placed over the manubrium sterni, the left arm electrode is placed over the V_5 position, and the ground electrode is placed on the left shoulder. The CS_5 modification is very similar to the CM_5, but the right arm electrode is placed on the right shoulder.

If more than one lead can be monitored, lead II (right arm to left leg) as well as V_5 is recommended because changes in the inferior wall are more accurately reflected by inferior leads (Kistner, Miller and Epstein, 1977). This is particularly important in patients who have disease of the right coronary artery. Being parallel to the P wave vector, lead II is also best for monitoring rhythm disturbances.

In all cases the electrocardiogram should be standardized to 1 cm deflection for each millivolt. A horizontal or down-sloping ST segment depression of 1 mm or more in any lead is a positive sign of the presence of myocardial ischaemia. However, this objective evidence of myocardial ischaemia is relatively insensitive. The absence of ST segment depression does not rule out the presence of ischaemia entirely. Additional monitoring is necessary.

The heart rate

Heart rate alone is the most important determinant of myocardial work (see 'Determinants of myocardial work' in Chapter 2). As heart rate increases, all the frequency-dependent factors affecting myocardial work increase. Kitamura and his co-workers (1972) found a good correlation between heart rate and the oxygen cost of myocardial work in healthy subjects; and Detry, Piette and Brasseur (1970) found similar correlation between heart rate and the magnitude of ST segment depression in patients with ischaemic heart disease (correlation coefficients better than 0.88 in both studies). In patients with ischaemic heart disease, a heart rate beyond 90 per minute represents not only excessive myocardial work, but also a critical reduction of the duration of diastole during which significant coronary blood flow occurs (see 'Coronary blood flow in the ischaemic heart' in Chapter 2). On the other hand, cardiac output falls when heart rate is below 50 per minute. Therefore heart rate should be kept within the range of 50–90 per minute in these patients.

The rate–pressure product

The product of heart rate and systolic blood pressure (rate–pressure product) correlates with myocardial work even better than heart rate alone in healthy patients as well as in those with ischaemic heart disease (Kitamura et al., 1972; Gobel et al., 1978). Robinson (1967) as well as Cokkinos and Voridis (1976) reported that the precipitation of angina in patients suffering from chronic myocardial ischaemia could be related consistently to a critical rate–pressure product. This critical product was essentially constant in each patient regardless of whether it was produced by a relatively greater increase of heart rate or of systolic blood pressure. Nelson et al. (1974) showed that this correlation held true whether systolic blood pressure was obtained directly by intra-arterial measurement or indirectly by auscultation. In order to prevent myocardial ischaemia, the rate–pressure product of patients with ischaemic heart disease should be kept below this critical value during operation.

Products ranging between 12 000 and 20 000 have been recommended as acceptable for these patients under anaesthesia. These values are only arbitrary. In fact, the management of these patients can be individualized. The resting heart rate and blood pressure of each patient will yield a product representing myocardial work at rest. After moderate exercise (not to the point of angina), the higher rate–pressure product obtained is a measure of the increase in myocardial work which can be tolerated. Exercise to the point of angina in a cardiac investigation unit can be used to obtain the absolute maximum rate–pressure product which is tolerable. These simple procedures should be done during the preoperative visit. The documented resting and tolerable rate–pressure products are valuable guides for the management of these patients under anaesthesia. Since an increase in heart rate increases myocardial work and reduces subendocardial blood flow, an increase in heart rate leads to a more severe degree of ischaemia than does an increase in blood pressure (Loeb *et al.*, 1978). Therefore, not only should the rate–pressure product of these patients be kept within the tolerable limits defined, but also the heart rate should be kept below 90 per minute.

The triple products

In the hope of finding better indirect indices of myocardial work, the use of triple products (heart rate × systolic pressure × pulmonary capillary wedge pressure, and heart rate × systolic pressure × systolic ejection period) have been explored. These triple products are disappointing. Nelson *et al.* (1974) found that their correlation with myocardial work was not as good as that of heart rate alone. Furthermore, to obtain pulmonary capillary wedge pressure or ejection period, cannulation of the pulmonary or a systemic artery is necessary. These invasive procedures limit the application of the triple products even further.

The tension time index (TTI)

The tension time index was proposed by Sarnoff, Braunwald and their colleagues (1958) to be a major determinant of myocardial work. It is obtained from the area under the systolic portion of the arterial pressure curve as illustrated in Fig. 6.1. However, Nelson and his group (1974) showed that this index correlated poorly with myocardial work in man. It is an invasive measurement and arterial cannulation is required. To obtain the area under the curve, cumbersome planimetry is necessary unless equipment for electronic integration and instant display is available.

The endocardial viability ratio (EVR)

The area between the diastolic portion of the arterial pressure curve and the left ventricular filling pressure, as illustrated in Fig. 6.1, is termed the diastolic pressure time index (DPTI). It was found by Buckberg *et al.* (1972) to be an index of myocardial blood flow in dogs with normal coronary arteries. If the tension time index (TTI) is an index of myocardial work, the ratio of DPTI:TTI (i.e. the endocardial viability ratio) will be a measure of the adequacy of myocardial blood flow in relation to myocardial work. The reduction of this ratio to a critical value will result in myocardial ischaemia. This is particularly true for the subendocardium, which has a smaller circulatory reserve than the subepicardium. The normal endocardial viability ratio is 1 or above. Subendocardial ischaemia will occur when this ratio falls to 0.75 or below (Philips *et al.*, 1975). Again, this is an invasive monitor. Furthermore, the accuracy of tension time index and diastolic pressure time index as indices of myocardial work and myocardial blood supply in patients with ischaemic heart disease is being questioned.

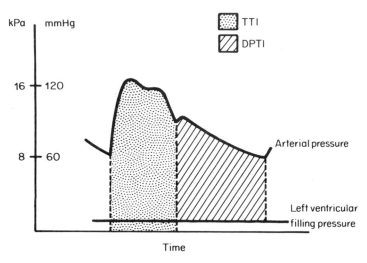

Fig. 6.1   The tension time index (TTI) and the diastolic pressure time index (DPTI). Tension time index is an index of myocardial work, and the diastolic pressure time index is an index of myocardial blood supply. The ratio of DPTI:TTI is the endocardial viability ratio (EVR).

Invasive haemodynamic monitoring

Equipment for the direct measurement of arterial pressure via an indwelling catheter, for the indirect measurement of left ventricular filling pressure via a Swan–Ganz pulmonary arterial catheter and for the measurement of cardiac output by the thermodilution method are now available commercially. As yet, there is no general agreement on the indications for invasive haemodynamic monitoring. There are serious complications associated with all these invasive procedures. The decision to use them should depend on the experience of the clinician and the supportive staff, and on the benefit to the patient. Dogmatism must be avoided.

Direct measurement of arterial blood pressure

Peripheral arteries, including the radial artery at the wrist, the brachial artery at the elbow and the dorsalis pedis artery of the foot, can be cannulated with a 20 to 23 gauge plastic cannula for direct arterial blood pressure monitoring. The left axillary and the femoral arteries have also been used. Cannulation of the radial artery is the most popular. Adequate collateral flow from the ulnar artery to supply the entire hand should be demonstrated by the Allen's test (Allen, 1929) before its cannulation. The test involves manual occlusion of both the radial and the ulnar arteries while the patient makes a tight fist. When the pressure on the ulnar artery alone is released with the hand and fingers relaxed in a neutral position, rapid capillary filling of the radial aspect of the hand, particularly the thenar eminence and the thumb, is a sign of adequate collateral circulation from the ulnar artery. Complications of direct radial arterial blood pressure monitoring include thrombosis of the cannulated artery (Bedford and Wollman, 1973), local ischaemia (Downs *et al.*, 1973), local infection and septicaemia (Rose, 1979) and peripheral and cerebral embolism (Lowenstein, Little and Lo, 1971). When proper care is exercised, these complications are rare (Davis and Stewart, 1980).

Direct arterial blood pressure monitoring with special reference to surgical patients suffering from chronic myocardial ischaemia should be considered in the following circumstances, both during operation and in the post-operative period.

1. Recent myocardial infarction, particularly within the last 3 months.
2. Unstable angina.
3. Pulmonary oedema and congestive heart failure.
4. Major arrhythmias.
5. A classification of IV in the cardiac risk index (see 'Assessment of the cardiac status and preparation of the patient' in Chapter 5).
6. Major and extensive operations (e.g. pancreatectomy, major peripheral vascular, thoracic and intracranial operations).
7. Respiratory failure.
8. Other severe concomitant illness (e.g. renal failure, unstable diabetes and multiple trauma) requiring intensive care postoperatively.
9. Vasodilator therapy with potent intravenous agents (nitroprusside and glyceryl trinitrate).

Central venous pressure and left ventricular filling pressure

Central venous pressure is an indirect measurement of right atrial pressure and right ventricular filling pressure. It ranges between 0.5 and 1 kPa (4–8 mmHg) from the mid-axillary line in patients breathing spontaneously. It is a reasonable index of blood volume and right ventricular function. Even in normal healthy individuals, it is a relatively poor index of left ventricular function. This is because the normal right ventricular function curve is steeper and lies to the left of the normal left ventricular function curve (Forrester *et al.*, 1971). When a fluid load is given to such a normal individual (Fig. 6.2), the stroke volume of the right and left ventricles will rise equally (from A to B). As can be seen, the filling pressures of the right and left

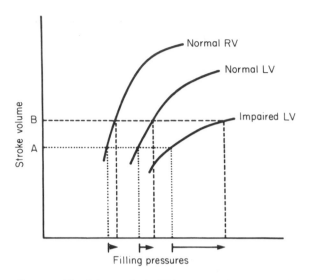

Fig. 6.2   The right ventricular (RV) and the left ventricular (LV) function curves. This diagram illustrates the discrepancy between changes in right ventricular filling pressure and left ventricular filling pressure following a fluid load. When left ventricular function is impaired, this discrepancy is further exaggerated.

ventricles change in the same direction, but the rise in the left ventricular filling pressure is larger than that of the right ventricle due to the position of the respective ventricular function curves. When left ventricular function alone is impaired, the discrepancy between the rise in the right and the left ventricular filling pressures is even greater with the same fluid load (Fig. 6.2). Paradoxically, when left ventricular function is unstable (Fig. 6.3), a deterioration of left ventricular function (from C to D) is accompanied by a fall in both left and right ventricular outputs, a rise in left ventricular filling pressure, but a fall in right ventricular filling pressure. Hence central venous pressure correlates poorly with left ventricular filling pressure in patients with poor ventricular function, and bears no relationship to changes in left ventricular filling pressure in the presence of disparity of the ventricles.

Civetta, Gabel and Laver (1971) found that disparity of left and right ventricular functions was common in surgical patients with ischaemic heart disease, particularly in victims of multiple trauma and in patients with advanced cirrhosis or severe peritonitis. Similar disparity was observed in patients with ischaemic heart disease during cross-clamping of the abdominal aorta. In these situations, measurement of left ventricular filling pressure provides better information on left ventricular function than central venous pressure. In the absence of mitral valve disease, pulmonary artery diastolic pressure (pulmonary artery end-diastolic pressure), mean pulmonary capillary wedge pressure (pulmonary artery wedge pressure or pulmonary artery occlusion pressure) and mean left atrial pressure are equal. They are acceptable indirect measurements of left ventricular end-diastolic pressure, which is the true left ventricular filling pressure. The normal range is from

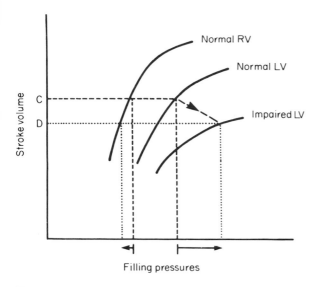

Fig. 6.3   The right ventricular (RV) and left ventricular (LV) function curves. When the left ventricle is unstable, the onset of left ventricular impairment is followed by a rise in left ventricular filling pressure but a fall in right ventricular filling pressure.

0.8 to 1.6 kPa (6–12 mmHg) in patients breathing spontaneously.

With the introduction of the flow-directed balloon-tipped (Swan–Ganz) catheter (Swan *et al.*, 1970), catheterization of the pulmonary artery and indirect measurement of left ventricular filling pressure by pulmonary arterial blood pressures (diastolic and wedge) has been made simple. A good correlation between pulmonary capillary wedge pressure and left atrial pressure has been demonstrated by several studies (Fitzpatrick, Hampson and Burgess, 1972; Lappas *et al.*, 1973; Humphrey *et al.*, 1976). If the catheter fails to wedge into position, the pulmonary artery diastolic pressure is still a reasonable, though less accurate, measurement of left atrial pressure. However, the interpretation of pulmonary capillary wedge pressure or pulmonary artery diastolic pressure is not always simple, especially in the following circumstances.

1. In patients with mitral stenosis, pulmonary arterial blood pressures (diastolic and wedge) and left atrial pressure are higher than left ventricular filling pressure.

2. In the presence of pulmonary hypertension, pulmonary diastolic pressure correlates poorly with left atrial pressure and left ventricular filling pressure (Fitzpatrick, Hampson and Burgess, 1972).

3. The correlation of mean wedge pressure and left atrial pressure is excellent up to 1.3 kPa (10 mmHg). The error increases beyond this point, but the correlation is still reasonable. At a pressure of 3.5 kPa (26 mmHg) and above, the correlation is poor (Walston and Kendall, 1973).

4. If the catheter tip is allowed to migrate to a region of the lung where the alveolar pressure is greater than the pulmonary venous pressure (zone 1 and

zone 2), wedge pressure will reflect alveolar pressure and not left atrial pressure (Pace, 1977). Furthermore, this error is inconsistent if the patient is allowed to change position or when positive pressure is applied to the airway.

5. In patients with chronic obstructive pulmonary disease who have a high intrathoracic pressure during active expiration, the measured wedge pressure overestimates the left atrial pressure (Rice et al., 1974). The authors suggested that a correction could be made in such a case by subtracting the mean intrathoracic pressure (obtained by measurement of oesophageal pressure) from the measured wedge pressure to obtain the 'effective wedge pressure'. Alternatively, the wedge pressure can be measured during a period of apnoea at the end of expiration with the glottis opened. These manoeuvres are recommended in patients whose intrathoracic pressure fluctuates more than 2.7 kPa (20 mmHg) during inspiration and expiration.

6. In the presence of acute myocardial infarction and in other situations when left ventricular compliance is low (e.g. left ventricular hypertrophy and other myopathies), *left ventricular filling* is dependent on *left atrial systole* (Rahimtoola et al., 1972). Therefore *mean left atrial pressure* is lower than left ventricular end-diastolic pressure, and pulmonary arterial pressure (diastolic and wedge) are poor measurements of the left ventricular filling pressure. Nevertheless, in this situation pulmonary capillary wedge pressure is still a true reflection of pulmonary venous pressure and will give warning of pulmonary congestion.

7. During controlled ventilation, when peak inflation pressure is 2 kPa (20 cmH$_2$O) or more, Schapira and Daum (1974) observed a large discrepancy between pulmonary capillary wedge pressure and left atrial pressure. Similar discrepancies exist between wedge pressure and left atrial pressure when positive end-expiratory pressure is applied, particularly when it is 1 kPa (10 cmH$_2$O) or more (Hobelmann et al., 1974; Lozman et al., 1974). Furthermore, increased intrathoracic pressure has a deleterious effect on venous return and cardiac output. Measurements made when controlled ventilation is discontinued temporarily do not reflect the true haemodynamic state of that patient when ventilation is controlled. This is also true in the case of positive end-expiratory pressure (Geer, 1977). There are no simple solutions in these situations. The best compromise is to make measurements during the end-expiratory phase over several cycles to obtain an averaged value (Berryhill, Benumoff and Rauscher, 1978). The pulmonary artery pressures (diastolic and wedge) thus obtained still may not reflect true left ventricular filling pressure. Therefore the trend of the pulmonary artery pressures is more important than absolute values.

Indications for the measurement of left ventricular filling pressure via a pulmonary arterial catheter varies between centres. Some are very liberal in its use; others are extremely conservative. Although the Swan–Ganz catheter has simplified this measurement, it still involves catheterization of the right heart and the pulmonary artery. Reported complications include ventricular arrhythmias (Shaw, 1979) and heart block (Abernathy, 1974), thromboembolism and pulmonary infarction (Foote, Schabel and Hodges, 1974), aseptic and bacterial endocarditis (Greene, Fitzwater and Clemmer, 1975; Pace and Horton, 1975), perforation of the pulmonary artery (Chun and Ellestad, 1971), intracardiac knotting of the catheter (Lipp, O'Donoghue and Resnekov, 1971), damage to the pulmonary valve (O'Toole *et al.*, 1979) and inadvertent catheterization of the carotid artery (P. J. Bradwell, 1979, personal communication). The incidence of these complications may have been under-reported.

On the other hand, the measurement of central venous pressure is simpler. It has served more than a generation of physicians well. In a group of patients with ischaemic heart disease, Mangano (1980) found that central venous pressure and pulmonary capillary wedge pressure correlated well in those with normal ventricular function. He suggested that monitoring of pulmonary capillary wedge pressure was necessary, and monitoring of central venous pressure was of little value, only in a subgroup of patients who had abnormal ventricular function preoperatively. The indications for monitoring pulmonary artery pressures in patients with ischaemic heart disease during operation and in the postoperative period are:

1. Recent history of myocardial infarction, particularly when the patient is still in the hospital phase of his convalescence.
2. Unstable angina.
3. Pulmonary oedema and congestive heart failure.
4. Operations of the abdominal aorta.
5. Extensive operations (e.g. total pancreatectomy or oesophagectomy).
6. Critically ill patients, particularly those with multiple trauma, advanced cirrhosis and generalized peritonitis or sepsis, and those in shock.
7. Vasodilator therapy.

The measurement of cardiac output

The use of a 7 Fr multi-purpose Swan–Ganz catheter equipped with a thermistor close to its tip has made the measurement of cardiac output by the thermodilution technique accessible to the clinical anaesthetist (Weisel, Berger and Hechtman, 1975). The determination of cardiac output also enables the anaesthetist to calculate other derived haemodynamic variables; the more important ones are stroke volume, stroke work, systemic vascular resistance and pulmonary vascular resistance. These derived variables can be calculated according to the formulae in Table 6.1.

In order to make the comparison between individuals possible, cardiac output, stroke volume and left ventricular stroke work can be divided by the surface area of the patient to give cardiac index, stroke index and left ventricular stroke work index. Left ventricular stroke work (external work) or its index is one of the factors determining myocardial work. Systemic vascular resistance is directly related to left ventricular afterload — another determinant of myocardial work. Furthermore, the determination of vascular resistance gives insight into the state of the systemic and pulmonary circulations.

The indicator used in this thermodilution method is cold 5% dextrose solution. At present there are several portable thermodilution cardiac output

Table 6.1 Derived haemodynamic variables

Formulae	Normal values	
	Old unit	SI unit
$SV = \dfrac{CO}{HR} \times 1000$	60–80 ml/beat	60–80 ml/beat
$LVSW = (\overline{AP} - \overline{PCWP}) \times SV \times 0.0136$	70–100 g·m/beat	0.7–1 J/beat
$SVR = \dfrac{\overline{AP} - CVP}{CO} \times 80$	900–1500 dyne·sec/cm^5	90–150 kPa·s·l^{-1}
$PVR = \dfrac{\overline{PAP} - \overline{PCWP}}{CO} \times 80$	90–150 dyne·sec/cm^5	9–15 kPa·s·l^{-1}
$\overline{P} = \dfrac{SP + DP \times 2}{3}$		

The conversion factor used to change stroke work from the old unit to the SI unit is 10^{-2} (approximate); the conversion factor used to change vascular resistance is 10^{-1} (exact).

$\overline{AP}$, mean arterial pressure; CO, cardiac output; CVP, central venous pressure; DP, diastolic pressure; HR, heart rate; LVSW, left ventricular stroke work; $\overline{P}$, mean pressure; $\overline{PAP}$, mean pulmonary artery pressure; $\overline{PCWP}$, mean pulmonary capillary wedge pressure; PVR, pulmonary vascular resistance; SP, systolic pressure; SV, stroke volume; SVR, systemic vascular resistance.

computers available at a reasonable cost. But there are practical problems limiting their accuracy (Weil, 1977):

1. A non-axial position of the catheter will introduce errors into the measurement of pulmonary capillary wedge pressure as well as cardiac output.

2. Fluctuations in the temperature of pulmonary arterial blood during controlled ventilation of the critically ill patient is a significant source of error.

3. Heat gained by the injectate from the wall of the catheter and its environs is another source of error. The size of this error is variable when injection is done by different operators at different speed.

4. The computation of cardiac output is often interfered with by delayed return of the temperature of the catheter and the endocardial surface of the heart to baseline value.

It is estimated that an error of more than 10 per cent in the measurement of cardiac output by the thermodilution technique is expected when it is performed by the occasional operator (Weil, 1977). Indications for the measurement of cardiac output by the thermodilution method are similar to those for the measurement of pulmonary artery pressures.

The measurement of contractility

There are many semi-quantitative indices of myocardial contractility, but an exact measurement remains elusive. Indices involving the measurement of left ventricular pressure (e.g. the rate of rise of left ventricular pressure — dp/dt) cannot be obtained except during catheterization of the left heart. Their clinical application is extremely limited. The non-invasive index, pre-ejection phase (PEP), can only be obtained when simultaneous recordings of the electrocardiogram, the phonocardiogram and the carotid *pulse waveform* are made. If arterial pressure is measured directly, its *pressure waveform* can be used in place of the carotid pulse waveform. From these recordings, total electromechanical systole (QS_2) and the left ventricular ejection time (LVET) are obtained as illustrated in Fig. 6.4. Total electromechanical systole is the interval from the onset of the Q wave to the onset of the second heart sound, and left ventricular ejection time is measured from the upstroke of the arterial pulse to the dicrotic notch. The pre-ejection phase, the interval between the onset of the Q wave to the onset of ventricular ejection, is obtained by subtracting left ventricular ejection time from total electromechanical systole. Martin *et al.* (1971) reported that changes in the pre-ejection phase (PEP) were inversely proportional to changes in myocardial contractility. Reitan *et al.* (1972) found that $1/PEP^2$ was linearly related to a directly measured index of contractility (maximum blood flow acceleration at the aortic root). However, the pre-ejection phase is also influenced by heart rate (Weissler, 1977) and adjustment has to be made accordingly. These cumbersome steps in obtaining the pre-ejection phase, together with a lack of equipment for instant display of this variable, have limited its application in clinical practice.

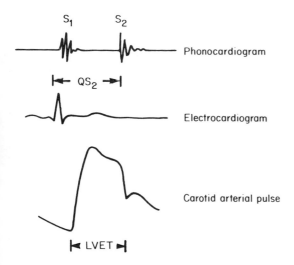

Fig. 6.4   The determination of the pre-ejection phase (PEP) from a simultaneous tracing of the phonocardiogram, the electrocardiogram and the carotid arterial pulse. Total electro-mechanical systole (QS_2) is the interval between the onset of the Q wave and the onset of the second heart sound; left ventricular ejection time (LVET) is the interval between the upstroke of the arterial pulse to the dicrotic notch. PEP is the difference between QS_2 and LVET.

If cardiac output and left ventricular filling pressure are being measured, contractility can be estimated from the position occupied by the ventricle on the ventricular function curves as illustrated in Fig. 6.5. (For the calculation of stroke work index, see 'The measurement of cardiac output' in this chapter.) When contractility is within normal limits, stroke work index should be normal when left ventricular filling pressure is normal (Sarnoff, 1955). When filling pressure is within normal range, contractility is depressed if stroke work index is below normal and *vice versa*.

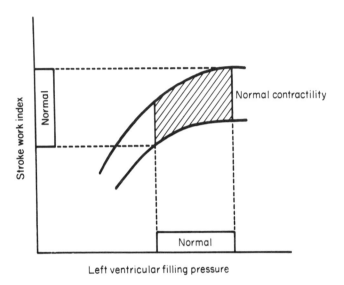

Fig. 6.5   The determination of contractility. Contractility is normal if stroke work index is normal both at the upper and lower limits of normal left ventricular filling pressure.

Practical monitoring

In monitoring, undue emphasis should never be placed on the measurement of a single variable. All measured variables should be correlated. The clinical picture of the patient is just as important. For patients with ischaemic heart disease, heart rate, systolic and diastolic arterial blood pressures as well as the electrocardiogram should be monitored, and the rate–pressure product calculated. Invasive haemodynamic monitoring techniques need not be routine, but should be instituted when indicated.

Heart rate alone is a reasonable index of myocardial work. A better index is the rate–pressure product obtained by multiplying the heart rate by the systolic blood pressure. Its predictive value is the same whether systolic blood pressure is obtained by direct measurement or by auscultation. In order to avoid myocardial ischaemia, the rate–pressure product should be kept well below the critical value at which the patient develops angina. Heart rate should be kept below 90 per minute, and the systolic blood pressure should be kept below an upper limit defined by the patient's heart rate and the critical rate–pressure product. The diastolic blood pressure is an index of coronary arterial perfusion. It should be kept above 8 kPa (60 mmHg).

In conjunction with the heart rate and rate–pressure product, electro-cardiographic monitoring of lead V_5 (and lead II when possible) supplies objective evidence of the presence or absence of myocardial ischaemia. Conventional lead V_5 is preferred, but the modified precordial leads CM_5 and CS_5 are acceptable. If the electrodes of these leads are close to the field of operation, they can be covered with sterile waterproof self-adhesive plastic drapes.

When the operation is extensive, blood loss should be closely monitored. Periodic measurements of haemoglobin concentration, serum electrolytes, arterial blood gases and buffer base are indicated during prolonged operations. Haemoglobin concentration should be kept at or near normal. Arterial oxygen tension should be maintained at not less than 8 kPa (60 mmHg). Acid–base disturbance of respiratory or metabolic origin should be corrected.

References

Abernathy, W. S. (1974). Complete heart block caused by the Swan–Ganz catheter. *Chest* **65**, 349.

Allen, E. V. (1929). Thromboangiitis obliterans: methods of diagnosis of chronic occlusive arterial lesions distal to the wrist with illustrative cases. *American Journal of the Medical Sciences* **178**, 237.

Bedford, R. F. and Wollman, H. (1973). Complications of percutaneous radial-artery cannulation: an objective prospective study in man. *Anesthesiology* **38**, 228.

Berryhill, R. E., Benumof, J. L. and Rauscher, L. A. (1978). Pulmonary vascular pressure reading at the end of exhalation. *Anesthesiology* **49**, 365.

Blitt, C. D. (1980). Monitoring the cardiovascular system during anaesthesia. In: *Anesthesia and the Patient with Heart Disease*, pp. 19–37. Ed. by B. R. Brown Jr., F. A. Davis: Philadelphia.

Buckberg, G. D., Fixler, D. E., Archie, J. P. and Hoffman, J. I. E. (1972). Experimental subendocardial ischemia in dogs with normal coronary arteries. *Circulation Research* **30**, 67.

Chun, G. M. H. and Ellestad, M. H. (1971). Perforation of the pulmonary artery by a Swan–Ganz catheter. *New England Journal of Medicine* **284**, 1041.

Civetta, J. M., Gabel, J. C. and Laver, M. B. (1971). Disparate ventricular function in surgical patients. *Surgical Forum* **22**, 136.

Cokkinos, D. V. and Voridis, E. M. (1976). Constancy of pressure–rate product in pacing-induced angina pectoris. *British Heart Journal* **38**, 39.

Davis, F. M. and Stewart, J. M. (1980). Radial artery cannulation: a prospective study in patients undergoing cardiothoracic surgery. *British Journal of Anaesthesia* **52**, 41.

Detry, J. M. R., Piette, F. and Brasseur, L. A. (1970). Hemodynamic determinants of exercise ST-segment depression in coronary patients. *Circulation* **42**, 593.

Downs, J. B., Rackstein, A. D., Klein, E. F. Jr and Hawkins, I. F. Jr (1973). Hazards of radial-artery catheterization. *Anesthesiology* **38**, 283.

Fitzpatrick, G. F., Hampson, L. G. and Burgess, J. H. (1972). Bedside determination of left atrial pressure. *Canadian Medical Association Journal* **106**, 1293.

Foëx, P. and Prys-Roberts, C. (1974). Anaesthesia and the hypertensive patient. *British Journal of Anaesthesia* **46**, 575.

Foote, G. A., Schabel, S. I. and Hodges, M. (1974). Pulmonary complications of the flow-directed balloon-tipped catheter. *New England Journal of Medicine* **290**, 927.

Forrester, J. S., Diamond, G., McHugh, T. J. and Swan, H. J. C. (1971). Filling pressures in the right and left sides of the heart in acute myocardial infarction. *New England Journal of Medicine* **285**, 190.

Geer, R. T. (1977). Interpretation of pulmonary-artery wedge pressure when PEEP is used. *Anesthesiology* **46**, 383.

Gobel, F. L., Nordstrom, L. A., Nelson, R. R., Jorgensen, C. R. and Wang, Y. (1978). The rate–pressure product as an index of myocardial oxygen consumption during exercise in patients with angina pectoris. *Circulation* **57**, 549.

Greene, J. F. Jr, Fitzwater, J. E. and Clemmer, T. P. (1975). Septic endocarditis and indwelling pulmonary artery catheters. *Journal of the American Medical Association* **233**, 891.

Hobelmann, C. F. Jr, Smith, D. E., Virgilio, R. W., Shapiro, A. R. and Peters, R. M. (1974). Left atrial and pulmonary artery wedge pressure difference with positive end-expiratory pressure. *Surgical Forum* **25**, 232.

Humphrey, C. B., Oury, J. H., Virgilio, R. W., Gibbons, J. A., Folkerth, T. L., Shapiro, A. R. and Fosburg, R. G. (1976). An analysis of direct and indirect measurements of left atrial filling pressure. *Journal of Thoracic and Cardiovascular Surgery* **71**, 643.

Kaplan, J. A. and King, S. B. III (1976). The precordial electrocardiographic lead (V$_5$) in patients who have coronary-artery disease. *Anesthesiology* **45**, 570.

Kistner, J. R., Miller, E. D. Jr and Epstein, R. M. (1977). Malignant hyperthermia during regional anesthesia. *Anesthesiology* **47**, 75.

Kitamura, K., Jorgensen, C. R., Gobel, F. L., Taylor, H. L. and Wang, Y. (1972). Hemodynamic correlates of myocardial oxygen consumption during upright exercise. *Journal of Applied Physiology* **32**, 516.

Lappas, D., Lell, W. A., Gabel, J. C., Civetta, J. M. and Lowenstein, E. (1973). Indirect measurement of left-atrial pressure in surgical patients — pulmonary-capillary wedge and pulmonary-artery diastolic pressures compared with left-atrial pressure. *Anesthesiology* **38**, 394.

Lipp, H., O'Donoghue, K. and Resnekov, L. (1971). Intracardiac knotting of a flow-directed balloon catheter. *New England Journal of Medicine* **284**, 220.

Loeb, H. S., Saudye, A., Croke, R. P., Talano, J. V., Klodnycky, M. L. and Gunnar, R. M. (1978). Effects of pharamcologically-induced hyper tension on myocardial ischemia and coronary hemodynamics in patients with fixed coronary obstruction. *Circulation* **57**, 41.

Lowenstein, E., Little, J. W. III and Lo, H. H. (1971). Prevention of cerebral embolization from flushing radial-artery cannulas. *New England Journal of Medicine* **285**, 1414.

Lozman, J., Powers, S. R. Jr, Older, T., Dutton, R. E., Roy, R. J., English, M., Marco, D. and Eckert, C. (1974). Correlation of pulmonary wedge and left atrial prssures: a study in the patient receiving positive end expiratory pressure ventilation. *Archives of Surgery* **109**, 270.

Mangano, D. T. (1980). Monitoring pulmonary arterial pressure in coronary-artery disease. *Anesthesiology* **53**, 364.

Martin, C. E., Shaver, J. A., Thompson, M. E., Reddy, P. S. and Leonard, J. J. (1971). Direct correlation of external systolic time intervals with internal indices of left ventricular function in man. *Circulation* **44**, 419.

Mason, R. E., Likar, I., Biern, R. O. and Ross, R. S. (1967). Multiple-lead exercise electrocardiography: experience in 107 normal subjects and 67 patients with angina pectoris, and comparison with coronary cinearterio-graphy in 84 patients. *Circulation* **36**, 517.

Nelson, R. R., Gobel, F. L., Jorgensen, C. R., Wang, K., Wang, Y. and Taylor, H. L. (1974). Hemodynamic predictors of myocardial oxygen consumption durng static and dynamic exercise. *Circulaton* **50**, 1179.

O'Toole, J. D., Wurtzbacher, J. J., Wearner, N. E. and Jain, A. C. (1979). Pulmonary-valve injury and insufficiency during pulmonary-artery catheterization. *New England Journal of Medicine* **301**, 1167.

Pace, N. L. (1977). A critique of flow-directed pulmonary arterial catheterization. *Anesthesiology* **47**, 455.

Pace, N. L. and Horton, W. (1975). Indwelling pulmonary artery catheters: their relationship to aseptic thrombotic endocardial vegetations. *Journal of the American Medical Associaton* **233**, 893.

Philips, P. A., Marty, A. T., Miyamoto, A. M. and Brewer, L. A. III (1975). A clinical method for detecting subendocardial ischemia after cardiopulmonary bypass. *Journal of Thoracic and Cardiovascular Surgery* **69**, 30.

Rahimtoola, S. H., Loeb, H. S., Ehsani, A., Sinno, M. Z., Chuquimia, R., Lal, R., Rosen, K. M. and Gunnar, R. M. (1972). Relationship of pulmonary artery to left ventricular diastolic pressures in acute myocardial infarction. *Circulation* **46**, 283.

Reitan, J. A., Smith, N. T., Borison, V. S. and Kadis, L. B. (1972). The cardiac pre-ejection period: a correlate of peak ascending aortic blood-flow acceleration. *Anesthesiology* **36**, 76.

Rice, D. L., Awe, R. J., Gaasch, W. H., Alexander, J. K. and Jenkins, D. E. (1974). Wedge pressure measurement in obstructive pulmonary disease. *Chest* **66**, 628.

Robinson, B. F. (1967). Relation of heart rate and systolic blood pressure to the onset of pain in angina pectoris. *Circulation* **35**, 1073.

Rose, H. D. (1979). Gas gangrene and *Clostridium perfringens* septicemia associated with the use of an indwelling radial artery catheter. *Canadian Medical Association Journal* **121**, 1595.

Sarnoff, S. J. (1955). Myocardial contractility as described by ventricular function curves; observations on Starling's law of the heart. *Physiological Reviews* **35**, 107.

Sarnoff, S. J., Braunwald, E., Welch, G. H. Jr., Case, R. B., Stainsby, W. N. and Macruz, R. (1958). Hemodynamic determinants of oxygen consumption of the heart with special reference to the tension-time index. *American Journal of Physiology* **192**, 148.

Schapira, M. and Daum, S. (1974). Hemodynamics of the pulmonary circulation in patients on intermittent positive pressure breathing with a Bird respirator. *Anesthesia and Analgesia . . . Current Researches* **53**, 31.

Shaw, T. J. I. (1979). The Swan–Ganz pulmonary artery catheter. *Anaesthesia* **34**, 651.

Swan, H. J. C., Ganz, W., Forrester, J., Marcus, H., Diamond, G. and Chonette, D. (1970). Catheterization of the heart in man with use of a flow-directed balloon-tipped catheter. *New England Journal of Medicine* **283**, 447.

Walston, A. II and Kendall, M. E. (1973). Comparison of pulmonary wedge and left atrial pressure in man. *American Heart Journal* **86**, 159.

Weil, M. H. (1977). Measurement of cardiac output. *Critical Care Medicine* **5**, 117.

Weisel, R. D., Berger, R. L. and Hechtman, H. B. (1975). Measurement of cardiac output by thermodilution. *New England Journal of Medicine* **292**, 682.

Weissler, A. M. (1977). Current concepts in cardiology: systolic-time intervals. *New England Journal of Medicine* **296**, 321.

7

Anaesthetic techniques

Due to the precarious blood supply of the ischaemic myocardium, anaesthesia in patients with ischaemic heart disease should offer optimal conditions for the scheduled operation and minimal disturbance of circulatory functions. *The principles and practice of anaesthesia in these patients are not different from those in any other surgical patients;* but special attention should be paid to maintaining an adequate coronary blood supply to meet the metabolic needs of myocardial work.

In the intraoperative period there are many factors which will disturb this precarious blanace of myocardial blood flow and myocardial work. Tachycardia and hypertension will increase myocardial work; hypotension will reduce coronary blood flow; anaemic and hypoxaemic hypoxia will disrupt oxidative energy metabolism; arrhythmias will interfere with both coronary and systemic circulatory dynamics. Many of these factors are precipitated by the anaesthetic technique and the surgical procedure. They can be anticipated and prevented. Should these complications occur, they should be corrected without delay. In the following sections and in the next chapter, attention is directed to the prevention and the treatment of these complications.

Regional anaesthesia versus general anaesthesia

In many instances a regional technique would seem ideal. However, many patients are anxious at being 'awake' during even minor procedures; and fear is a major cause of tachycardia and hypertension. The use of heavy sedation to supplement regional anaesthesia, on the other hand, can cause excessive respiratory and circulatory depression. Arterial hypotension is a known complication of spinal anaesthesia as well as of general anaesthesia. Steen, Tinker and Tarhan (1978) found that there was no difference in the incidence of a repeated myocardial infarction following transurethral prostatic resection, whether the operation was done under spinal or general anaesthesia. On the contrary, Backer, Tinker and Robertson (1979) reported that patients with ischaemic heart disease who had regional anaesthesia (retrobulbar block and infiltration) for ophthalmic procedures had a much lower incidence of postoperative myocardial infarction than expected. These findings suggest that regional anaesthesia is safe for at least one type of operation. There should be others equally suitable for regional techniques. Until there is evidence to suggest the contrary, a regional technique is acceptable in patients with ischaemic heart disease, provided the following conditions are met.

1. The patient must be a willing subject. He should be fully informed of the technique involved and its possible complications. Care should be exercised to identify the unduly anxious patient who 'requests' regional anaesthesia because he has fears about general anaesthesia. The apparent confidence in regional technique of such a patient is most likley misguided.

2. The operative site can be anaesthetized easily with simple regional techniques (e.g. retrobulbar block for ophthalmic operations, brachial plexus block for operations on the forearm, and saddle block for extra-peritoneal genitourinary operations). Analgesia provided by the technique must be total. There is little merit in supplementing inadequate regional anaesthesia with heavy sedation.

3. The anaesthetist is experienced with the chosen technique and can do it with minimal discomfort to the patient.

4. Patient comfort can be ensured by careful positioning during operation. Regional techniques should be used only in operations which can be finished within 1–1½ hours. Lying in one position for a prolonged period can be extremely uncomfortable.

Due to its inotropic and chronotropic properties, adrenaline should not be used to increase the duration of action of the local anaesthetic. During the operation a *mild* degree of sedation is advisable, and the attendance of the anaesthetist to monitor the patient is mandatory.

If one or more of the said conditions cannot be met, general anaesthesia would provide better conditions for the operation. Under general anaesthesia the reaction of the circulation to noxious stimuli and to depressants is exaggerated in patients with ischaemic heart disease. Wide swings of heart rate and blood pressure are common. The critical periods during which these disturbances may occur are:

1. During induction of anaesthesia.
2. From induction to the commencement of the operation.
3. During the operation.
4. During emergence.

During induction of anaesthesia

This is a labile period during which respiratory depression and poor airway control can result in inadvertent hypoxaemia. Some intravenous agents (e.g. thiopentone and tubocurarine) can cause a fall in coronary perfusion pressure; others (e.g. ketamine and pancuronium), tachycardia and hypertension. The pressor response to direct laryngoscopy and endotracheal intubation is a well recognized phenomenon. It is particularly marked in poorly sedated hypertensive patients and in patients with chronic myocardial ischaemia. Systolic blood pressures above 27 kPa (200 mmHg) and heart rates in excess of 120 per minute have been observed.

From induction to the commencement of the operation

Both the hypertensive patient and the patient with ischaemic heart disease have poor control of blood pressure and heart rate. During this period when stimulation is minimal, there is a tendency for blood pressure and heart rate to fall, sometimes to alarmingly low values.

During the operation

Tachycardia and hypertension in response to noxious stimuli is common during this period. However, in the lightly anaesthetized patient bradycardia and hypotension (vagal responses to specific surgical stimulus) also can occur.

During emergence

Tachycardia and hypertension again are common reactions to the presence of the endotracheal tube, to intraoral suction and to pain. This is another period during which inadvertent hypoxaemia can occur.

The prevention of the said complications begins with good general management of the patient under anaesthesia. There should be a keen sense of anticipation of the patient's reaction to drugs and surgical stimuli. Anaesthetic agents should be used wisely. Close attention should be paid to the patient's airway, ventilation, oxygenation, and fluid and blood replacement.

The choice of anaesthetic agents

Current general anaesthetic techniques usually involve a multiplicity of agents. Most anaesthetic agents, either alone or in combination, are circulatory depressants (see Chapter 4). Patients with normal ventricular function can tolerate a mild to moderate degree of myocardial depression, but patients in heart failure tolerate myocardial depressants poorly. Therefore the choice of anaesthetic agents should be made accordingly.

Patients with normal ventricular function

Since circulatory depression reduces myocardial work, a mild to a moderate degree of circulatory depression is advantageous, provided that ventricular function is normal and systemic circulation will not be compromised. Ketamine, an agent with potent pressor effects, is in fact unacceptable in patients with ischaemic heart disease (see 'Ketamine' in Chapter 4). Otherwise, the choice of anaesthetic agents and techniques should rest with the experience of the anaesthetist, the anaesthetic history of the patient and the type of operation. All intravenous drugs (anaesthetics, narcotics and muscle relaxants) should be given slowly to avoid the circulatory effects of a high serum concentration attained transiently after a rapid bolus injection. The major volatile agents (halothane, enflurane and isoflurane) have similar circulatory actions (see 'Inhalational agents' in Chapter 4). They can be administered according to the needs of the patient.

Patients with poor ventricular function

When ventricular function is marginal, further depression of myocardial function may result in ventricular dilation and heart failure. Since narcotic analgesics have minimal myocardial effects (see 'Narcotic analgesics' in Chapter 4), the use of a narcotic analgesic (up to 2 mg/kg of morphine or 50–100 μg/kg of fentanyl) can be used for induction and maintainance of anaesthesia to the advantage of these patients. During induction the chosen agent is given slowly until the patient is not responding to the command to breathe. Pancuronium can be used to facilitate intubation and controlled ventilation. Small increments of diazepam, or a low concentration of nitrous oxide with or without a volatile agent, can be used as adjuvants to maintain amnesia. However, even a low concentration of these adjuvants can cause hypotention in these patients. In this respect the inhalational agents have a distinct advantage over diazepam. If they are tolerated poorly, these inhalational agents can be discontinued and the operation can proceed under the cover of at least profound analgesia if not aneasthesia.

Special considerations

Pre-oxygenation

The protective value of maintaining myocardial oxygenation has been mentioned (see 'Oxygen therapy' in Chapter 3). Pre-oxygenation is commonly performed in conjunction with the so-called 'crash induction' technique. The advantage of pre-oxygenation is equally applicable to induction of general anaesthesia for elective operations. Pre-oxygenation for 3–5 minutes will prevent the development of hypoxaemia for 4–5 minutes after the onset of apnoea (Nolan, 1967; Cole and Stoelting, 1971). This precaution is especially beneficial to patients with ischaemic heart disease, whose coronary blood flow and myocardial work may fluctuate widely due to changes in blood pressure and heart rate during induction of anaesthesia.

Laryngoscopy and endotracheal intubation

Due to an exaggerated pressor response, arrhythmias and ventricular failure following endotracheal intubation have been reported in hypertensive patients (Fox et al., 1977). Similarly, the pressor response to laryngoscopy and endotracheal intubation is exaggerated in patients with ischaemic heart disease. Transient ST segment depression indicating myocardial ischaemia as a result of this exaggerated response has been observed. This harmful response should be abolished. Although a number of methods have been proposed, not one of them is universally effective. The commonly used methods and their effectiveness in attenuating this pressor response are:

1. King *et al.* (1951) found that this pressor response was abolished by increasing the depth of anaesthesia during induction. Although this method is acceptable in healthy patients, it should be practised with extreme care in patients with ischaemic heart disease because of the danger of circulatory depression.

2. Denlinger, Ellison and Ominsky (1974) reported that the application of topical lignocaine to the trachea under direct laryngoscopy after the induction of general anaesthesia only attenuated this pressor response, but did not abolish it altogether.

3. Stoelting (1977) considered the pressor response to direct laryngoscopy and that to endotracheal intubation separately. He reported that the application of viscous lignocaine (25 ml of 2% solution) as a mouthwash and gargle 10 minutes before the induction of anesthesia would abolish the large rise in blood pressure associated with laryngoscopy, but it was found to have no effect on the increase in heart rate. Similar attenuation of the blood pressure response to direct laryngoscopy was observed in patients who had 1.5 mg/kg of lignocaine intravenously 90 seconds before the start of the procedure. Only the additional application of lignocaine, 2 mg/kg, to the larynx and trachea would attenuate the rise in blood pressure following endotracheal intubation.

4. Prys-Roberts and his co-workers (1973) showed that this pressor response to laryngoscopy and intubation was attenuated by the pretreatment of hypertensive patients with a beta-adrenergic antagonist (practolol, 1.5 mg/kg orally every 6 hours for 48 hours or 0.4 mg/kg intravenously following induction of anaesthesia).

5. In another study, Stoelting (1979) gave his patients sodium nitroprusside, 1–2 μg/kg, 15 seconds before laryngoscopy was attempted. He concluded that this method was successful in attenuating the hypertensive response to laryngoscopy and intubation but had no effect on the increase in heart rate. Undoubtedly the timing of the injection will be affected by the circulation time of the patient. (This aspect was not taken into account in this report.) Furthermore, sodium nitroprusside should not be administered intravenously without continuous monitoring of arterial pressure. This method cannot be recommended as standard practice.

6. It was reported that the administration of droperidol, 150 μg/kg intravenously 5 minutes before the induction of anaesthesia, would attenuate the hypertensive response (Curran, Crowley and O'Sullivan, 1980), but the droperidol itself caused an unacceptable tachycardia.

The most practical solution to this nagging problem is the application of topical lignocaine to the pharynx, the larynx and the trachea (Stoelting, 1977). In order to obtain maximum benefit from this method, the pharynx and larynx should be anaesthetized with viscous lignocaine used as a mouthwash and gargle. After induction of light general anaesthesia and under direct laryngoscopy, lignocaine spray is applied to the supraglottic structures and the trachea immediately before endotracheal intubation. Laryngoscopy should be done skilfully and gently. Fentanyl, 100–200 μg, given intravenously with induction of anaesthesia will moderate this pressor response even further.

Artificial ventilation versus spontaneous respiration

In patients with normal ventricular function, the decision to control ventilation or not should rest with the type of operation, the status of the patient's respiratory function and the choice of anaesthetic agents. In patients with heart failure, artificial ventilation is indicated.

Whether respiration is spontaneous or controlled, it is important to maintain normocapnia. Hypocapnia has two serious side-effects in patients with ischaemic heart disease:

1. An arterial carbon dioxide tension of 2.7–3.3 kPa (20–25 mmHg) reduces cardiac output (Prys-Roberts *et al.*, 1972), increases coronary vascular resistance (Case and Greenberg, 1976) and reduces coronary blood flow (Case, Greenberg and Moskowitz, 1975). Furthermore, respiratory alkalosis shifts the oxygen-haemoglobin dissociation curve to the left and reduces oxygen availability to the tissue. Both myocardial ischaemia (Neill and Hattenhauer, 1975) and refractory arrhythmias (Ayres and Grace, 1969) associated with hyperventilation and hypocapnia have been reported.

2. For each 1.3 kPa (10 mmHg) fall in arterial carbon dioxide tension, serum potassium concentration decreases by as much as 0.5 mmol/l (Edwards, Winnie and Ramamurthy, 1977). Many patients with ischaemic heart disease are being treated with diuretics. They have a reduced total body potassium store and are ill-equipped to cope with a large flux in extracellular potassium. If they are also being treated with digitalis, the consequence of hypokalaemia can be serious (see 'Factors enhancing the cardiotoxic effects of digitalis' in Chapter 11).

Moderate hypercapnia, on the other hand, stimulates the myocardium via the sympathetic nervous system. (Tenney, 1956; Skovsted, Price and Price, 1972) but depresses it by a direct effect (Noble, Trenchard and Guz, 1966; Ng, Levy and Zieske, 1967). At arterial carbon dioxide tensions of up to 9.3 kPa (70 mmHg), the stimulant action predominates in man (Blackburn *et al.*, 1972). However, there is no evidence that an arterial carbon dioxide tension of 6.0–6.7 kPa (45–50 mmHg), which is found in anaesthetized patients breathing spontaneously, is harmful.

Parenteral fluids

Glucose, a substrate of myocardial metabolism, can be given intravenously. It can supply part of the energy requirement of the heart by anaerobic glycolysis (see 'Energy metabolism of the myocardium' in Chapter 2). Therefore intravenous solutions containing 5% dextrose should be used in the operating theatre. The administration of 5% dextrose should start the night before the scheduled operation to ensure against depletion of intracellular glycogen store.

Anaemia is a major cause of acute myocardial ischaemia and heart failure. All patients should have a normal haemoglobin concentration before coming to the operating theatre. Blood loss during operation should be closely monitored. The use of a large volume of balanced salt solution to replace blood loss is to be discouraged (Moore and Shires, 1967). When blood loss is more than 10 per cent of the patient's blood volume, replacement with whole blood is indicated.

Large volumes of fluid may be sequestered in the operative site and in the lumen of the intestine (Shires, Williams and Brown, 1961). Third-space loss assumes significance only when there is extensive surgical dissection, paralytic ileus, multiple trauma or extensive burns. It should be replaced with lactated Ringer's solution. Central venous pressure or left ventricular filling pressure measurement is indicated to guide therapy.

During emergence

To avoid tachycardia and hypertension, the patient should be allowed to emerge undisturbed. Early extubation is warranted when possible. The administration of lignocaine, 1 mg/kg intravenously 2 minutes before extubation, is reported to be successful in aborting the pressor response to extubation (Bidwai *et al.*, 1979). Oxygen should be administered by mask during emergence to prevent inadvertent hypoxaemia due to diffusion hypoxia, airway obstruction or hypoventilation.

References

Ayres, S. M. and Grace, W. J. (1969). Inappropriate ventilation and hypoxemia as causes of cardiac arrhythmias. *American Journal of Medicine* **46**, 495.

Backer, C. L., Tinker, J. H. and Robertson, D. M. (1979). Myocardial reinfarction following local anaesthesia. *Anesthesiology* **51** Suppl, S61.

Bidwai, A. V., Bidwai, V. A., Rogers, C. R. and Stanley, T. H. (1979). Blood-pressure and pulse-rate responses to endotracheal extubation with and without prior injection of lidocaine. *Anesthesiology* **51**, 171.

Blackburn, J. P., Conway, C. M., Leigh, J. M., Lindop, M. J. and Reitan, J. A. (1972). Pa_{CO_2} and the pre-ejection period: the Pa_{CO_2}/inotropy response curve. *Anesthesiology* **37**, 268.

Case, R. B. and Greenberg, H. (1976). The response of canine coronary vascular resistance to local alterations in coronary arterial P_{CO_2}. *Circulation Research* **39**, 558.

Case, R. B., Greenberg, H. and Moskowitz, R. (1975). Alteration in coronary sinus pO_2 & O_2 saturation resulting from pCO_2 changes. *Cardiovascular Research* **9**, 167.

Cole, W. L. and Stoelting, V. K. (1971). Blood gases during intubation following two types of oxygenation. *Anesthesia and Analgesia . . . Current Researches* **50**, 68.

Curran, J., Crowley, M. and O'Sullivan, G. (1980). Droperidol and endotracheal intubation: attenuation of pressor response to laryngoscopy and intubation. *Anaesthesia* **35**, 290.

Denlinger, J. K., Ellison, N. and Ominsky, A. J. (1974). Effects of intratracheal lidocaine on circulatory responses to tracheal intubation. *Anesthesiology* **41**, 409.

Edwards, R., Winnie, A. P. and Ramamurthy, S. (1977). Acute hypocapneic hypokalemia: an anesthetic complication. *Anesthesia and Analgesia . . . Current Researches* **56**, 786.

Fox, E. J., Sklar, G. S., Hill, C. H., Villanueva, R. and King, B. D. (1977). Complications related to the pressor response to endotracheal intubation. *Anesthesiology* **47**, 524.

King, B. D., Harris, L. C. Jr, Greifenstein, F. E., Elder, J. D. Jr and Dripps, R. D. (1951). Reflex circulatory responses to direct laryngoscopy and tracheal intubation performed during general anesthesia. *Anesthesiology* **12**, 556.

Moore, F. D. and Shires, G. T. (1967). Moderation. *Annals of Surgery* **166**, 300.

Neill, W. A. and Hattenhauer, M. (1975). Impairment of myocardial O_2 supply due to hyperventilation. *Circulation* **52**, 854.

Ng, M. L., Levy, M. N. and Zieske, H. A. (1967). Effects of changes of pH and of carbon dioxide tension on left ventricular performance. *American Journal of Physiology* **213**, 115.

Noble, M. I. M., Trenchard, D. and Guz, A. (1966). Effect of changes in Pa_{CO_2} and Pa_{O_2} on cardiac performance in conscious dogs. *Journal of Applied Physiology* **22**, 147.

Nolan, R. T. (1967). Pre-oxygenation and thiopentone–suxamethonium induction. *British Journal of Anaesthesia* **39**, 794.

Prys-Roberts, C., Foëx, P., Greene, L. T. and Waterhouse, T. D. (1972). Studies of anaesthesia in relation to hypertension. IV: The effects of artificial ventilation on the circulation and pulmonary gas exchanges. *British Journal of Anaesthesia* **44**, 335.

Prys-Roberts, C., Foëx, P., Biro, G. P. and Roberts, J. G. (1973). Studies of anaesthesia in relation to hypertension. V: Adrenergic beta-receptor blockade. *British Journal of Anaesthesia* **45**, 671.

Shires, T., Williams, J. and Brown, F. (1961). Acute change in extracellular fluids associated with major surgical procedures. *Annals of Surgery* **154**, 803.

Skovsted, P., Price, M. L. and Price, H. L. (1972). The effects of carbon dioxide on preganglionic sympathetic activity during halothane, methoxyflurane, and cycloproprane anesthesia. *Anesthesiology* **37**, 70.

Steen, P. A., Tinker, J. H. and Tarhan, S. (1978). Myocardial reinfarction after anesthesia and surgery. *Journal of the American Medical Association* **239**, 2566.

Stoelting, R. K. (1977). Circulatory changes during direct laryngoscopy and tracheal intubation: influence of duration of laryngoscopy with or without prior lidocaine. *Anesthesiology* **47**, 381.

Stoelting, R. K. (1979). Attenuation of blood pressure response to laryngoscopy and tracheal intubation with sodium nitroprusside. *Anesthesia and Analgesia . . . Current Researches* **58,** 116.

Tenney, S. M. (1956). Sympatho-adrenal stimulation by carbon dioxide and the inhibitory effect of carbonic acid on epinephrine response. *American Journal of Physiology* **187,** 341.

8

The management of hypertension, hypotension and arrhythmias

Despite the special precautions reviewed in the previous chapter, hypertension, hypotension and arrhythmias can still occur during operation. These are serious complications in patients with ischaemic heart disease. They can precipitate acute myocardial ischaemia and circulatory failure. They require immediate attention. First and foremost in the management of these problems is a review of the patient's medical history and the course of events under anaesthesia. A precipitating cause directly related to the anaesthetic technique or the surgical procedure is common. These complications are self-limiting when the precipitating cause is corrected. If they persist, active treatment is necessary.

The treatment of sinus tachycardia and hypertension

Sinus tachycardia and systolic hypertension in response to noxious stimuli are frequent complications. Both increase myocardial work, but tachycardia alone also reduces coronary blood flow. Under anaesthesia the heart rate of a patient with ischaemic heart disease should not be allowed to rise beyond 90 per minute, and the systolic blood pressure should be kept below an upper limit defined by the rate–pressure product found tolerable by the patient during the preoperative visit (see 'Indices of myocardial ischaemia and myocardial work' in Chapter 6). If these limits are exceeded, the patient's anaesthetic requirements should be reviewed, and the depth of anaesthesia increased unless it is contraindicated. When in doubt, the surgeon should be asked to stop the operation temporarily. A test dose of fentanyl, 50–100 μg intravenously, can be given. The return of heart rate and blood pressure towards normal is a good indication that anaesthesia was inadequate.

If anaesthesia is judged adequate but tachycardia or hypertension persists, the use of propranolol or a vasodilator is indicated. The sparing effects of propranolol and vasodilators on myocardial work are summarized in Table 8.1 (see 'Beta-adrenergic antagonists' and 'Vasodilators' in Chapter 3).

Propranolol is indicated for the treatment of tachycardia with or without hypertension, but a vasodilator should be used when hypertension occurs alone without tachycardia. Propranolol and a vasodilator often have to be given concurrently to obtain satisfactory control of both heart rate and blood pressure. There are many vasodilators available, but nitroprusside and glyceryl trinitrate are, by far, the most popular. Nitroprusside and glyceryl trinitrate are potent agents. Continuous direct measurement of blood

Table 8.1   The effects of propranolol and vasodilators on the major determinants of myocardial work

	Propranolol	Vasodilators
Heart rate	Decreased	No change or increased
Systolic pressure	Decreased	Decreased
Filling pressure	No change or mildly increased	Decreased
Contractility	Decreased	No change

pressure and monitoring of central venous pressure are advisable during their administration. In the critically ill patient, monitoring of left ventricular filling pressure is indicated.

Propranolol

This is a beta-adrenergic antagonist (Shand, 1975). It is the agent of choice for tachycardia (heart rate above 90 per minute) with or without hypertension. It should be remembered that the circulatory effects of propranolol and many anaesthetic agents are additive (see Chapter 4). It is contra-indicated if there is pre-existing hypotension, heart block, congestive heart failure or bronchospasm. It must be discontinued should hypotension, heart block, heart failure or bronchospasm develop during its administration. When it is given intravenously, the first milligram should be administered in divided doses over 10 minutes. Side-effects are unlikely to develop if they are not observed after 1 mg. Subsequent increments of 0.5 mg each can be given, up to a total dose of 0.1 mg/kg as necessary.

Sodium nitroprusside

Sodium nitroprusside is a potent vasodilator with a short duration of action and low incidence of tachyphylaxis. It acts on vascular smooth muscles of both arterial resistance and venous capacitance vessels (Miller *et al.*, 1976), but has no known effect on cardiac muscle (Adams *et al.*, 1973). It will return elevated arterial pressure and left ventricular filling pressure towards normal, improve cardiac output and decrease myocardial work (see 'Vasodilators' in Chapter 3). However, there is some indication that sodium nitroprusside will affect unfavourably the collateral flow to ischaemic regions of the heart (Chiariello *et al.*, 1976). Although sodium nitroprusside will dilate coronary collateral vessels (Capurro, Kent and Eptsein, 1977), its simultaneous vasodilating effect on arteriolar resistance vessels may encourage a 'coronary steal'. Despite this paradox, sodium nitroprusside is a popular vasodilator. It has been used successfully to improve ventricular function without evidence of increasing myocardal ischaemia, except after acute myocardial infarction.

Sodium nitroprusside is available commercially as Nipride. Fifty milligrams are usually dissolved in 500 ml of 5% dextrose in water to give a light brown solution of 100μg/ml. Because it will decompose under sunlight or artificial light, its container and delivery tubing should be wrapped in opaque material. Only freshly prepared solutions should be used. The use of a minidrip delivery set is mandatory, and a constant infusion device is recommended. Start the infusion at a rate of 0.5μg/kg per minute and increase it in steps to obtain the desired effect. The hypotensive effects of sodium nitroprusside and halothane, and possibly enflurane, are additive.

Cyanide and thiocyanate, the intermediate and final products of metabolism of sodium nitroprusside, are highly toxic. Deaths attributed to cyanide poisoning following the use of sodium nitroprusside have been reported (Jack, 1974; Davies, Kadar *et al.*, 1975). The plasma cyanide level following sodium nitroprusside administration is related to the total dose and its rate of infusion. The following guidelines are recommended so that the danger of cyanide poisoning can be minimized.

1. *Not more than* 1 mg/kg in 1 hour of infusion (Michenfelder and Theye, 1977).
2. *Not more than* 1.5 mg/kg in 2–3 hours of infusion (Vesey, Cole and Simpson, 1976).
3. *Not more than* 0.5 mg/kg per hour in long-term therapy (Michenfelder and Tinker, 1977).

When the projected dose exceeds those mentioned, the patient must be regarded as resistant to the hypotensive effect of nitroprusside. The infusion must be stopped, and an alternative vasodilator used.

The development of severe metabolic acidosis, a rising mixed venous oxygen content and a narrowing of arterial venous oxygen differences are early indications of cyanide toxicity (Davies, Greiss *et al.*, 1975). Therefore frequent measurements of arterial and mixed venous oxygen content and buffer base should be done. As most of the cyanide is tissue bound, blood cyanide level is seldom helpful. Blood thiocyanate level should be determined daily during long-term administration. A level of 1.7 mmol/litre (10 mg/100 ml) is toxic.

Glyceryl trinitrate

Glyceryl trinitrate is another short-acting vasodilator which acts predominantly on venous capacitance vessels (Miller *et al.*, 1976). It reduces venous return to the heart, decreases left ventricular filling pressure and alleviates pulmonary congestion. In higher doses, intravenous glyceryl trinitrate will also reduce arteriolar resistance. Glyceryl trinitrate also has direct effects on the coronary microcirculation. Cowan *et al.* (1969) presented conclusive evidence indicating that glyceryl trinitrate increases myocardial blood flow in man. Cohen and his associates (1973) noted a prolonged dilation of coronary collaterals following the administration of glyceryl trinitrate in dogs; other authors observed a redistribution of coronary blood flow from normally perfused to underperfused areas of the heart in patients with isolated stenosis of the coronary arteries (Cohn *et al.*, 1977; Mehta and

Pepine, 1978). Unlike sodium nitroprusside, it has been demonstrated that glyceryl trinitrate reduces ischaemic injury, even after acute myocardial infarction (Chiariello *et al.*, 1976). Being a non-toxic agent, it is fast becoming the most popular vasodilator for patients with ischaemic heart disease.

Commercial preparation of glyceryl trinitrate for parenteral injection is not yet universally available, but a sterile solution for intravenous use can be prepared in the hospital pharmacy by dissolving glyceryl trinitrate tablets in water or saline and filtering the solution through a 0.22 μm bacterial filter (Fahmy, 1978). Final dilution to an appropriate concentration can be made with normal saline or 5% dextrose in water. Such a solution will contain other components of the tablet (lactose adsorbate and water-soluble stabilizers). No adverse side-effects have been reported from its use. Since glyceryl trinitrate is adsorbed or absorbed by plastic (Crouthamel, Dorsch and Shangraw, 1978), its solution should be stored in glass bottles. A minidrip delivery set should be used for intravenous infusion. Start with an initial infusion rate of 0.5 μg/kg per minute and adjust it to obtain the desired effect. When the infusion rate is slow, some loss of potency through absorption by the delivery tubing is inevitable. Only solutions prepared the same day should be used.

Phentolamine

Phentolamine, an alpha-adrenergic blocking agent, has a duration of action of 15–20 minutes. It has a more potent action on arteriolar resistance than venous capacitance vessels (Miller *et al.*, 1976). Stern *et al.* (1978) found that patients receiving phentolamine had a higher heart rate than those receiving sodium nitroprusside or glyceryl trinitrate. Capurro, Kent and Epstein (1977) reported that phentolamine had a deleterious effect on coronary collateral function in dogs. Interpretation of these findings is difficult. In practice, phentolamine has been used successfully in the management of congestive heart failure, with minimal increase in heart rate (Majid, Sharma and Taylor, 1971) and no adverse effects on myocardial oxygenation (Chatterjee *et al.*, 1973).

Phentolamine hydrochloride or mesylate is available as a lyophilized powder which is soluble in water or physiological saline. It can be given either as a single bolus (0.5–1 mg) for transient effects or as an infusion (10 μg/kg per minute) for long-term therapy. If tachycardia is a problem, propranolol can be used to control it.

Chlorpromazine

This phenothiazine has pronounced cardiovascular effects. It has been used successfully for the treatment of hypertensive crisis in patients after cardiac surgery (Stinson *et al.*, 1975). The cardiovascular effects of chlorpromazine are complex (Baldessarini, 1980). The most prominent feature is a reduction in systemic and pulmonary vascular resistance due to alpha-adrenergic blockade. Tachycardia is another consistent feature, which is either reflex in nature or the result of an atropine-like effect. Chlorpromazine should be given in increments of 2.5 mg intravenously for the treatment of hypertension. Its effect is noticeable in 5–10 minutes. If no response is observable after 20 mg, it can be regarded as ineffective. Propranolol should be used to control the heart rate if tachycardia is a problem.

Hydrallazine

Hydrallazine is another direct relaxant of arteriolar smooth muscle which has been found useful in the control of arterial hypertension. Its circulatory effects are similar to those of chlorpromazine, but it does not cause orthostatic hypotension (Koch-Weser, 1976). Reflex tachycardia is pronounced and almost always requires the concurrent administration of propranolol. Hence hydrallazine should not be used when propranolol is contraindicated. Hydrallazine, up to 0.5 mg/kg, can be given slowly intravenously. This dose can be repeated in 15 minutes if an effect is not seen. The usual dose is 20–40 mg. Patients with renal failure require a lower dose. Maximal effect lasts from 10 to 80 minutes.

The treatment of hypotension

Blood flow across narrowed segments of coronary arteries is pressure dependent (see 'Coronary blood flow in the ischaemic heart' in Chapter 2). Therefore, even a minor degree of diastolic hypotension (diastolic blood pressure below 8 kPa or 60 mmHg) can precipitate myocardial ischaemia in patients with ischaemic heart disease. If hypotension is profound or if it is accompanied by ST segment depression, it should be treated actively. Identification and elimination of the precipitating cause is important. Acute myocardial infarction, arrhythmias and drug interactions as well as anaesthetic misadventures (e.g. hypoxia, excessive airway pressure, pneumothorax and mismatched transfusion) should be ruled out. Infusion of vasodilator should be discontinued. Blood loss and third-space loss should be reviewed, and deficits replaced. Vagal reflexes, obstruction of the inferior vena cava by the exploring hand of the surgeon or dislocation of the heart by surgical retractors are also common causes which can be rectified promptly.

The inspired oxygen fraction should always be increased when hypotension is a complication. If hypotension persists and coexists with a slow heart rate, the level of anaesthesia should be lightened. When this is not possible or when improvement is not forthcoming, support of the circulation with vasoactive drugs is indicated.

Atropine

Atropine, 2–3 mg, given intravenously in increments of 0.4 mg each, is the drug of choice when hypotension and bradycardia coexist. As heart rate increases, blood pressure usually improves.

Isoprenaline and adrenaline

Isoprenaline is a beta-adrenergic agonist. It has potent inotropic and chronotropic properties and causes peripheral vasodilation. The dose of this potent vasoactive drug should be titrated against its effects. An initial infusion rate of $2-5\mu g$ per minute is recommended. A solution containing 1 mg in 250 ml of 5% dextrose in water (i.e. a final concentration of $4\mu g/ml$) is a convenient dilution. Adrenaline is another potent beta-adrenergic agonist, but it also has alpha effects which increase with increasing dose. The recommended initial rate of infusion is $5\mu g$ per minute. Both isoprenaline and adrenaline can cause a marked increase in heart rate. They have been largely replaced by dopamine in recent years.

Dopamine

Dopamine, like noradrenaline and adrenaline, is an endogenous catecholamine (Goldberg, 1974). Its action on the heart is beta-adrenergic in nature. Unlike the other catecholamines, a therapeutic concentration of dopamine dilates the renal, mesenteric, coronary and cerebral microcirculation via dopaminergic receptors. At higher concentrations the effect of dopamine on the peripheral circulation is uniformly vasoconstrictive. It has a less prominent effect on heart rate than isoprenaline and adrenaline. The recommended initial rate of infusion is $2-5\mu g/kg$ per minute. The dose can be increased in steps to obtain the desired circulatory response. When the dose is in excess of $50\mu g/kg$ per minute, its alpha effect on the peripheral circulation predominates. A convenient dilution is 200 mg in 250 or 500 ml of 5% dextrose in water, to give a final concentration of 800 or $400\mu g/ml$, respectively.

Dobutamine

Dobutamine, a synthetic agent, has pharmacological actions similar to those of dopamine (Sonnenblick, Frishman and LeJemtel, 1979). Its effect on heart rate is even less than that of dopamine. An intravenous infusion should begin with $2.5\mu g/kg$ per minute.

Pure alpha-adrenergic agents

The pure alpha agonists include noradrenaline, phenylephrine and methoxamine. They increase blood pressure by peripheral vasoconstriction. Since the left ventricle has to eject against a higher arterial resistance, an added workload is imposed on the ischaemic heart. Therefore, indication for the use of a pure alpha agonist is rare. When hypotension is accompanied by a low central venous pressure or left ventricular filling pressure and a low systemic vascular resistance, volume expansion is indicated. Phenylephrine can be given in $50\mu g$ increments to increase blood pressure temporarily while fluid is being replaced. It can also be used to counteract the effects of an excessive dose of a vasodilator. In both situations the goal is to return the coronary perfusion pressure to a more acceptable level (a diastolic pressure of 8 kPa or 60 mmHg), and not necessarily towards absolutely normal values. Prolonged infusion of an alpha agent is never indicated.

The treatment of arrhythmias

Depending on the method of monitoring, the reported incidence of arrhythmias in the operating theatre varies between 20 and 60 per cent (Dodd, Sims and Bone, 1962; Kuner *et al.*, 1967; Vanik and Davis, 1968). Most authors agreed that the incidence of arrhythmias was increased in patients who had endotracheal anaesthesia and in those with pre-existing heart disease.

In the environment of the operating theatre, there are many factors which can precipitate abnormal cardiac rhythms, even in the well managed patients. Most of these factors have been mentioned in previous chapters. They are summarized below for clarity.

1. *Halothane* is associated with a high incidence of nodal bradycardia. Ventricular arrhythmias are also common if the *arterial carbon dioxide tension* is allowed to rise above normal or if *adrenaline* is used to infiltrate the operative site. The incidence of nodal rhythm in patients anaesthetized with *enflurane* is just as high, but enflurane is more compatible with the use of adrenaline.

2. Sinus bradycardia or transient asystole following repeated doses of *suxamethonium* is not rare. Cardiac arrest following the administration of suxamethonium in patients suffering from severe burns, multiple trauma or neurosurgical illness has been reported.

3. Following a large bolus of *pancuronium* or *ketamine*, sinus tachycardia is invariable.

4. Bradycardia is not uncommon following the administration of a large dose of *morphine* or *fentanyl*.

5. Sinus tachycardia and ventricular arrhythmias in response to *direct laryngoscopy* and *endotracheal intubation* are common, but bradycardia and transient asystole have been observed also.

6. Both sinus tachycardia in response to noxious *surgical stimuli* and profound bradycardia in response to other surgical manipulations (e.g. traction on extraocular muscles and pressure on the carotic sinus) have been reported.

In addition, organic heart disease, hypoxaemia, hypokalaemia, acid–base disturbances and drug interaction are complicating factors in criticilly ill patients, while digitalis intoxication is still a common cause of arrhythmias in cardiac patients (see Chapter 11).

Whether an arrhythmia requires active treatment depends on an accurate diagnosis of the rhythm disturbance and on its effects on circulatory function. Fortunately, the majority of arrhythmias encountered in anaesthetized patients are not serious (Vanik and Davis, 1968). An arrhythmia is serious if it is the cause of haemodynamic instability, if it disturbs the balance of myocardial blood flow and myocardial work, or if it is the forerunner of life-threatening ventricular arrhythmias.

Arrhythmias due to underlying organic heart disease are always serious. They should have been identified and treated before the scheduled operation (see 'Arrhythmias and their control' in Chapter 5). Most of the arrhythmias not related to organic heart disease are self-limiting when the precipitating cause is identified and eliminated. Only the treatment of arrhythmias commonly encountered in the operating theatre are discussed below.

Sinus and atrial tachycardias

Healthy adults can tolerate a heart rate of 160–180 per minute, but patients with ischaemic heart disease behave differently. As their heart rate increases towards the maximum tolerable limit, not only is myocardial work increased and diastolic myocardial blood flow decreased, but ventricular filling also declines, and cardiac output is compromised. The extent of the fall in cardiac output depends on the degree of ventricular impairment. Therefore sinus and atrial tachycardias are two of the most serious arrhythmias to be encountered in this group of patients. During an attack of sinus or atrial tachycardia, carotid sinus massage can slow the heart rate; but its effect is only transient in sinus tachycardia, and this procedure is contraindicated in patients with carotid artery disease or cerebral vascular disease. The administration of edrophonium, 10 mg intravenously, and repeated when necessary, often will bring these tachycardias under control. Otherwise, propranolol can be used as described earlier (see 'The treatment of sinus tachycardia and hypertension' in this chapter). If the atrial tachycardia is paroxysmal in nature and is characterized by an abrupt onset (paroxysmal atrial tachycardia), direct current cardioversion should be tried when pharmacological agents fail.

Atrial flutter and atrial fibrillation

Not infrequently, these arrhythmias are seen in older patients during or after intrathoracic procedures. The development of congestive heart failure is another possible cause of a sudden onset of atrial fibrillation. Treatment is necessary when the ventricular response is fast. If the patient is not already digitalized, rapid digitalization to control the ventricular rate between 70 and 80 per minute is indicated. Digoxin, 1 mg, can be given intravenously over a period of 10–20 minutes. If it is ineffective, propranolol in small increments can also be used, provided that heart failure is not a complication. Direct current cardioversion is another alternative.

Sinus bradycardia

The haemodynamic consequence of profound sinus bradycardia is a fall in cardiac output. When blood volume is normal, most anaesthetized patients tolerate a heart rate of 60 per minute, and some of them tolerate a heart rate as low as 50 per minute. Arterial hypotension accompanying sinus brady-cardia is an indication that cardiac output is impaired. Atropine, 2–3 mg given intravenously in divided doses, is the treatment of choice. An isoprenaline infusion of 2–5 μg per minute or an adrenaline infusion of 5 μg per minute are alternatives. If profound sinus bradycardia is refractory to pharacological measures, the introduction of a transvenous pacemaker for artificial pacing is indicated.

Nodal rhythm

Atrial contraction during normal sinus rhythm can contribute up to 30 per cent of the stroke volume in a small number of patients. When these patients develop nodal rhythm, cardiac output is reduced and blood pressure falls. The decline in cardiac output and blood pressure is particularly noticeable during an attack of nodal bradycardia or nodal tachycardia. Nodal rhythm usually does not require treatment unless it is accompanied by arterial hypotension. A large number of patients anaesthetized with halothane or enflurane have nodal rhythm. Sinus rhythm will return if the concentration of the volatile agent is reduced or if these inhalational agents are replaced. The treatment of nodal bradycardia or nodal tachycardia is similar to that of sinus bradycardia or sinus tachycardia, respectively.

Ventricular premature beats

Isolated ventricular premature beats are benign and do not require any treatment. Frequent but unifocal ventricular contractions in the presence of a very slow supraventricluar rhythm are likely escape beats. They will disappear when the supraventricular rhythm is increased with the administration of atropine. Otherwise, frequent ventricular premature beats (more than 5 per minute), those which come in runs of three or more, those which are multifocal in origin and those which fall on the T wave of the preceding beat are harbingers of ventricular tachycardia and ventricular fibrillation. They require immediate attention. The most effective treatment is intravenous lignocaine, 1–1.5 mg/kg, which can be repeated in 5–10 minutes if necessary. If the ventricular premature beats recur after the initial treatment, a lignocaine infusion of 2–4 mg per minute should be administered. Propranolol is also effective but is not the drug of first choice.

References

Adams, A. P., Clarke, T. N. S., Edmonds-Seal, J., Foëx, P., Prys-Roberts, C. and Roberts, J. (1973). Effects of sodium nitroprusside on myocardial contractility and haemodynamics. *British Journal of Anaesthesia* **45**, 120.

Baldessarini, R. J. (1980). Drugs and the treatment of psychiatric disorders. In: *The Pharmacological Basis of Therapeutics*, 6th edn., pp. 391–447. Ed. by A. G. Gilman, L. S. Goodman and A. Gilman. Macmillan: New York, Toronto, London.

Capurro, N. L., Kent, K. M. and Epstein, S. E. (1977). Comparison of nitroglycerin-, nitroprusside-, and phentolamine-induced changes in coronary collateral function in dogs. *Journal of Clinical Investigation* **60**, 295.

Chatterjee, K., Parmley, W. W., Ganz, W., Forrester, J., Walinsky, P., Crexells, C. and Swan, H. J. C. (1973). Hemodynamic and metabolic responses to vasodilator therapy in acute myocardial infarction. *Circulation* **48,** 1183.

Chiariello, M., Gold, H. K., Leinbach, R. C., Davis, M. A. and Maroko, P. R. (1976). Comparison between the effects of nitroprusside and nitroglycerin on ischemic injury during acute myocardial infarction. *Circulation* **54,** 766.

Cohen, M. V., Downey, J. M., Sonnenblick, E. and Kirk, E. S. (1973). The effects of nitroglycerin on coronary collaterals and myocardial contractility. *Journal of Clinical Investigation* **52,** 2836.

Cohn, P. F., Maddox, D., Holman, B. L., Markis, J. E., Adams, D. F. and See, J. R. (1977). Effect of sublingually administered nitroglycerin on regional myocardial blood flow in patients with coronary artery disease. *American Journal of Cardiology* **39,** 672.

Cowan, C., Duran, P. V., Corsini, G., Goldschlager, N. and Bing, R. J. (1969). The effects of nitroglycerin on myocardial blood flow in man — measured by coincidence counting and bolus injections of rubidium. *American Journal of Cardiology* **24,** 154.

Crouthamel, W. G., Dorsch, B. and Shangraw, R. (1978). Loss of nitroglycerin from plastic intravenous bags. *New England Journal of Medicine* **299,** 262.

Davies, D. W., Greiss, L., Kadar, D. and Steward, D. J. (1975). Sodium nitroprusside in children: observations on metabolism during normal and abnormal responses. *Canadian Anaesthetists' Society Journal* **22,** 553.

Davies, D. W., Kadar, D., Steward, D. J. and Munro, I. R. (1975). A sudden death associated with the use of sodium nitroprusside for induction of hypotension during anaesthesia. *Canadian Anaesthetists' Society Journal* **22,** 547.

Dodd, R. B., Sims, W. A. and Bone, D. J. (1962). Cardiac arrhythmias observed during anesthesia and surgery. *Surgery* **51,** 440.

Fahmy, N. R. (1978). Nitroglycerin as a hypotensive drug during general anesthesia. *Anesthesiology* **49,** 17.

Goldberg, L. I. (1974). Dopamine — clinical uses of an endogenous catecholamine. *New England Journal of Medicine* **291,** 707.

Jack, R. D. (1974). Toxicity of sodium nitroprusside. *British Journal of Anaesthesia* **46,** 952.

Koch-Weser, J. (1976). Hydralazine. *New England Journal of Medicine* **295,** 320.

Kuner, J., Enescu, V., Utsu, F., Boszormenyi, E., Bernstein, H. and Corday, E. (1967). Cardiac arrhythmias during anesthesia. *Diseases of the Chest* **52,** 580.

Majid, P. A., Sharma, B. and Taylor, S. H. (1971). Phentolamine for vasodilator treatment of severe heart-failure. *Lancet* **ii,** 719.

Mehta, J. and Pepine, C. J. (1978). Effect of sublingual nitroglycerin on regional flow in patients with and without coronary disease. *Circulation* **58,** 803.

Michenfelder, J. D. and Theye, R. A. (1977). Canine systemic and cerebral effects of hypotension induced by hemorrhage, trimethaphan, halothane, or nitroprusside. *Anesthesiology* **46,** 188.

Michenfelder, J. D. and Tinker, J. H. (1977). Cyanide toxicity and thiosulfate protection during chronic administration of sodium nitroprusside in the dog: Correlation with a human case. *Anesthesiology* **47**, 441.

Miller, R. R., Vismara, L. A., Williams, D. O., Amsterdam, E. A. and Mason, D. T. (1976). Pharmacological mechanisms for left ventricular unloading in clinical congestive heart failure: differential effects of nitroprusside, phentolamine, and nitroglycerin on cardiac function and peripheral circulation. *Circulation Research* **39**, 127.

Shand, D. G. (1975). Propranolol. *New England Journal of Medicine* **293**, 280.

Sonnenblick, E. H., Frishman, W. H. and LeJemtel, T. H. (1979). Dobutamine: a new synthetic cardioactive sympathetic amine. *New England Journal of Medicine* **300**, 17.

Stern, M. A., Gohlke, H. K., Loeb, H. S., Croke, R. P. and Gunnar, R. M. (1978). Hemodynamic effects of intravenous phentolamine in low output cardiac failure: dose–response relationships. *Circulation* **58**, 157.

Stinson, E. B., Holloway, E. L., Derby, G., Oyer, P. E., Hollingsworth, J., Griepp, R. B. and Harrison, D. C. (1975). Comparative hemodynamic responses to chlorpromazine, nitroprusside, nitroglycerin, and trimethaphan immediately after open-heart operations. *Circulation* **51** and **52**, Suppl. I, I–26.

Vanik, P. E. and Davis, H. S. (1968). Cardiac arrhythmias during halothane anesthesia. *Anesthesia and Analgesia . . . Current Researches* **47**, 299.

Vesey, C. J., Cole, P. V. and Simpson, P. J. (1976). Cyanide and thiocyanate concentrations following sodium nitroprusside infusion in man. *British Journal of Anaesthesia* **48**, 651.

9

Postoperative management

The stress of anaesthesia and the surgical operation extends well into the postoperative period. With the return of consciousness, tachycardia and hypertension in response to pain are common cardiovascular complications. During the first hours of recovery, poor airway control and residual respiratory depression are leading causes of hypoxaemia. Shivering during this period will increase metabolic demand; the patient who has depressed respiratory and cardiac functons is ill-equipped to cope with this added stress. Blood loss and fluid loss due to the operation may continue into the postoperative phase and have to be replaced. The metabolic response to trauma demands vigilance in the administration of fluid and electrolytes. Some of these patients may require long-term support of respiratory and circulatory functions. Therefore the intraoperative and the postoperative management of these patients require equal diligence. If intensive monitoring and treatment are necessary, the patient should be admitted to a critical care area.

Monitoring

The principles of monitoring are the same both during operation and in the postoperative period (see Chapter 6). In general, monitoring techniques instituted during operation should be continued in the immediate postoperative phase. On arrival in the recovery area after a major operation, blood should be sampled for the determination of haemoglobin concentration, serum electrolytes, blood glucose, serum urea and creatinine, blood gas tensions and buffer base. The establishment of postoperative baseline values in these variables is necessary for the continuing care of the patient.

Postoperative analgesia

As in other surgical patients, good postoperative management includes adequate pain relief. During the immediate postoperative period, the use of a narcotic analgesic intravenously in small doses (e.g. morphine, 1–2 mg every 15 minutes as necessary) will allow careful titration of its analgesic effect against its respiratory depressant effect. Epidural analgesia is an excellent form of pain relief where it is indicated.

119

Parenteral maintenance fluid

Antidiuresis is part of the metabolic response to trauma. Fluid balance should be carefully monitored in the postoperative period. Patients with cardiac disease are easy victims of fluid and sodium excess. The volume of maintenance fluid should be limited to 25–30 ml/kg on the day of operation. This can be increased to 30–35 ml/kg per day in the next 2 days (Randall, 1976). The normal kidney has a large capacity to conserve sodium. Since the normal daily sodium requirement is 1–2 mmol/kg, this daily requirment will be met if the calculated maintenance fluid is given as 0.3% saline and 3.3% dextrose in water. Although the ability of the kidney to conserve potassium is limited, the catabolic phase following an operation is accompanied by mobilization of a considerable amount of intracellular potassium. Little potassium is required by the surgical patient in the first 2 postoperative days unless a deficit can be demonstrated. The normal daily requirment of 0.5–1 mmol/kg can be added to the maintenance fluid in subsequent days, provided renal function is normal. In addition to normal maintenance, blood loss and abnormal fluid and electrolyte losses (e.g. drains, nasogastric suction, translocated fluids, increased insensible loss due to fever or hyperventilation) should be replaced.

Respiratory care

Although artificial ventilation of the lungs poses few limitations, it is difficult to set hard and fast rules for mechanical support of ventilation in the postoperative period. The decision should rest with the cardiopulmonary status of the patient, the nature of the operation and recovery from the effects of anaesthetics. When in doubt, ventilaton should be controlled for a few hours until all physiological variables have stabilized. If artificial respiration is not indicated, oxygen by face mask or nasal prongs should be administered until the patient has regained full control of his airway.

Many patients with ischaemic heart disease who are heavy cigarette smokers also have chronic bronchitis and chronic obstructive pulmonary disease. They are prone to respiratory complications (Tarhan et al., 1973). Therefore it is important to emphasize early ambulation and deep breathing exercise during recovery. For those developing pulmonary complications, chest physiotherapy, incentive spirometry and intermittent positive pressure breathing with the application of aerosol are indicated.

Circulatory care

The practice of protecting the ischaemic myocardium should be continued in the postoperative period; arrhythmias should be monitored and treated; the circulation should be supported when necessary. Patients with a history of previous myocardial infarction deserve special attention (see 'Myocardial infarction and anaesthesia' in Chapter 5). The incidence of another myocardial infarction in the first postoperative week is much higher in this group of patients. Tarhan et al. (1972) reported an incidence of 37 per cent in those who had a history of myocardial infarction within 3 months before the operation, an incidence of 16 per cent if the previous myocardial infarction had occurred 4–6 months before the operation, and an incidence of 5 per cent if the previous myocardial infarction had occurred 7 months before the operation or longer. Not only is the incidence of postoperative myocardial infarction higher in this group of patients, but also the mortality after acute myocardial infarction in the postoperative period is higher. The overall mortality was 54 per cent (Tarhan *et al.*, 1972); and the majority of deaths occurred within 48 hours after the infarction, presumably due to arrhythmias. Many of these infarcts are silent and without pain. Therefore these patients should be admitted to a special care area where continuous electrocardiographic monitoring is available for at least 48 hours. They should have serial 12-lead electrocardiograms and cardiac enzyme assays done for the same period. Arrhythmias should be treated with anti-arrhythmic agents, and heart failure treated aggressively with digitalis, diuretics and vasodilators.

References

Randall, H. T. (1976). Fluid, electrolye and acid–base balance. *Surgical Clinics of North America* **56**, 1019.

Tarhan, S., Moffitt, E. A., Taylor, W. F. and Giuliani, E. R. (1972). Myocardial infarction after general anesthesia. *Journal of the American Medical Association* **220**, 1451.

Tarhan, S., Moffitt, E. A., Sessler, A. D., Douglas, W. W. and Taylor, W. F. (1973). Risk of anesthesia and surgery in patients with chronic bronchitis and chronic obstructive pulmonary disease. *Surgery* **74**, 720.

10

Beta-adrenergic antagonists

Propranolol is the first effective and safe beta-adrenergic antagonist to gain wide acceptance (Black *et al.*, 1964). Since its introduction in 1964, contradictory opinions have been expressed on the anaesthetic management of patients on chronic therapy. Although Viljoen, Estafanous and Kellner (1972) as well as Ayscue (1972) recommended the withdrawal of this agent for 24 hours to 2 weeks before elective operations, others have shown that it was safe to anaesthetize patients on chronic therapy even when it was given 6 hours before cardiac (Caralps *et al.*, 1974; Korpiva, Brown and Pappas, 1978) or other operations (Kaplan and Dunbar, 1976; Haidinyak and Didier, 1977). Beta-adrenergic antagonists are potent myocardial depressants. It has been estimated that not less than 9 per cent of inpatients on propranolol had adverse reactions, and nearly a third of these were life-threatening cardiac complications (Greenblatt and Koch-Weser, 1973). It is likley that the real difference in the experience of these authors lies not in substance but in the method of selection and preparation of their patients. With better understanding of the pharmacology of the beta-adrenergic system and its blockade, and of the interaction of beta antagonists with anaesthetic agents, it is possible to approach this controversy more rationally.

Besides propranolol there are now a number of other beta-adrenergic antagonists available. They include acebutolol, atenolol, metoprolol, nadolol, oxprenolol, pindolol, sotalol and timolol. Cardioselectivity is claimed for some of these, and intrinsic agonist activity for others. However, the pharmacology of beta blockade by these agents in patients with cardiovascular disease is similar (Davidson *et al.*, 1976; Thadani *et al.*, 1979). Propranolol is still by far the most popular member of the family and is the only agent which can be given intravenously. Therefore the *patient on propranolol* will be discussed as a *prototype* in this chapter.

The beta-adrenergic mechanism and its blockade

Adrenaline, the naturally occurring beta agonist, is a messenger molecule capable of combining with specific receptor sites on the myocardial cell membrane surface (Fig. 10.1). Such an interaction will result in the activation of the enzyme adenyl cyclase, which catalyses the conversion of ATP to cyclic AMP. Cyclic AMP in turn catalyses the conversion of inactive kinase to active kinase. The alteration of cellular mechanisms by active kinase leads to the chronotropic and inotropic effects of adrenaline (Butcher, 1968; Wiklund, 1974).

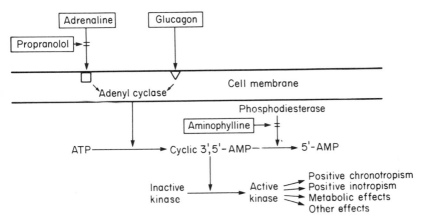

Fig. 10.1   The beta-adrenergic mechanism and its blockade. This diagram also illustrates the mechanism of action of glucagon and aminophylline. (Please refer to text for details.)

Propranolol is an adrenaline analogue capable of combining with beta-adrenergic receptors without activating adenyl cyclase. It is a competitive antagonist (Epstein and Braunwald, 1966a) similar to the action of curare at the myoneural junction. This blockade can be overcome by increasing the concentration of the agonist.

The cyclic AMP–kinase-mediated chronotropic and inotropic effects can be activated by agents other than beta-adrenergic agonists (Fig. 10.1). Glucagon, when combined with specific surface receptors, will also activate adenyl cyclase and lead to the conversion of ATP to cyclic AMP and the conversion of inactive kinase to active kinase (Sutherland, Robison and Butcher, 1968). Aminophylline, by inhibiting phosphodiesterase, will retard the enzymatic breakdown of cyclic AMP and will increase the effect of beta-adrenergic agents (Rall and West, 1963).

Actions on the cardiovascular system

Since the introduction of propranolol, the indications for beta blockade have grown to include ischaemic heart disease, obstructive cardiomyopathy, supraventricular and ventricular arrhythmias, essential hypertension, phaeochromocytoma, thyrotoxicosis, certain tremors and psychiatric disorders, and glaucoma. The majority of patients treated with beta antagonists are those with ischaemic heart disease and hypertensive cardiovascular disease.

Propranolol alleviates symptoms and signs of myocardial ischaemia and improves the exercise tolerance of patients with ischaemic heart disease. As a result of beta-adrenergic blockade, heart rate, cardiac output, myocardial contractility, ventricular systolic pressure and its rate of rise are reduced. Consequently, the oxygen cost of myocardial work falls. On the contrary, ventricular volume and ejection time are increased, and myocardial energy requirements rise. The sum total of all these effects is a net reduction in myocardial work, which is beneficial to the patient with myocardial ischaemia (Epstein and Braunwald, 1966a). By virtue of its activity as a beta antagonist on the excitable and conducting tissues of the heart and its quinidine-like activity on myocardial cell membrane, propranolol is found useful in the treatment of arrhythmias (Epstein and Braunwald, 1966b; Gibson and Sowton, 1969).

Propranolol is a potent inhibitor of renin secretion by the kidneys. Its anti-hypertensive action is most effective in patients with high or normal plasma renin activity (Bühler et al., 1973; Hollifield et al., 1976). Since inhibition of renin secretion will reduce aldosterone secretion, propranolol will prevent the compensatory salt and water retention accompanying vasodilator therapy. Therefore propranolol is often combined with a diuretic (Hollifield et al., 1976) or a vasodilator (Zacest, Gilmore and Koch-Weser, 1972) in the control of hypertension. Other anti-hypertensive actions of propranolol include a decrease in cardiac output (Frohlich et al., 1968; Lydtin et al., 1972) and cerebral effect in high doses (Stern, Hoffman and Braun, 1971; Myers et al., 1975).

Absorption and fate

Propranolol is completely absorbed from the gastrointestinal tract (Paterson et al., 1970) and it is eliminated almost entirely by metabolism in the liver (Bond, 1967). Hepatic extraction during its transfer from the gut to the systemic circulation (presystemic or 'first pass' hepatic elimination) is high (Shand and Rangno, 1972). The outcome is a low bio-availability. When absorbed, 90–95 per cent is bound to plasma protein (Evans, Nies and Shand, 1973). After oral but not after intravenous administration, an equipotent active metabolite with a shorter half-life, 4-hydroxypropranolol can be detected (Fitzgerald and O'Donnell, 1971). However, at the end of a 6-hourly dose interval after oral administration, the effect of this metabolite can be ignored.

A plasma level of 50–100 μg/ml at the end of a 6-hourly oral dose interval is therapeutic and will confer a high degree of beta blockade (Shand, 1974). The oral dose required by patients varies widely. Several factors are responsible (Nies and Shand, 1975):

    1. There may be a seven- to twentyfold difference in plasma level of

propranolol among different individuals after the same oral dose (Shand, Nuckolls and Oates, 1970; Shand, 1974). This large variation is the result of different rates of presystemic hepatic extraction.

2. Only the unbound fraction is free to combine with receptor molecules. The difference in protein binding of 90–95 per cent (Evans, Nies and Shand, 1973) may seem small, but it means a twofold difference (5–10 per cent) in the availability of the active unbound fraction.

3. There may be a genuine difference in receptor sensitivity among different individuals (George and Dollery, 1973).

4. The underlying mechanism of action may be different. For example, hypertensive patients with high or normal plasma renin activity require only a modest dose of propranolol. In some other patients doses up to 2000 mg are necessary (Zacharias et al., 1972). The anti-hypertensive action of propranolol in this second group of patients is probably through its central nervous system effect (Stern, Hoffman and Braun, 1971; Myers et al., 1975) rather than the lowering of plasma renin activity.

5. Propranolol is a competitive antagonist. Its effect depends, to a large extent, on the underlying sympathetic tone which differs from patient to patient and may vary with the daily activities of the patient (Shand, 1975).

6. Poor compliance of some patients is also a factor to be considered (Nies and Shand, 1975). They may not be taking the prescribed dose regularly.

With intravenous administration, presystemic hepatic elimination does not occur, and only a fraction of the oral dose is necessary to produce a similar degree of beta blockade. No active metabolites are detectable after intravenous administration.

Both bound and unbound fractions of propranolol are extracted and metabolized by the liver (Evans and Shand, 1973). The plasma half-life is 3–6 hours after oral administration and 2–3 hours after intravenous administration (Shand, 1975). Coltart et al. (1973) reported that 24 hours was required for the complete elimination of propranolol and its metabolites from the myocardium, while others found no detectable cardiac beta-adrenergic blockade by propranolol or its metabolites as early as 18 hours, and certainly no longer than 48 hours after withdrawal from chronic therapy (Faulkner et al., 1973; Romagnoli and Keates, 1975). However, as the rate of hepatic extraction of propranolol is very sensitive to hepatic blood flow, beta blockade itself, by decreasing cardiac output and hepatic blood flow, will reduce and delay the elimination of propranolol (Nies, Evans and Shand, 1973a, b). Similarly, the action of propranolol is prolonged in patients with uncompensated congestive heart failure, in whom it is also contraindicated.

Contraindications and adverse reactions

The contraindications and adverse reactions to propranolol are similar (Greenblatt and Koch-Weser, 1973). It is contraindicated in patients who have bronchospasm, congestive heart failure, hypotension, bradycardia and heart blocks. Its administration should be discontinued should any of these develop during therapy. Propranolol is administered in small increments until a maintenance dose is established. Adverse reactions usually occur early in the course of therapy and are not related to the magnitude of the maintenance dose. Once the maintenance dose is reached, life-threatening complications are unlikely unless there is a change in the underlying disease.

Anaesthetic considerations

Preoperative assessment and preparation of the patient

During the preoperative assessment of patients on propranolol, their medical history and cardiac disability should be reviewed. The combined circulatory depressant effect of beta blockade and anaesthesia is a constant threat to these patients. Profound bradycardia and hypotension is more likely to occur in patients on a toxic dose of the agent. Therefore an effort should be made to determine the adequacy of treatment and the possibility of toxicity. Unfortunately, the daily maintenance dose varies from individual to individual because of differences in receptor sensitivity, pharmacokinetic factors and compliance with treatment. Therefore the daily dose is not a reliable guide to the degree of beta blockade. A thorough examination of the cardiovascular system is helpful.

The optimally treated patient

The usual oral maintenance dose varies between 80 and 320 mg per day. The patient on an optimum dose of propranolol has a good exercise tolerance, his blood pressure is well controlled, and he has no anginal symptoms, congestive heart failure, orthostatic hypotension or electrocardiographic evidence of heart block. The resting heart rate is around 60 per minute, and it will increase by 10 per cent or more after routine activities. However, profound bradycardia and hypotension can still occur in the optimally treated patient under the additional depressant effects of anaesthesia, although this is rare.

For such a patient there is little reason for withholding or even reducing the maintenance dose before non-cardiac operations. If the operation is scheduled in the morning, the usual evening dose should be allowed the night before; if the operation is scheduled late in the day, the morning dose should be given on the day of operation. Atropine should be omitted from the premedication, but should be available in the operating room.

The patient with propranolol toxicity

Clinical features of propranolol toxicity include symptomatic and inappropriate bradycardia, orthostatic hypotension, reduced exercise tolerance, congestive heart failure and evidence of impaired atrioventricular conduction on the electrocardiogram. The frankly toxic patient is usually obvious and is treated, but the mildly toxic patients who have escaped attention are likely to cause concern. Unless propranolol is withdrawn or the dose reduced or supplementary measures taken, life-threatening cardiac complications are likely in such a patient during operation.

In preparing the toxic patient for surgery, withdrawal of propranolol should be gradual because abrupt cessation can be associated with acute coronary insufficiency in some patients (Alderman *et al.*, 1974; Mizgala and Counsell, 1976). The underlying mechanism of this withdrawal rebound phenomenon is multifactorial (Shand and Wood, 1978). Receptor hypersensitivity to catecholamine plays a significant role. This hypersensitive period lasts up to 2 weeks after withdrawal (Nattel, Rangno and Van Loon, 1979). During withdrawal the patient should be observed closely in hospital, and care must be taken in the use of exogenous catecholamine. The return of anginal symptoms, arrhythmias or uncontrolled hypertension are indications for re-institution of propranolol therapy to the last symptom-free dose.

If gradual withdrawal is not possible because the operation is urgent, supportive treatment is necessary. Digitalization is indicated for congestive heart failure; implantation of a temporary artificial pacemaker is indicated for bradycardia or heart block. The management of bradycardia and hypotension is discussed in a later section.

The inadequately treated patient

Some patients would benefit from the introduction of propranolol therapy or from an increase in the dose. These include patients with angina and a high resting heart rate, patients with atrial fibrillation or atrial flutter and a fast ventricular rate not controlled by digitalis, patients with significant ventricular premature beats, and hypertensive patients with high or normal plasma renin activity. If time permits, the oral route is preferred; in an emergency, intravenous propranolol is necessary.

Intravenous propranolol should be given slowly according to a schedule proposed by Shand (1975). The first milligram should be given over 10–15 minutes in increments of 0.1–0.2 mg each. During this period the patient should be observed closely for serious side-effects. If there are no adverse reactions after 1 mg, it is unlikely that they will occur, and the dose can be increased when necessary at a rate of 0.5–1 mg every 5 minutes to a total dose of 0.1 mg/kg.

Management during operation

Basic monitoring should include blood pressure, heart rate and electrocardiography. Invasive haemodynamic monitoring should be instituted when indicated. During anaesthesia the decision to control ventilaton or not should rest with the surgical requirements and the cardiorespiratory status of the patient (see Part III: 'Anaesthesia in Patients with Ischaemic Heart Disease'). The combined effect of anaesthetic agents and beta blockade on circulatory function is predictable, and the choice of agents should be made accordingly.

Suxamethonium

This is a cholingeric agent. An increase in heart rate is the usual response in adults to a first dose of suxamethonium sufficient for tracheal intubation (see 'Suxamethonium' in Chapter 4), even when they are on propranolol. Cardiac slowing can occur following subsequent doses. As its muscarinic effect on the beta-blocked heart is a cause for concern, it is best reserved for situations when it is absolutely indicated. Atropine should be available immediately.

The curares

Hypotension following tubocurarine can be alarming, particularly when halothane is being used (see 'Tubocurarine' in Chapter 4). The administration of tubocurarine is best avoided in patients on propranolol. Theoretically its ganglionic blocking effect can make the sympathetic blockade on the beta-blocked heart pharmacologically complicated. Dimethyl tubocurarine, on the other hand, has no ganglionic blocking activity and is associated with a lower incidence of hypotension (see 'Dimethyl tubocurarine' in Chapter 4). It is a good choice when it is available (Zaidan *et al.*, 1977).

Pancuronium

Pancuronium is known for its pressor effects (see 'Pancronium' in Chapter 4). It is also a satisfactory agent for tracheal intubation. The increase in heart rate and blood pressure can be minimized by a slow rate of administration, and it is unlikely to vitiate the beneficial effect of propranolol.

Narcotic analgesics

There has been no clinical report of specific adverse interaction between narcotic analgesics and propranolol to date. The myocardial effect of morphine alone is insignificant in man (see 'Morphine' in Chapter 4). Hypotension following the administration of morphine is mediated by dilation of arterial resistance and venous capacitance vessels. In dogs it has been found that the circulatory effect of morphine and propranolol was simply additive.

Inhalational agents

There is always some concern about the combined circulatory depressant effect of inhalational anaesthetics and propranolol (see 'Inhalational anaesthetics' in Chapter 4). Of the two major agents, enflurane is a more potent circulatory depressant than halothane. In dogs the depressant effect of halothane and propranolol is simply additive, while the combination of enflurane and propranolol is less compatible. For these reasons, halothane is deemed a safer agent in these patients. Similar studies indicate that the newer agent, isoflurane, is better tolerated than halothane in the presence of moderate to profound beta-adrenergic blockade by propranolol; but the combined depressant effect of methoxyflurane and practolol seems unacceptable.

Neostigmine

The muscarinic effect of this agent on the heart is potent. Sprague (1975) has reported a case of profound bradycardia following the administration of neostigmine in a patient taking propranolol to control paroxysmal atrial tachycardia. Atropine and neostigmine should not be given combined in a bolus to patients on propranolol. Atropine, 0.6 mg, should be given first; then neostigmine is given in small increments, alternating with further increments of atropine when required. To avoid an excess of neostigmine, the use of the peripheral nerve stimulator is most helpful. Close observation of the heart rate and blood pressure during this period is mandatory.

Postoperative management

Very little is written about the continuation of propranolol therapy in the postoperative period. Since catastrophe and death can strike as early as 24 hours after abrupt withdrawal, it is only logical that the surgical patient should be allowed to go back to his maintenance dose as early as possible. For patients who have to abstain from oral intake postoperatively, the intravenous route should be considered. Rotem (1976) used a continuous infusion of propranolol 5% dextrose in water at an initial rate equal to 10 per cent of the patient's usual daily oral dose over 24 hours. This infusion rate was further adjusted according to the haemodynamic response of the patient. As hepatic blood flow is reduced in the haemodynamically unstable patient, the hepatic extraction and elimination of propranolol is reduced due to haemodynamic-drug interaction (Nies, Evans and Shand, 1973b). The intravenous infusion of propranolol in the critically ill surgical patient should be observed closely in an intensive care area, as frequent adjustment of the rate may be necessary.

The management of profound bradycardia and hypotension

Most anaesthetized patients can tolerate a heart rate as low as 50 per minute. They will not become hypotensive unless they are hypovolaemic. However, there is always the risk of profound bradycardia and hypotension in all patients under the combined effect of beta blockade and anaesthesia. The anaesthetist should be prepared for these complications. There are many pharmacological agents which can counteract the negative chronotropic and negative inotropic effects of beta-adrenergic blockade; but atropine and beta agonists are, by far, the most effective (see 'The Treatment of Hypotension' in Chapter 8).

Pharmacological principles

Atropine

Atropine, the drug of choice when bradycardia is present, should be given in 0.6 mg increments to a total of 2–3 mg as necessary. It is a vagolytic agent which allows residual sympathetic stimulation of the heart to emerge.

Beta-adrenergic agents

Propranolol is a competitive antagonist. Its action can be reversed by the use of a beta agonist. Isoprenaline, a pure agonist, is the agent of choice. It should be given as a continuous intravenous infusion: start with 2–5μg per minute and adjust the rate to obtain the desired effects. Extremely high doses may be needed.

Adrenaline is predominantly a beta agonist with some alpha effect on skin and visceral vascular beds. Due to this alpha effect, it may be more efficacious in maintaining blood pressure. The initial infusion rate is 5μg per minute.

The action of dopamine on the heart is beta-adrenergic in nature, but it has a lesser effect on heart rate than isoprenaline and adrenaline. The recommended initial rate of infusion is 2–5μg/kg per minute, which can be increased in steps to obtain the desired circulatory response.

Dobutamine is a synthetic agent. Its effect on heart rate is even less than that of dopamine. An intravenous infusion can start at 2.5μg/kg per minute.

Alpha-adrenergic agents

Vasopressors with pure alpha effects (noradrenaline, methoxamine and phenylephrine) increase peripheral vascular resistance without any direct effect on the myocardium. If the beta-blocked and depressed heart is unable to cope with the increase in afterload, cardiac function will deteriorate rapidly. These agents are not recommended.

Xanthines

Aminophylline blocks the enzymatic breakdown of cyclic AMP by phosphodiesterase (Rall and West, 1963). Since cyclic AMP-mediated activation of kinase is an important step in the beta-adrenergic mechanism, aminophylline has beta-like activity. It works best when given in conjunction with a betaagonist. The recommended dose is 4–6 mg/kg given intravenously over 15 minutes.

Cardiac glycosides

Digitalis improves myocardial contractility by increasing the cytoplasmic pool of calcium during excitation-contraction coupling. Except in the presence of bradycardia and AV block, rapid digitalization with intravenous digoxin is useful in patients not already digitalized.

Calcium salts

The exact mechanism by which calcium salts improve myocardial contractility remains speculative. It is proposed that calcium salts exert their positive inotropic effect by increasing the sarcoplasmic pool of calcium ions as well. It antagonizes the negative inotropic effect of halothane in man (Denlinger et al., 1975). It is also effective, though less potent, in dogs anaesthetized with halothane and pretreated with beta antagonists (Prys-Robers et al., 1976). Calcium chloride or calcium gluconate, 0.5–1.0 g, can be administered slowly intravenously under electrocardiographic monitoring.

Glucagon

Glucagon can activate adenyl cyclase by interacting with specific and non-beta-adrenergic receptors (Sutherland, Robison and Butcher, 1968); thus it bypasses beta blockade (Glick et al., 1968). It has both chronotropic and inotropic effects in man even in the presence of beta-adrenergic blockade, catecholamine depletion and full digitalization (Parmley, Glick and Sonnenblick, 1968). Its action is not always predictable, and it has been reported to be ineffective (Viljoen, Estafanous and Kellner, 1972). It should be tried in combination with other agents. A bolus of 5–10 mg should be given intravenously and followed by an infusion of 1 mg per minute (Kaplan and Dunbar, 1976). Side-effects of glucagon administration include nausea and vomiting, hypoglycaemia (a result of depletion of glycogen store after prolonged administration) and a minor fall in serum potassium (Parmley, 1971).

Other measures

Besides pharmacological measures, the depth of anaesthesia should be reduced when possible to minimize central nervous system and myocardial depression. Surgical manipulation of viscera should be stopped to avoid evoking unwanted vagal reflexes, and fluid administration should be increased to meet blood loss and third-space loss when indicated. It should be remembered that in the presence of beta blockade, tachycardia may not occur even when hypovolaemia is severe. On the other hand, the beta-blocked heart can be overloaded rapidly. If more than a modest amount of intravenous fluid is used, central venous pressure or pulmonary capillary wedge pressure should be monitored.

References

Alderman, E. L., Coltart, D. J., Wettach, G. E. and Harrison, D. C. (1974). Coronary artery syndromes after sudden propranolol withdrawal. *Annals of Internal Medicine* **81**, 625.

Ayscue, Q. A. (1972). The experts opine. *Survey of Anesthesiology* **16**, 484.

Black, J. W., Crowther, A. F., Shanks, R. G., Smith, L. H. and Dornhorst, A. C. (1964). A new adrenergic beta-receptor angatonist. *Lancet* **i**, 1080.

Bond, P. A. (1967). Metabolism of propranolol (Inderal) a potent, specific β-adrenergic receptor blocking agent. *Nature* **213**, 721.

Bühler, F. R., Laragh, J. H., Vaughan, E. D. Jr, Brunner, H. R., Gavras, H. and Baer, L. (1973). Antihypertensive action of propranolol: specific antirenin responses in high and normal renin forms of essential, renal, renovascular and malignant hypertension. *American Journal of Cardiology* **32**, 511.

Butcher, R. W. (1968). Role of cyclic AMP in hormone actions. *New England Journal of Medicine* **279**, 1378.

Caralps, J. M., Mulet, J., Wienke, H. R., Moran, J. M. and Pifarre, R. (1974). Results of coronary artery surgery in patients receiving propranolol. *Journal of Thoracic and Cardiovascular Surgery* **67**, 526.

Coltart, D. J., Cayen, M. N., Stinson, E. B., Davies, R. O. and Harrison, D. C. (1973). Determination of the safe period for withdrawal of propranolol therapy. *Circulation* **48**, Suppl. IV, IV–7.

Davidson, C., Thadani, U., Singleton, W. and Taylor, S. H. (1976). Comparison of antihypertensive activity of beta-blocking drugs during chronic treatment. *British Medical Journal* **2**, 7.

Denlinger, J. K., Kaplan, J. A., Lecky, J. H. and Wollman, H. (1975). Cardiovascular responses to calcium administered intravenously to man during halothane anesthesia. *Anesthesiology* **42**, 390.

Epstein, S. E. and Braunwald, E. (1966a). Beta-adrenergic receptor blocking drugs: mechanisms of action and clinical applications. *New England Journal of Medicine* **275**, 1106.

Epstein, S. E. and Braunwald, E. (1966b). Beta-adrenergic receptor blocking drugs: mechanisms of action and clinical applications. *New England Journal of Medicine* **275**, 1175.

Evans, G. H. and Shand, D. G. (1973). Disposition of propranolol. VI. Independent variation in steady-state circulating drug concentrations and half-life as a result of plasma drug binding in man. *Clinical Pharmacology and Therapeutics* **14**, 494.

Evans, G. H., Nies, A. S. and Shand, D. G. (1973). The disposition of propranolol. III. Decreased half-life and volume of distribution as a result of plasma binding in man, monkey, dog and rat. *Journal of Pharmacology and Experimental Therapeutics* **186**, 114.

Faulkner, S. L., Hopkins, J. T., Boerth, R. C., Young, J. L. Jr, Jellett, L. B., Nies, A. S., Bender, H. W. and Shand, D. G. (1973). Time required for complete recovery from chronic propranolol therapy. *New England Journal of Medicine* **289**, 607.

Fitzgerald, J. D. and O'Donnell, S. R. (1971). Pharmacology of 4-hydroxy-propranolol, a metabolite of propranolol. *British Journal of Pharmacology* **43**, 222.

Frohlich, E. D., Tarazi, R. C., Dustan, H. P. and Page, I. H. (1968). The paradox of beta-adrenergic blockade in hypertension. *Circulation* **37**, 417.

George, C. F. and Dollery, C. T. (1973). Plasma concentrations and pharmacological effect of β-receptor blocking drugs. In: *Pharmacology and the Future of Man*, Proc. 5th Int. Cong. Pharmacology, San Francisco 1972, Vol. 3, pp. 86–97. Karger: Basel.

Gibson, D. and Sowton, E. (1969). The use of beta-adrenergic receptor blocking drugs in dysrhythmias. *Progress in Cardiovascular Diseases* **12**, 16.

Glick, G., Parmley, W. W., Wechsler, A. S. and Sonnenblick, E. H. (1968). Glucagon: its enhancement of cardiac performance in the cat and dog and persistence of its inotropic action despite beta-receptor blockade with propranolol. *Circulation Research* **22**, 789.

Greenblatt, D. J. and Koch-Weser, J. (1973). Adverse reactions to propranolol in hospitalized medical patients: a report from the Boston Collaborative Drug Surveillance Program. *American Heart Journal* **86**, 478.

Haidinyak, J. G. and Didier, E. P. (1977). Case history number 95: anesthetics and propranolol. *Anesthesia and Analgesia . . . Current Researches* **56**, 283.

Hollifield, J. W., Sherman, K., Vander Zwagg, R. and Shand, D. G. (1976). Proposed mechanisms of propranolol's antihypertensive effect in essential hypertension. *New England Journal of Medicine* **295**, 68.

Kaplan, J. A. and Dunbar, R. W. (1976). Propranolol and surgical anesthesia. *Anesthesia and Analgesia . . . Current Researches* **55**, 1.

Kopriva, C. J., Brown, A. C. D. and Pappas, G. (1978). Hemodynamics during general anesthesia in patients receiving propranolol. *Anesthesiology* **48**, 28.

Lydtin, H., Kusus, T., Daniel, W., Schierl, W., Ackenheil, M., Kempter, H., Lohmoller, G., Niklas, M. and Walter, I. (1972). Propranolol therapy in essential hypertension. *American Heart Journal* **83**, 589.

Mizgala, H. F. and Counsell, J. (1976). Acute coronary syndrome following abrupt cessation of oral propranolol therapy. *Canadian Medical Association Journal* **114**, 1123.

Myers, M. G., Lewis, P. J., Reid, J. L. and Dollery, C. T. (1975). Brain concentration of propranolol in relation to hypotensive effect in the rabbit with observations on brain propranolol levels in man. *Journal of Pharmacology and Experimental Therapeutics* **192**, 327.

Nattel, S., Rangno, R. E. and Van Loon, G. (1979). Mechanisms of propranolol withdrawal phenomena. *Circulation* **59**, 1158.

Neis, A. S. and Shand, D. G. (1975). Clinical pharmacology of propranolol. *Circulation* **52**, 6.

Nies, A. S., Evans, G. H. and Shand, D. G. (1973a). Regional hemodynamic effects of beta-adrenergic blockade with propranolol in the unanesthetized primate. *American Heart Journal* **85**, 97.

Nies, A. S., Evans, G. H. and Shand, D. G. (1973b). The hemodynamic effects of beta adrenergic blockade on the flow-dependent hepatic clearance of propranolol. *Journal of Pharmacology and Experimental Therapeutics* **184**, 716.

Parmley, W. W. (1971). The role of glucagon in cardiac therapy. *New England Journal of Medicine* **285**, 801.

Parmley, W. W., Glick, G. and Sonnenblick, E. H. (1968). Cardiovascular effects of glucagon in man. *New England Journal of Medicine* **279**, 12.

Paterson, J. W., Conolly, M. E., Dollery, C. T., Hayes, A. and Cooper, R. G. (1970). The pharmacodynamics and metabolism of propranolol in man. *Pharmacologia Clinica* **2**, 127.

Prys-Roberts, C., Roberts, J. G., Foëx, P., Clarke, T. N. S., Bennett, M. J. and Ryder, W. A. (1976). Interaction of anesthesia, beta-receptor blockade, and blood loss in dogs with induced myocardial infarction. *Anesthesiology* **45**, 326.

Rall, T. W. and West, T. C. (1963). The potentiation of cardiac inotropic responses of norepinephrine by theophylline. *Journal of Pharmacology and Experimental Therapeutics* **139**, 269.

Romagnoli, A. and Keats, A. S. (1975). Plasma and atrial propranolol after preoperative withdrawal. *Circulation* **52**, 1123.

Rotem, C. E. (1976). Propranolol therapy in the perioperative period. *Canadian Medical Association Journal* **114**, 188.

Shand, D. G. (1974). Individualization of propranolol therapy. *Medical Clinics of North America* **58**, 1063.

Shand, D. G. (1975). Propranolol. *New England Journal of Medicine* **293**, 280.

Shand, D. G. and Rangno, R. E. (1972). The disposition of propranolol. I. Elimination during oral absorption in man. *Pharmacology* **7**, 159.

Shand, D. G. and Wood, A. J. J. (1978). Propranolol withdrawal syndrome — why? *Circulation* **58**, 202.

Shand, D. G., Nuckolls, E. M. and Oates, J. A. (1970). Plasma propranolol levels in adults with observations in four children. *Clinical Pharmacology and Therapeutics* **11**, 112.

Sprague, D. H. (1975). Severe bradycardia after neostigmine in a patient taking propranolol to control paroxysmal atrial tachycardia. *Anesthesiology* **42**, 208.

Stern, S., Hoffman, M. and Braun, K. (1971). Cardiovascular responses to carotid and vertebral artery infusions of propranolol. *Cardiovascular Research* **5**, 425.

Sutherland, E. W., Robison, G. A. and Butcher, R. W. (1968). Some aspects of the biological role of adenosine 3′, 5′-monophosphate (cyclic AMP). *Circulation* **37**, 279.

Thadani, U., Davidson, C., Singleton, W. and Taylor, S. H. (1979). Comparison of the immediate effects of five ‡-adrenoreceptor-blocking drugs with different ancillary properties in angina pectoris. *New England Journal of Medicine* **300**, 750.

Viljoen, J. F., Estafanous, G. and Kellner, G. A. (1972). Propranolol and cardiac surgery. *Journal of Thoracic and Cardiovascular Surgery* **64**, 826.

Wiklund, R. A. (1974). Cyclic nucleotides. *Anesthesiology* **41**, 490.

Zacest, R., Gilmore, E. and Koch-Weser, J. (1972). Treatment of essential hypertension with combined vasodilation and beta-adrenergic blockade. *New England Journal of Medicine* **286**, 617.

Zacharias, F. J., Cowen, K. J., Prestt, J., Vickers, J. and Wall, B. G. (1972). Propranolol in hypertension: a study of long-term therapy, 1964–1970.

American Heart Journal **83,** 755.

Zaidan, J., Philbin, D. M., Antonio, R. and Savarese, J. (1977). Hemo-dynamic effects of metocurine in patients with coronary artery disease receiving propranolol. *Anesthesia and Analgesia . . . Current Researches* **56,** 255.

11

Digitalis toxicity

The cardiotonic effect of cardiac glycosides has been known to man since the Romans (Moe and Farah, 1975). They are not only the most useful drugs in the treatment of congestive heart failure, but also some of the most toxic agents in the pharmacopoeia. Despite the purity of modern preparations and vigorous standards of bio-availability, digitalis toxicity remains a common problem affecting a fifth to a quarter of all treated patients (Beller *et al.*, 1971; Evered and Chapman, 1971).

While digitalized patients pose no new anaesthetic problems, toxic patients behave differently. During operation and in the postoperative period, there are many factors — including fluid, electrolyte and acid–base disturbances, hypoxaemia, abnormal renal function and drug interactions — which can accentuate this life-threatening complication. In the following discussion, the pharmacology of digitalis, factors enhancing its toxic action and the anaesthetic implication of digitalis toxicity are reviewed. ('Digitalis' is used synonymously to represent all cardiac glycosides in this chapter.)

The molecular basis of the inotropic and cardiotoxic effects of digitalis

It is now realized that digitalis has inotropic effects on both normal and failing hearts. Its inotropic effects increase linearly as a function of dose, and cardiotoxicity occurs at a higher dose range without affecting contractility. There is considerable overlap between therapeutic and cardiotoxic serum concentrations (Smith, 1975). The inotropic and toxic actions of digitalis are mediated through the inhibition of the transmembranous active transport of sodium and potassium (Langer, 1972). The toxic action is merely a more advanced stage of the same process.

In the resting cardiac cell there is a resting membrane potential of approximately -90 mV. There is also a transmembranous ionic concentration difference with a high intracellular potassium and a high extracellular sodium concentration. This ionic concentration difference is maintained by the selective permeability of the membrane and by an ATP dependent membrane transport system known as the sodium–potassium pump (Bonting, Simon and Hawkins, 1961; Schwartz, 1962; Whittam, 1962); sodium ions are actively returned to the extracellular fluid in exchange for potassium ions (Fig. 11.1). Sodium is also coupled to calcium in another membrane transport system in which sodium efflux is linked to calcium influx (Baker *et al.*, 1969). This sodium–calcium transport system is relatively inactive when the intracellular sodium concentration is low.

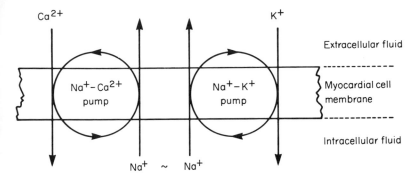

Fig 11.1   The sodium–potassium and the sodium–calcium transport systems of myocardial cell membrane. Normally the sodium–calcium transport system is inactive, but it is stimulated by an increase in intracellular sodium concentration.

The role of calcium ions in excitation-contraction coupling is summarized in Fig. 11.2. In the myocardial cell there are interdigitating actin and myosin filaments. In the resting state, interaction between actin and myosin is inhibited by a troponin–tropomyosin complex (Katz, 1970). With the

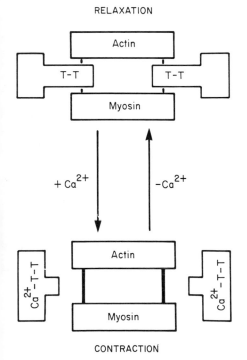

Fig. 11.2   The role of calcium in the contraction of cardiac muscle. Calcium binding of the troponin–tropomyosin complex (T–T) releases the inhibition on actin–myosin interaction and activates a myosin–ATPase.

development of depolarization and a change in the permeability of the cell membrane, the intracellular calcium ion concentration increases as a result of the influx of calcium ions from the extracellular fluid and the release of bound calcium from the sarcoplasmic pool. Calcium binding of the troponin–tropomyosin complex releases its inhibition on actin–myosin interaction. Cross-bridges form across the filaments and concentration occurs. Furthermore, a myosin-ATPase is stimulated. ATP is hydrolysed to ADP, releasing the energy necessary for contraction.

Digitalis inhibits the ATP-dependent sodium–potassium pump (Matsui and Schwartz, 1968; Schwartz, Allen and Harigaya, 1969) and leads to a net loss of potassium and a net gain of sodium in the intracellular compartment. This increase in intracellular sodium ionic concentration stimulates the sodium–calcium transport system. Consequently, calcium uptake and turnover is enhanced (Lüllmann and Holland, 1962; Grossman and Furchgott, 1964; Langer and Serena, 1970), the efficiency of excitation-contration coupling improves, and myocardial contractility increases.

Cardiotoxicity of digitalis is the result of a more advanced stage of inhibition of the sodium–potassium membrane transport and an excessive loss of intracellular potassium. At this stage the configuration of the action potential is affected. Disorders of impulse formation and impulse conduction ensue.

The action potential of a typical automatic or conducting cardiac cell can be described in five phases (solid line in Fig. 11.3): phase 0 is the phase of deplarization, while 1, 2 and 3 are phases of repolarization, and phase 4 is the resting period during which there is a slow rate of depolarization (pre-potential or diastolic depolarization). The prepotential is the result of a small net movement of sodium into the cell (a sodium leak). When the prepotential reaches a threshold value (threshold potential), phase 0 begins. The sequence of depolarization (sodium influx) and repolarization (potassium efflux) is repeated.

With digitalization, the configuration of the action potential is changed (broken line in Fig. 11.3): the resting potential is less negative than normal and approaches the threshold potential, the rate of phase 4 depolarization or sodium leak is increased (Rosen et al., 1973). There is an accompanying increase in automaticity and an enhanced activity of secondary pacemaker tissues (ectopic activities). With toxic doses, ventricular excitability (responsiveness to electrical stimulus) is depressed. At the same time the rate of phase 0 depolarization is slowed, and the velocity of impulse conduction depressed (Moe and Méndez, 1951; Swain and Weidner, 1957; Fisch et al., 1964; Przybyla et al., 1974). With the exception of atrioventricular nodal tissue, digitalis also shortens the duration of the action potential, mostly by shortening the effective refractory period (Méndez and Méndez, 1953; Morrow, Gaffney and Braunwald, 1963). This combination of increased automaticity, depressed impulse conduction and shortened effective refractory period predisposes to the development of re-entrant arrhythmias (Langer, 1972).

Digitalis also has a vagomimetic effect on the sinoatrial and atrioventricular nodes (Fisch et al., 1964). A toxic concentration will suppress the pacemaker

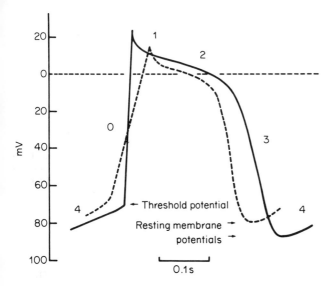

Fig. 11.3 A comparison of the action potentials of a normal (solid line) and a digitalized (broken line) automatic or conducting cardiac cell. The resting potential of the digitalized cell is less negative; the rate of phase 4 depolarization is increased; the rate of phase 0 depolarization is decreased. With the exception of atrioventricular nodal tissue, the effective refractory period of the digitalized cell is also shortened.

activity of the sinus node and depress atrioventricular nodal conduction. These vagal effects can be reversed by the administration of atropine.

The clinical manifestations of digitalis intoxication

Digitalis intoxication affects many systems (von Capeller, Copeland and Stern, 1959; Lely and Van Enter, 1970; Moe and Farah, 1975). These systemic manifestations are non-specific, but their presence should suggest the possibility of cardiotoxicity.

Gastrointestinal signs

Gastrointestinal complaints are among the early indications of digitalis intoxication. Anorexia, nausea and vomiting are the commonest. They arise from the effect of digitalis on the chemoreceptor trigger zone of the medulla and are not direct effects on the gastrointestinal tract. Other symptoms include diarrhoea and abdominal discomfort.

Neurological signs

Early neurological symptoms include general malaise, easy fatigability and headache. Paraesthesia and neuralgia are also common. More severe central nervous system intoxication will result in confusion, delirium and convulsions. Psychiatric manifestations ranging from anxiety and depression to frank psychosis may also be present.

Ophthalmic signs

The typical yellow vision, though commonly quoted in standard medical textbooks, is relatively rare (Marcus and Gordon, 1978). Other visual disturbances include photophobia, halos around objects, light flashes, scotomata and blurring of vision.

Dermatological signs

Skin reactions are rare and are not necessarily a manifestation of true toxicity. Gynaecomastia has been reported in male patients and in post-menopausal female patients (von Capeller, Copeland and Stern, 1959).

Cardiac signs

Other systemic complaints do not always precede cardiac complications. Arrhythmia is the first evidence of digitalis toxicity in one-third of all patients (von Capeller, Copeland and Stern, 1959). Although no particular arrhythmia is pathognomonic of digitalis toxicity, ventricular extrasystole (particularly bigemini) and various degrees of heart blocks are more common than others (Irons and Orgain, 1966). Other arrhythmias include sinus, atrial, junctional and ventricular tachycardias, sinus bradycardia, sinoatrial arrest and block, and atrial and ventricular fibrillations. More than one type of arrhythmia can coexist in the same patient. Depression of the ST segment and inversion of the T wave seen in the digitalized patient are non-specific changes and do not indicate toxicity.

Precipitation of congestive heart failure or worsening of existing heart failure is a common and a very deceptive complication of digitalis toxicity. Misinterpretation can be fatal. Toxicity should be suspected if heart failure is intractable despite digitalis.

Factors enhancing the cardiotoxic effects of digitalis

Many factors increase the sensitivity of the heart to the arrhythmogenic effect of digitalis. They are partly responsible for the overlap of the therapeutic and toxic serum concentrations. Many of these factors are correctable.

Electrolyte disturbances

The most common electrolyte disturbance enhancing digitalis toxicity is hypokalaemia (Kleiger *et al.*, 1966; Steiness and Olesen, 1976). The depletion of intracellular potassium and an abnormal ratio between the intracellular and extracellular concentrations of potassium are determining factors (Brater and Morrelli, 1977). The use of diuretics is a common cause. Furthermore, the myocardial uptake of digitalis is increased by hypokalaemia (Binnion and Morgan, 1971; Hall *et al.*, 1977), while binding to the sodium–potassium pump is inhibited by hyperkalaemia (Matsui and Schwartz, 1968). Therefore enhancement of digitalis toxicity can still be seen when serum potassium is at the lower limit of normal, and hyperkalaemia endows some protection. In the surgical population, gastrointestinal pathology is often accompanied by loss of fluid and electrolytes, and rapid correction of fluid depletion and acid–base abnormalities is accompanied by redistribution of potassium. These patients are vulnerable to digitalis intoxication. Similarly, in patients with chronic renal failure, digitalis cardiotoxicity can evolve during dialysis when the serum potassium is returned to lower values.

Only very high serum calcium concentrations (7.5 mmol/l or more) will increase the sensitivity of the heart to digitalis (Nola, Pope and Harrison, 1970). Hypercalcaemia should be suspected in surgical patients with metastatic breast or bronchogenic carcinomas, hyperparathyroidism, hyperthyroidism, milk alkali syndrome and Paget's disease of bone. But serum calcium concentration this high is rare. Hypomagnesaemia, also a complication of diuretic therapy (Ware, 1975), will increase the arrhythmogenic effects of digitalis (Kleiger *et al.*, 1966; Seller, 1971). Blood pH *per se* has no effect; but acute metabolic alkalosis, accompanied by a shift in extracellular potassium, enhances the sensitivity of the heart to digitalis, while acidosis offers some protection (Bliss, Fishman and Smith, 1963).

Respiratory disease and hypoxaemia

Patients with chronic obstructive lung disease or respiratory insufficiency and patients with acute hypoxaemia are very sensitive to digitalis (Beller and Smith, 1972; Green and Smith, 1977). Since ventilation/perfusion abnormalities are always complications of anaesthesia, the development of hypoxaemia and hypercarbia, which enhance digitalis toxicity, is a real possibility in the anaesthetized patient.

Neuroendocrine factors

Beta-adrenergic stimulation of the heart increases digitalis-induced arrhythmias (Becker *et al.*, 1962). Whether depletion of myocardial catecholamine with reserpine offers any protection is not settled (Lown *et al.*, 1961; Roberts *et al.*, 1963). The thyroid function of the patient influences the sensitivity of the heart by an unknown mechanism (Lawrence *et al.*, 1977): the hypothyroid patient is sensitive, and the hyperthyroid patient resistant (Frye and Braunwald, 1961; Doherty and Perkins, 1966).

Physiological status

Age is an important consideration when prescribing digitalis. Children have a remarkable tolerance and geriatric patients are very sensitive (Hermann, 1966). It is often said that digoxin 0.25 mg per day is excessive in many patients over the age of 65 years. Since digitalis is also bound to skeletal muscle, its requirement is reduced in patients with loss of muscle mass. This may be one of the reasons for the increased sensitivity in the aged.

Renal function

Digoxin, the most popular member of the group, is almost entirely excreted unchanged by the kidney. Elimination is by glomerular filtration and tubular secretion (Steiness, 1974). Renal excretion is closely related to the renal clearance of creatinine (Doherty *et al.*, 1975). Hence impaired renal function is the most important cause of digoxin intoxication. In severe renal failure this can occur even in the presence of hyperkalaemia and hypermagnesaemia. However, digoxin is still a popular choice for patients with renal failure because of the predictability of its pharmocokinetics (Gault *et al.*, 1976). Its plasma half-life is prolonged from a normal of 36 hours to 3½–5 days in advanced renal failure. The maintenance dose should be reduced to a quarter to a half of normal accordingly.

Hepatic function

Digitoxin, the secnd most popular member of the group, is broken down by the liver to inactive metabolites which are then excreted by the kidney. The plasma half-life is 5–7 days. Its hepatic metabolism is enhanced by all agents which induce the proliferation of hepatic microsomal enzymes (Solomon *et al.*, 1971). If enzyme-inducing agents given to these patients concurrently are stopped, digitoxin requirement will be reduced and toxicity may develop. If liver function is impaired or if hepatic blood flow is reduced, the maintenance dose should be decreased.

Type and severity of heart disease

It is paradoxical that the more severe the heart disease, the more sensitive the heart is to digitalis intoxication (Smith, 1975). Cardiotoxicity is more common in patients who need digitalis most. Patients with ischaemic heart disease, particularly after an acute myocardial infarction, are especially sensitive.

Digitalis–quinidine interaction

Hager *et al.* (1979) reported that when digoxin and quinine were given to patients concurrently, the total body clearance, renal clearance and volume of distribution of digoxin were reduced, but its half-life remained unchanged. These changes in the pharmacokinetics of digoxin are reflected in higher plasma concentrations (Ejvinsson, 1978). On the contrary, similar interaction between digitoxin and quinidine does not occur (Ochs *et al.*, 1980). Although the clinical significance of these findings has not been fully assessed, it is suggested that the dose of digoxin be reduced when quinidine is administered.

Anaesthetic agents

The effects of anaesthetic agents on digitalis-induced cardiotoxicity vary (see Chapter 4). Halothane, enflurane, ketamine, droperidol, Thalamonal (Innovar) and tubocurarine increase the tolerance of the heart to digitalis-induced arrhythmias; but thiopentone and fentanyl have no effect. On the other hand, suxamethonium-, neostigmine- (Ivankovic *et al.*, 1971) and diazepam-induced ventricular arrhythmias have been reported in digitalized subjects. Clinical reports of interactions between anaesthetic agents and digitalis are anecdotal in nature. Most of the quoted findings were obtained from animal experiments. These findings do not necessarily imply that the use of these anaesthetic agents is contraindicated in the digitalized patient.

The use of serum concentration assay

Due to the non-specificity of the systemic and cardiac toxic manifestations of digitalis, attempts have been made to improve the diagnosis of toxicity by the assay of serum concentration. Radioimmunoassay of digoxin or digitoxin serum concentration is now a well established technique (Smith, Butler and Haber, 1969; Smith, 1970).

The therapeutic concentration of digoxin is between 0.5 and 2.5 ng/ml (Doherty, 1978). In the range of 2.0–3.0 ng/ml the therapeutic and toxic concentrations overlap. The absolute serum concentration of digoxin may vary from laboratory to laboratory. Spuriously high levels may be reported in the presence of haemolysis and hyperbilirubinaemia, and if the specimen is drawn less than 4 hours after an intravenous dose or 8 hours after an oral dose (Marcus, 1976; Doherty, 1978). On the contrary, spuriously low levels may be reported if the patient has hypoalbuminaemia, uraemia, or if he has been exposed to iodine-125 within the last 24 hours (Marcus, 1976).

The therapeutic serum concentration of digitoxin is approximately ten times that of digoxin (Smith, 1975). The range of overlap between non-toxic and toxic concentrations tends to be even greater than that of digoxin. The antibodies used are immunospecific for each cardiac glycoside. Failure to identify the proper cardiac glycoside to be assayed will lead to improper interpretation and potentially fatal mistakes (Edmonds, Howard and Trainer, 1972).

The wide range of overlap between therapeutic and toxic levels has cast doubts on the usefulness of serum concentration alone in the diagnosis of digitalis toxicity (Ingelfinger and Goldman, 1976; Smith, 1978). It certainly should not be used as a routine diagnostic test, but it is indicated in the following situations (Huffman, 1976).

1. When digitalization is contemplated in a patient whose drug history is unobtainable.
2. To determine whether a patient is receiving digoxin or digitoxin.
3. In the patient who shows unexpected sensitivity or resistance to digitalis.
4. In the patient who has developed clinical signs suggestive of digitalis toxicity. It is useful in differentiating between arrhythmias due to digitalis toxicity or intrinsic heart disease.

Anaesthetic implications

All cardiac glycosides have a low therapeutic ratio and many factors can enhance their toxic action in the surgical patient. The seriousness of digitalis cardiotoxicity demands a careful preoperative assessment of all digitalized patients.

The diagnosis of digitalis toxicity must still be based on clinical acumen in which the history of medication, the type and dose of digitalis preparation employed, factors affecting pharmocokinetics, factors known to affect the sensitivity of the heart, and the systemic and electrocardiographic evidence of toxicity are considered together with the serum concentration. Only the disappearance of symptoms and signs of toxicity following the withdrawal of digitalis is absolute proof of intoxication.

Whether to proceed with anaesthesia in the toxic patient depends entirely on the urgency of the operation. Elective operations should be postponed until cardiotoxcity subsides; even the mildly toxic patient can behave unpredictably during the operation and in the postoperative period. To proceed without waiting for digitalis toxicity to subside is to court disaster. When the operation is urgent, this urgency outweighs all other risks. Cardiotoxicity should be treated aggressively without delay. When it is under control, anaesthesia and operation can proceed. A little time well spent in the preoperative preparation of the patient will save endless anxiety afterwards.

No single anaesthetic agent is contraindicated in the digitoxic patient, but agents nown to induce arrhythmias in digitalized patients should be given with caution. During the operation special attention should be paid to the monitoring of cardiac rhythm and circulatory dynamics; normal renal function and fluid, electrolye and acid–base balance should be maintained.

The management of digitalis toxicity

The treatment of cardiotoxicity can be graded according to its severity and urgency. When the arrhythmia is relatively benign and in the absence of ventricular irritability, haemodynamic disturbance and urgency, the following measures are usually adequate.

1. Withhold digitalis and diuretics.
2. Correct hypokalaemia. Give potassium salt, 4–8 g per day, in divided doses.
3. Identify and eliminate all other correctable factors which enhance digitalis toxicity.

Generally speaking, toxicity will subside in 2–3 days, and the dosage of digitalis, diuretic and potassium supplement can be adjusted.

In the more urgent situation and when cardiotoxicity is severe, aggressive treatment is necessary. Naturally, digitalis and diuretics should be withdrawn, and factors enhancing toxicity eliminated. The pharmacological treatment of digitalis-induced arrhythmias varies according to the nature of the rhythm disturbance (Chou, 1970; Bigger and Strauss, 1972; Marcus and Gordon, 1978).

The treatment of tachyarrhythmias and extrasystoles

Supraventricular and ventricular tachyarrhythmias and ventricular premature contractions associated with digitalis toxicity can be controlled with a number of anti-arrhythmic agents.

Potassium salts

Hypokalaemia must be corrected. In the presence of ventricular extrasystoles, potassium should be administered even when the serum potassium concentration is in the lower range of normal. This is an attempt to replace potassium depletion and to reverse the electrophysiological process of digitalis cardiotoxicity. Potassium chloride, 20–40 mmol, diluted to 100 ml in 5% dextrose solution, can be given intravenously over 1–2 hours under constant electrocardiographic monitoring. Further supplements can be given according to scrum potassium level. However, potassium itself, like digitalis, will prolong atrioventricular conduction. It is contraindicated in the presence of second or third degree heart block. It is also contraindicated in the presence of renal failure.

Lignocaine

Lignocaine is the drug of choice in the treatment of digitalis-induced ventricular irritability (Hilmi and Regan, 1968; Mason et al., 1970). In therapeutic concentrations it reduces the enhanced automaticity of subsidiary pacemakers without affecting myocardial contractility and atrioventricular conduction. However, it is not very useful in the treatment of supraventricular arrhythmias. The recommended dose is 1 mg/kg given as a bolus followed by 2–4 mg per minute in a continuous intravenous infusion of appropriate dilution (e.g. 1 g in 500 ml of 5% dextrose solution, giving 2 mg/ml.

Phenytoin

Phenytoin is another agent which reduces ventricular irritability without affecting contractility. It also suppresses supraventricular arrhythmias induced by digitalis, and has the added advantage of enhancing atrioventricular conduction which is slowed by digitalis (Conn, 1965; Helfant, Scherlag and Damato, 1967). It is the drug of choice in the treatment of supraventricular tachyarrhythmias with or without atrioventricular block. The recommended dose is 20 mg per minute, given through a fast-running intravenous infusion. It should be stopped when the arrhythmia is abolished or when undesirable effects appear (Bigger, Schmidt and Kutt, 1968). A total dose of 1000 mg should not be exceeded. Its effect is almost immediate.

If no response is seen after several minutes, it will probably be ineffective. During its administration, constant electrocardiographic and blood pressure monitoring is mandatory. Shortening of the PR and QT intervals is part of the therapeutic effect. The deterioration of ventricular arrhythmias, the development of atrioventricular block and the onset of drowsiness, nystagmus, vertigo, nausea or hypotension are toxic reactions to phenytoin or its solvent which is 40 per cent propylene glycol and 10 per cent ethanol.

Propranolol

The disadvantage of propranolol in the treatment of both ventricular and supraventricular arrhythmias induced by digitalis is the depression of myo-cardial contractility and a further prolongation of atrioventricular conduction (Turner, 1966). Therefore it is contraindicated in the presence of existing heart block or congestive heart failure, unless further supportive measures are instituted. Being less effective than lignocaine or phenytoin in the treatment of digitalis-induced ventricular tachycardias, it should not be regarded as the drug of first choice. When both lignocaine and phenytoin are unsuccessful, propranolol may be given intravenouly in small increments up to a total dose of 0.1 mg/kg (beware of complications).

If atrioventricular block is already present or develops before control is obtained, a transvenous pacemaker should be inserted before initiation of therapy or administration of further increments.

Other drugs

Procainamide is still a popular agent in the treatment of ventricular arrhyth-mias and some supraventricular arrhythmias, but its usefulness in the treatment of digitalis-induced tachyarrhythmias has largely been superseded by superior agents (Bigger and Heissenbuttel, 1969). However, some authors still find it useful in the treatment of some toxic arrhythmias, particularly paroxysmal atrial tachycardia with block in the absence of hypokalaemia (Marcus and Gordon, 1978). One hundred milligrams should be given slowly every 5 minutes until the arrhythmia is controlled. The total dose should not exceed 1000 mg. Since hypotension and excessive widening of the QRS complex or prolongation of the PR interval are warning signs of myocardial toxicity, patients should be monitored appropriately when procainamide is being administered.

Although bretylium tosylate, a sympatholytic agent, has been used in the treatment of digitalis-induced ventricular arrhythmias (Bacaner, 1968), it cannot be recommended because the initial release of catecholamines caused by this agent may actually aggravate digitalis toxicity (Abramowicz, 1978).

Cardioversion

Cardioversion is usually contraindicated in digitalis-induced tachyarrhyth-mias because even more severe and bizarre ventricular arrhythmias have occurred after countershock (Lown, 1967). However, direct-current countershock is sometimes necessary in tachyarrhythmias resistant to drug therapy. It is a desperate measure and should not be undertaken unless all correctable factors have been eliminated. When it is essential to proceed, low energy level and small graded increments should be employed: start with the lowest energy level possible and certainly not more than 25 joules (Bigger and Strauss, 1972). Lignocaine or phenytoin should be given immediately before cardioversion to suppress ventricular irritability often seen after cardioversion in the digitalized patient (Helfant, Scherlag and Damato, 1968; Chou, 1970). If propranolol is used instead of lignocaine or phenytoin, the prophylactic placement of a transvenous pacemaker is advisable.

The treatment of bradyarrhythmias and atrioventricular block

If time permits and if the patient's condition is stable, it is only necessary to withhold digitalis and allow the automatic and conducting tissues of the heart to recover. Potassium should not be administered unless hypokalaemia can be demonstrated. When the operation is urgent or when bradycardia is complicated by syncope, hypotension or heart failure, atropine, 0.6–1.2 mg, should be given intravenously. This will often restore normal sinus rhythm with an acceptable rate and blood pressure. When atropine is unsuccessful, the placement of a transvenous pacemaker (Leon-Sotomayor et al., 1962) is warranted before proceeding with anaesthesia and operation. Administration of catecholamines is contraindicated because they enhance ventricular irritability.

The treatment of concomitant congestive heart failure

Congestive heart failure is often a complication of digitalis toxicity. When this is secondary to an arrhythmia, it will improve when the arrhythmia is controlled. If myocardial disease is severe, withdrawal of digitalis should be accompanied by other means of circulatory support. The use of a peripheral vasodilator (e.g. sodium nitroprusside or glyceryl trinitrate) to reduce preload and afterload of the heart will improve its mechanical efficiency, enhance cardiac output and relieve pulmonary congestion (Braunwald, 1977).

The role of cholestyramine

About twenty-five to thirty per cent of digitoxin undergoes enterohepatic circulation. Orally administered cholestyramine (a steroid-binding resin), colestipol and activated charcoal can bind this portion of the cardiac glycoside and prevent its reabsorption (Caldwell, Bush and Greenberger, 1971; Huffman, 1976). Its half-life will be shortened and the serum concentration will fall. In contrast to previous findings, digoxin has also been reported to undergo significant enterohepatic circulation (Doherty et al., 1970; Caldwell and Cline, 1975). Cholestyramine, 4 g, three times a day, is a useful adjunct in the treatment of toxicity due to digitoxin and digoxin.

Experimental treatments of digitalis intoxication

Digitalis-specific antibody fragments of animal source have been used successfully in the treatment of massive digoxin overdose in attempted suicide (Smith *et al.*, 1976). Purified preparations of these antibodies with low antigenicity are being developed for general clinical use. The reversal of toxicity is rapid in onset because the binding of digitalis to cellular receptors is reversible.

In experimental animals, potassium canrenoate (Yeh, 1972), an aldosterone antagonist, has been shown to abolish the toxic electrophysiological manifestations of ouabain without abolishing its inotropic effect. This compound will be very useful in the treatment of digitalis toxicity if these animal data are found applicable to man.

References

Abramowicz, M. (Ed.) (1978). Bretylium (Bretylol) for ventricular arrhythmias. *Medical Letter on Drugs and Therapeutics* **20**, 105.

Bacaner, M. B. (1968). Treatment of ventricular fibrillation and other acute arrhythmias with bretylium tosylate. *American Journal of Cardiology* **21**, 530.

Baker, P. F., Blaustein, M. P., Hodgkin, A. L. and Steinhardt, R. A. (1969). The influence of calcium on sodium efflux in squid axons. *Journal of Physiology* **200**, 431.

Becker, D. J., Nonkin, P. M., Bennett, L. D., Kimball, S. G., Sternberg, M. S. and Wasserman, F. (1962). Effect of isoproterenol in digitalis cardiotoxicity. *American Journal of Cardiology* **10**, 242.

Beller, G. A. and Smith, T. W. (1972). Toxic effects of ouabain during normoxia and hypoxia in intact conscious dogs. *Circulation* **45** and **46**, Suppl. II, II–129.

Beller, G. A., Smith, T. W., Abelmann, W. H., Haber, E. and Hood, W. B. Jr (1971). Digitalis intoxication: a prospective clinical study with serum level correlations. *New England Journal of Medicine* **284**, 989.

Bigger, J. T. Jr and Heissenbuttel, R. H. (1969). The use of procaine amide and lidocaine in the treatment of cardiac arrhythmias. *Progress in Cardiovascular Diseases* **11**, 515.

Bigger, J. T. Jr and Strauss, H. C. (1972). Digitalis toxicity: drug interactions promoting toxicity and the management of toxicity. *Seminars in Drug Treatment* **2**, 147.

Bigger, J. T. Jr., Schmidt, D. H. and Kutt, H. (1968). Relationship between the plasma level of diphenylhydantoin sodium and its cardiac antiarrhythmic effects. *Circulation* **38**, 363.

Binnion, P. F. and Morgan, L. M. (1971). Effect of acute hypokalaemia on H-digoxin metabolism. *Cardiovascular Research* **5**, 431.

Bliss, H. A., Fishman, W. E. and Smith, P. M. (1963). Effect of alterations of blood pH on digitalis toxicity. *Journal of Laboratory and Clinical Medicine* **62**, 53.

Bonting, S. L., Simon, K. A. and Hawkins, N. M. (1961). Studies on sodium–potassium-activated adenosine triphosphatase. I. Quantitative distribution in several tissues of the cat. *Archives of Biochemistry and Biophysics* **95**, 416.

Brater, D. C. and Morrelli, H. F. (1977). Digoxin toxicity in patients with normokalemic potassium depletion. *Clinical Pharmacology and Therapeutics* **22**, 21.

Braunwald, E. (1977). Vasodilator therapy — a physiologic approach to the treatment of heart failure. *New England Journal of Medicine* **297**, 331.

Caldwell, J. H. and Cline, C. T. (1975). The biliary excretion of 3H-digoxin in man. *Clinical Research* **23**, 219A.

Caldwell, J. H., Bush, C. A. and Greenberger, N. J. (1971). Interruption of the enterohepatic circulation of digitoxin by cholestyramine. II. Effect of metabolic disposition of tritium-labelled digitoxin and cardiac systolic intervals in man. *Journal of Clinical Investigation* **50**, 2638.

Chou, T. C. (1970). Digitalis-induced arrhythmias. *Modern Treatment* **7**, 96.

Conn, R. D. (1965). Diphenylhydantoin sodium in cardiac arrhythmias. *New England Journal of Medicine* **272**, 277.

Doherty, J. E. (1978). How and when to use the digitalis serum levels. *Journal of the American Medical Association* **239**, 2594.

Doherty, J. E. and Perkins, W. H. (1966). Digoxin metabolism in hypo- and hyperthyroidism: studies with tritiated digoxin in thyroid disease. *Annals of Internal Medicine* **64**, 489.

Doherty, J. E., Bissett, J. K., Kane, J. J., deSoyza, N., Murphy, M. L., Flanigan, W. J. and Dalrymple, G. V. (1975). Tritiated digoxin: studies in renal disease in human subjects. *International Journal of Clinical Pharmacology and Biopharmacy* **12**, 89.

Doherty, J. E., Flanigan, W. J., Murphy, M. L., Bulloch, R. T., Dalrymple, G. L., Beard, O. W. and Perkins, W. H. (1970). Tritiated digoxin. XIV. Enterohepatic circulation, absorption, and excretion studies in human volunteers. *Circulation* **42**, 867.

Edmonds, T. T., Howard, P. I. and Trainer, T. D. (1972). Measurement of digitoxin and digoxin. *New England Journal of Medicine* **286**, 1266.

Ejvinsson, G. (1978). Effect of quinidine on plasma concentrations of digoxin. *British Medical Journal* **1**, 279.

Evered, D. C. and Chapman, C. (1971). Plasma digoxin concentrations and digoxin toxicity in hospital patients. *British Heart Journal* **33**, 540.

Fisch, C., Greenspan, K., Knoebel, S. B. and Feigenbaum, H. (1964). Effect of digitalis on conduction of the heart. *Progress in Cardiovascular Diseases* **6**, 343.

Frye, R. L. and Braunwald, E. (1961). Studies on digitalis. III. The influence of triiodothyronine on digitalis requirements. *Circulation* **23**, 376.

Gault, M. H., Jeffrey, J. R., Chirito, E. and Ward, L. L. (1976). Studies of digoxin dosage, kinetics and serum concentrations in renal failure and review of the literature. *Nephron* **17**, 161.

Green, L. H. and Smith, T. W. (1977). The use of digitalis in patients with pulmonary disease. *Annals of Internal Medicine* **87**, 459.

Grossman, A. and Furchgott, R. F. (1964). The effects of various drugs on calcium exchange in the isolated guinea-pig left auricle. *Journal of Pharmacology and Experimental Therapeutics* **145**, 162.

Hager, W. D., Fenster, P., Mayersohn, M., Perrier, D., Graves, P., Marcus, F. I. and Goldman, S. (1979). Digoxin–quinidine interaction: pharmacokinetic evaluation. *New England Journal of Medicine* **300**, 1238.

Hall, R. J., Gelbart, A., Silverman, M. and Goldman, R. H. (1977). Studies on digitalis-induced arrhythmias in glucose- and insulin-induced hypokalemia. *Journal of Pharmacology and Experimental Therapeutics* **201**, 711.

Helfant, R. H., Scherlag, B. J. and Damato, A. N. (1967). Protection from digitalis toxicity with the prophylactic use of diphenylhydantoin sodium: an arrhythmic-inotropic dissociation. *Circulation* **36**, 119.

Helfant, R. H., Scherlag, B. J. and Damato, A. N. (1968). Diphenylhydantoin prevention of arrhythmias in the digitalis-sensitized dog after direct-current cardioversion. *Circulation* **37**, 424.

Hermann, G. R. (1966). Digitoxicity in the aged: recognition, frequency, and management. *Geriatrics* **21**, 109.

Hilmi, K. I. and Regan, T. J. (1968). Relative effectiveness of antiarrhythmic drugs in treatment of digitalis-induced ventricular tachycardia. *American Heart Journal* **76**, 365.

Huffman, D. H. (1976). Clinical use of digitalis glycosides. *American Journal of Hospital Pharmacy* **33**, 179.

Ingelfinger, J. A. and Goldman, P. (1976). The serum digitalis concentration — does it diagnose digitalis toxicity? *New England Journal of Medicine* **294**, 867.

Irons, G. V. Jr and Orgain, E. S. (1966). Digitalis-induced arrhythmias and their management. *Progress in Cardiovascular Diseases* **8**, 539.

Ivankovic, A. D., Ruggiero, R. P., El-Etr, A. A. and Kaye, M. P. (1971). Effect of neostigmine on cardiac rhythm in digitalized dogs. *Anesthesia and Analgesia . . . Current Researches* **50**, 1079.

Katz, A. M. (1970). Contractile proteins of the heart. *Physiological Reviews* **50**, 63.

Kleiger, R. D., Seta, K., Vitale, J. J. and Lown, B. (1966). Effects of chronic depletion of potassium and magnesium upon the action of acetylstrophanthidin on the heart. *American Journal of Cardiology* **17**, 520.

Langer, G. A. (1972). Effects of digitalis on myocardial ionic exchange. *Circulation* **46**, 180.

Langer, G. A. and Serena, S. D. (1970). Effectsof strophanthidin upon contraction and ionic exchange in rabbit ventricular myocardium: relation to control of active state. *Journal of Molecular and Cellular Cardiology* **1**, 65.

Lawrence, J. R., Sumner, D. J., Kalk, W. J., Ratcliffe, W. A., Whiting, B., Gray, K. and Lindsay, M. (1977). Digoxin kinetics in patients with thyroid dysfunction. *Clinical Pharmacology and Therapeutics* **22**, 7.

Lely, A. H. and Van Enter, C. H. J. (1970). Large-scale digitoxin intoxication. *British Medical Journal* **3**, 737.

Leon-Sotomayor, L., Myers, W. S., Hyatt, K. H. and Hyman, A. L. (1962).

Digitalis-induced ventricular asystole treated by an intracardiac pacemaker. *American Journal of Cardiology* **10**, 298.

Lown, B. (1967). Electrical reversion of cardiac arrhythmias. *British Heart Journal* **29**, 469.

Lown, B., Ehrlich, L., Lipschultz. B. and Blake, J. (1961). Effect of digitalis in patients receiving reserpine. *Circulation* **24**, 1185.

Lüllman, H. and Holland, W. (1962). Influence of ouabain on an exchangeable calcium fraction, contractile force, and resting tension of guinea-pig atria. *Journal of Pharmacology and Experimental Therapeutics* **137**, 186.

Marcus, F. I. (1976). Current concepts of digoxin therapy. *Modern Concepts of Cardiovascular Disease* **45**, 77.

Marcus, F. I. and Gordon, A. E. (1978). Digitalis intoxication. In: *Cardiac Emergencies*, pp. 363–383. Ed. by D. T. Mason. Williams & Wilkins: Baltimore.

Mason, D. T., Spann, J. F. Jr, Zelis, R. and Amsterdam, E. A. (1970). The clinical pharmacology and therapeutic applications of the antiarrhythmic drugs. *Clinical Pharmacology and Therapeutics* **11**, 460.

Matsui, H. and Schwartz, A. (1968). Mechanism of cardiac glycoside inhibition of the $(Na^+—K^+)$-dependent ATPase from cardiac tissue. *Biochimica et Biophysica Acta* **151**, 655.

Méndez, R. and Méndez, C. (1953). The action of cardiac glycosides on the refractory period of heart tissues. *Journal of Pharmacology and Experimental Therapeutics* **107**, 24.

Moe, G. K. and Farah, A. E. (1975). Digitalis and allied cardiac glycosides. In: *The Pharmacological Basis of Therapeutics*, pp. 653–682. Ed. by L. S. Goodman and A. Gilman. MacMillan: New York, Toronto, London.

Moe, G. K. and Méndez, R. (1951). The action of several cardiac glycosides on conduction velocity and ventricular excitability in the dog heart. *Circulation* **4**, 729.

Morrow, D. H., Gaffney, T. E. and Braunwald, E. (1963). Studies on digitalis. VIII. Effect of autonomic innervation and of myocardial catecholamine stores upon the cardiac action of ouabain. *Journal of Pharmacology and Experimental Therapeutics* **140**, 236.

Nola, G. T., Pope, S. and Harrison, D. C. (1970). Assessment of the syngergistic relationship between serum calcium and digitalis. *American Heart Journal* **79**, 499.

Ochs, H. R., Pabst, J., Greenblatt, D. J. and Dengler, H. J. (1980). Noninteraction of digitoxin and quinidine. *New England Journal of Medicine* **303**, 672.

Przybyla, A. C., Paulay, K. L., Stein, E. and Damato, A. N. (1974). Effects of digoxin on atrioventricular conduction patterns in man. *American Journal of Cardiology* **33**, 344.

Roberts, J., Ita, R., Reilly, J. and Cairoli, V. J. (1963). Influence of reserpine and βTM 10 on digitalis-induced ventricular arrhythmia. *Circulation* **13**, 149.

Rosen, M. R., Gelband, H., Merker, C. and Hoffman, B. F. (1973). Mechanisms of digitalis toxicity: effects of ouabain on phase four of canine Purkinje fiber transmembrane potentials. *Circulation* **47**, 681.

Schwartz, A. (1962). A sodium and potassium-stimulated adenosine triphosphatase from cardiac tissues. I. Preparation and properties. *Biochemical and Biophysical Research Communications* **9**, 301.

Schwartz, A., Allen, J. C. and Harigaya, S. (1969). Possible involvement of cardiac Na+, K+-adenosine triphosphatase in the mechanism of action of cardiac glycosides. *Journal of Pharmacology and Experimental Therapeutics* **168**, 31.

Seller, R. H. (1971). The role of magnesium in digitalis toxicity. *American Heart Journal* **82**, 551.

Smith, T. W. (1970). Radioimmunoassay for serum digitoxin concentration: methodology and clinical experience. *Journal of Pharmacology and Experimental Therapeutics* **175**, 352.

Smith, T. W. (1975). Digitalis toxicity: epidemiology and clinical use of serum concentration measurements. *American Journal of Medicine* **58**, 470.

Smith, T. W. (1978). Digitalis: ions, inotropy and toxicity. *New England Journal of Medicine* **299**, 545.

Smith, T. W., Butler, V. P. Jr and Haber, E. (1969). Determination of therapeutic and toxic serum digoxin concentrations by radioimmunoassay. *New England Journal of Medicine* **281**, 1212.

Smith, T. W., Haber, E., Yeatman, L. and Butler, V. P. Jr (1976). Reversal of advanced digoxin intoxication with FAB fragments of digoxin-specific antibodies. *New England Journal of Medicine* **294**, 797.

Solomon, H. M., Reich, S., Spirt, N. and Abrams, W. B. (1971). Interactions between digitoxin and other drugs in vitro and in vivo. *Annals of the New York Academy of Sciences* **179**, 362.

Steiness, E. (1974). Renal tubular secretion of digoxin. *Circulation* **50**, 103.

Steiness, E. and Olesen, K. H. (1976). Cardiac arrhythmias induced by hypokalaemia and potassium loss during maintenance digoxin therapy. *British Heart Journal* **38**, 167.

Swain, H. H. and Weidner, C. L. (1957). A study of substances which alter intraventricular conduction in the isolated dog heart. *Journal of Pharmacology and Experimental Therapeutics* **120**, 137.

Turner, J. R. B. (1966). Propranolol in the treatment of digitalis-induced and digitalis-resistant tachycardias. *American Journal of Cardiology* **18**, 450.

Von Capeller, D., Copeland, G. D. and Stern, T. N. (1959). Digitalis intoxication: a clinical report of 148 cases. *Annals of Internal Medicine* **50**, 869.

Ware, M. (Ed.) (1975). Calcium, magnesium, and diuretics. *British Medical Journal* **1**, 170.

Whittam, R. (1962). The asymmetrical stimulation of a membrane adenosine triphosphatase in relation to active cation transport. *Biochemical Journal* **84**, 110.

Yeh, B. K. (1972). Digitalis toxicity: reversal by potassium canrenoate in canine Purkinje fibers. *Pharmacology* **31**, 584.

12

Artificial pacemaker

The technology of electrical pacing of the human heart with an implantable device has improved the prospect of long-term survival of many patients with cardiac arrhythmias. While the indications for artificial pacing of the human heart in disease of the sinus node and in second and third degree heart block are well established, the indications for artificial pacing in chronic bifascicular and trifascicular disease remain controversial (Kastor, 1978; McAnulty *et al.*, 1978). Permanently implanted artificial pacemakers *may be found* in patients with the following conditions.

1. Sinus node dysfunctions:
   (a) Sick sinus syndrome;
   (b) Hypertsensitive carotid sinus syndrome.
2. Abnormalities of atrioventricular conduction:
   (a) Acquired complete heart block with or without Stokes–Adams attacks;
   (b) Symptomatic congenital heart block;
   (c) Second degree heart block (Mobitz type II);
   (d) Atrial flutter or fibrillation with a slow ventricular rate.
3. Disease of branches of the His bundle:
   (a) Right bundle branch block with left anterior hemiblock (left axis deviation of −30 degrees or more);
   (b) Right bundle branch block with left posterior hemiblock (right axis deviation of +120 degrees or more);
   (c) Right bundle branch block with first degree heart block;
   (d) Left bundle branch block with first degree heart block;
   (e) Alternating or intermittent right and left bundle branch block or other patterns indicating trifascicular disease.
4. Paroxysmal supraventricular or ventricular tachyarrhythmias resistant to treatment with anti-arrhythmic agents (for conversion of tachyarrhythmias).

Although the modern implantable artificial pacemaker is a robust instrument, its power source will fail with time and other malfunctions can occur. In the environment of the operating theatre, extraneous electromagnetic signals can interfere with its normal function. When surgery is planned for a patient with such a device, it is necessary to be certain that it is functioning normally; it is equally important to take precautions to prevent and to deal with malfunctions.

The pacemaker system

The components of an implantable system include a pulse generator and flexible leads ending in bipolar or unipolar electrodes connecting the pulse generator to the myocardium (Keller, Gosselin and Lister, 1972; Tarjan, 1973). The pulse generator is a compact package (Fig. 12.1) consisting of four to six power cells in series and electrical circuits regulating its function. The reliable and long-life zinc–mercuric oxide battery was a commonly used power source in the past (Ruben, 1969), but the lithium salt battery has become more popular in recent years. With the leads introduced via the cephalic vein at either shoulder so that the electrodes are lodged against the endocardium at the apex of the right ventricle, the pulse generator can be implanted in a subcutaneous pocket in the infraclavicular region. Alternatively, the pulse generator can be implanted in the hypochondrium and the electrodes fixed to the epicardium via a small thoracotomy.

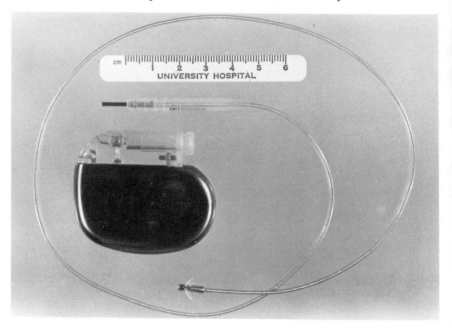

Fig 12.1   A ventricular-inhibited (demand) pacemaker and its endocardial lead and electrode by Medtronic of Canada, Ltd.

The pacemakers available today can be classified into the following categories (Lown and Kosowsky, 1970a, b, c; Chung, 1977).

1. Non-competitive pacemakers:
    (a) Ventricular-inhibited (demand) type;
    (b) Ventricular-triggered (standby or ventricular synchronous) type;
    (c) Atrial synchronous type.
2. Fixed rate (asynchronous) pacemakers.

3. Special purpose pacemakers.

Ever since the introduction of the first fixed rate (asynchronous) implantable cardiac pacemaker more than 20 years ago (Chardack, Gage and Greatbatch, 1960), many new models have been developed. They incorporate newer power source and improved circuit design, and have more sophisticated functions to deal with different types of arrhythmias. Unfortunately, equivalent models from different manufacturers are not standardized, even in basic pacing functions. In the following sections only the general features of these pacemakers are reviewed. The pacing rates quoted are from exemplary models.

The ventricular-inhibited (demand) pacemaker

This type of pacemaker is by far the most frequently implanted today. It is specifically designed for patients with intermittent heart block or other bradyarrhythmias. It generates a stream of impulses at a constant rate whenever the patient's ventricular rate is below a preset pacing rate (Fig. 12.2a). This automatic pacing rate is usually around 70 per minute. In the presence of spontaneous ventricular depolarizations, endogenous R waves of the QRS complexes are sensed via the electrodes and the pacemaker is inhibited. When the endogenous heart rate is above the automatic pacing rate, the pacemaker will only be on standby. This type of device can be converted to pace in the fixed rate (asynchronous) mode by the application of a magnet externally.

The ventricular-triggered (standby or ventricular synchronous) pacemaker

This type of pacemaker will stimulate the heart at an automatic pacing rate of around 70 per minute when spontaneous activity is slow or absent (Fig. 12.2b). In the presence of intrinsic ventricular activity, the sensed QRS complex will trigger the pulse generator to discharge an impulse immediately into the refractory period of the endogenous beat; therefore competition with intrinsic rhythm will not occur. It can be converted also to pace in the fixed rate (asynchronous) mode by the application of a magnet.

The atrial synchronous pacemaker

This pacemaker requires an atrial sensing electrode, a ventricular pacing electrode and normal atrial activity to function properly. It will sense normal atrial activity and discharge an impulse to the ventricle after a normal atrioventricular delay of 0.16 second (Fig. 12.2c). It has the advantage of being able to follow the rise and fall of normal atrial activity (e.g. during exercise). It also allows normal ventricular filling during atrial systole, which can improve cardiac output by as much as 30 per cent (Carleton, Passovoy and Graettinger, 1966). In order to avoid rapid ventricular stimulation in the presence of abnormally rapid atrial activity (e.g. atrial flutter), the pulse

(a) Ventricular inhibited

(b) Ventricular triggered

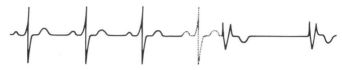

(c) Atrial synchronous

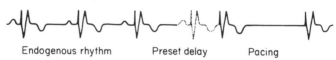

Endogenous rhythm   Preset delay   Pacing

Fig. 12.2   The normal function of three different types of pacemaker. (*a*) The ventricular-inhibited pacemaker is totally inhibited if the endogenous rhythm is above a preset rate. If the pacemaker has not sensed an endogenous ventricular beat after a predetermined delay, it will discharge and activate the ventricles at the preset rate. (*b*) The ventricular triggered pacemaker is activated by endogenous ventricular beats to discharge an impulse into the refractory period of each endogenous beat. Thus competition with endogenous rhythm will not occur. If the pacemaker has not sensed an endogenous ventricular beat after a preset delay, it will discharge and activate the ventricles at a preset rate. (*c*) For each atrial contraction sensed by the atrial synchronous pacemaker, it will discharge an impulse to activate the ventricles. If this pacemaker has not sensed an endogenous atrial contraction after a preset delay, it will discharge and activate the ventricles at a preset rate.

generator is programmed to step down to a discharge rate of 60 per minute when the sensed atrial impulse is above 125 per minute. As a fail-safe design, this type of device will pace at a fixed rate (usually 60 per minute) when atrial activity is absent.

The fixed rate (asynchronous) pacemaker

The fixed rate pacemaker was the first implantable pacemaker developed and is the simplest in design. It is suitable for older patients with established heart block, in whom a return to normal sinus rhythm and atrioventricular conduction is unlikely. It assumes total pacemaker function at a preset rate of 70–75 per minute. In the event of a return of normal intrinsic rhythm, competition between the intrinsic and the pacemaker rhythms will occur.

The special purpose pacemaker

The special purpose pacemaker is designed to convert supraventricular tachycardias to sinus rhythm with rapid atrial pacing (Lister *et al.*, 1973). On rare occasions it is also implanted to convert ventricular tachycardias (Bennett and Pentecost, 1971). It is used in selected patients who are resistant to medical therapy. It is permanently on standby and has to be switched on exernally. One model can be turned on by the application of a magnet. Another model consists of an implanted receiver which can be activated by an external transmitter generating a pulse-modulated radio-frequency carrier signal. The rate of stimulation of the second model is adjustable within the range of 50–400 per minute.

Bedside assessment of the patient with an implanted cardiac pacemaker

During the preoperative visit, the function of the pacemaker should be assessed together with the underlying disease and its progress. The commonest cause of pacemaker malfunction is failure of its power source. Fortunately, the power source of the modern pacemaker does not fail suddenly. When only one of the power cells is exhausted, the pacemaker will continue to function relatively normally; but total failure will follow shortly, and elective replacement should be done as soon as possible. Other pacemaker malfunctions leading to permanent or intermittent failure to pace or to sense include lead breakage and poor contact between the electrodes and the myocardium (e.g. from fibrosis or displacement). The migration of electrodes may also lead to the pacing of extra-cardiac tissues (e.g. the diaphragm). Malfunction may also be due to the pacemaker sensing non-physiological and other physiological electrical potentials.

Every patient with an implanted pacemaker carries a card issued by the manufacturer identifying the type of device, the model, the serial number, the type of leads, the date of implantation and the preset rate or the magnet rate of the pacemaker. The name, address and telephone number of the patient's physician are also identified. These patients are also examined regularly, though such quarterly or monthly visits to the pacemaker clinic do not entirely eliminate possible failure between visits. The function of the pacemaker can easily be determined clinically and with the help of simple hospital equipment. It should be checked during preoperative assessment.

The return of preimplantation symptoms or the development of new symptoms — syncope, palpitation, cardiac irregularity, congestive heart failure, chest pain or intractable hiccough — must be regarded as signs of pacemaker malfunction until proven otherwise. More subtle signs of impending power failure or other malfunctions can be detected at the bedside by obtaining an ECG rhythm tracing and counting the peripheral pulse. The method differs slightly with different types of pacemakers, and each is discussed separately.

The ventricular-inhibited (demand) pacemaker

A ventricular-inhibited (demand) pacemaker with a preset pacing rate of 72 per minute is used as an example. When functioning properly, this pacemaker should behave as follows.

1. It discharges pacing impulses regularly at the preset rate of 72 per

minute when the intrinsic rhythm is below this preset rate. The pacing rate
will not fall below 90 per cent of this preset rate (not less than 65 per minute).
A slow-down in rate of more than 10 per cent indicates failure of at least one
of its power cells.

2. A timely discharged pacing impulse always captures the ventricle.

3. When sensing properly, this pacemaker is inhibited by the R wave of
an endogenous beat for an interval consistent with a beat rate of
72 per minute (or within 10 per cent of this rate). When the intrinsic ventricular
rate is regularly above 72 per minute, its pacing function is totally inhibited.

4. In the presence of an irregular intrinsic rhythm, the pacemaker will
discharge intermittently: inhibited when the intrinsic rhythm is fast, and
pacing when the intrinsic rhythm is slow or absent.

The ECG signs of the normal functions and of some of the commoner
malfunctions of this ventricular-inhibited pacemaker are illustrated as
follows.

Example 1   The electrocardiogram in Fig. 12.3 is an example of this
ventricular-inhibited pacemaker functioning in the demand mode. Three
types of ventricular complexes can be identified. Beats 1, 8 and 9 are sinus
beats. Beats 2 to 6 are paced complexes. Beat 7 is a pseudofusion beat (i.e. a
normally conducted sinus beat whose QRS complex is distorted by a pacing
artefact). The patient's intrinsic cardiac rhythm in this electrocardiogram is
variable. When it slows, pacing function of the pacemaker is activated.

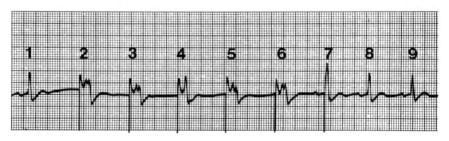

Fig. 12.3   Example 1. An electrocardiogram illustrating the normal functions of a ventricular-
inhibited (demand) pacemaker.

When it quickens, the pacemaker is inhibited. The interval between successive pacing impulses (beats 2 to 6) is 0.84 second each (rate of 72 per
minute). (The width of each small square on an ECG trace is 0.04 second.)
This indicates *normal power supply*. This type of pacemaker should discharge
at no less than 90 per cent of the preset rate (no less than 65 per minute)
when its power supply is normal. *Ventricular capture* occurs with every
pacing impulse (except when it falls on the R wave of the pseudofusion
beat). The interval between the pacing artefact of the second beat and the R
wave of the preceding sinus beat is also 0.84 second (rate of 72 per minute).
This indicates *proper sensing function*. A pseudofusion beat occurs when the
pacing impulse falls on the R wave of a normally conducted intrinsic beat,
and a fusion beat occurs when the pacing impulse and a conducted sinus
impulse both contribute to activate the ventricle. They occur by chance and

are not signs of malfunction.

Example 2   In this trace (Fig. 12.4) the patient's intrinsic cardiac rhythm is absent. The pacemaker assumes full pacing function. The interval between successive pacing impulses is 0.84 second each (rate of 72 per minute). It can be concluded that the power supply of this device is normal. Ventricular capture occurs with every pacing impulse. Sensing function cannot be ascertained from this trace.

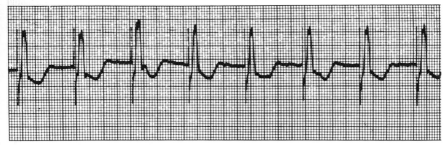

Fig. 12.4   Example 2. An electrocardiogram illustrating normal pacing function of a ventricular-inhibited (demand) pacemaker.

Example 3   In this example (Fig. 12.5) the patient has, for the moment, regained normal sinus rhythm with a rate of 83 per minute. No artificial pacemaker function can be identified on this trace. To assume that its function is normal and that pacing is only inhibited, is not fully justified. More information concering its pacing function should be sought.

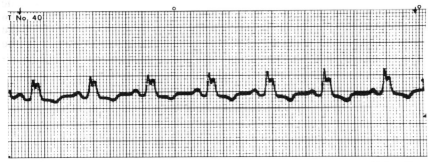

Fig. 12.5   Example 3. An electrocardiogram illustrating normal sinus rhythm with bundle branch block. No artificial pacemaker function can be identified.

Example 4   This electrocardiogram (Fig. 12.6) illustrates the *slow-down in pacing rate* associated with the *exhaustion of one of the power cells*. At implantation the interval between pacing artefacts of this demand unit was 0.84 second (rate of 72 per minute). Some months later this interval has increased to 0.94 second (rate of 64 per minute) as illustrated. A slow-down in rate of 10 per cent is a very reliable sign of the exhaustion of one of the power cells. Since the paper speed of diagnostic ECG machines may not be accurate to within 10 per cent, large errors can be introduced by obtaining the pacing rate in the illustrated manner. Counting the number of pacing artefacts or peripheral pulses over 1 minute will eliminate this source of error.

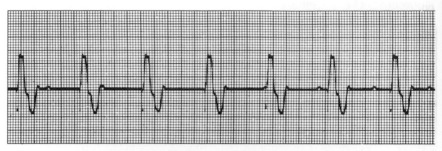

Fig. 12.6 Example 4. An electrocardiogram illustrating the slow-down in pacing rate of a ventricular-inhibited (demand) pacemaker following the exhaustion of one of its power cells. (Courtesy of Medtronic of Canada, Ltd)

Example 5   This trace (Fig. 12.7) is an example of *failure to capture.* In this electrocardiogram beats 1, 2, 5 and 6 are paced beats, while beat 4 is a spontaneous ventricular depolarization, and 3 is a pacing signal and its decay. This pacing signal falls outside the refractory period of beat 2 (from the Q wave to the upstroke of the T wave) and should have captured the ventricle. It has not. Failure to capture in this occasion is only intermittent. If it had been permanent, the patient would be left to cope with his intrinsic rhythm which might not be adequate. From this trace it can also be determined that the interval between successive pacing signals and the interval from the pacing artefact of beat 5 to the R wave of beat 4 (the intrinsic beat) are 0.84 second (rate of 72 per minute). These mean that both the power supply and the sensing function are normal

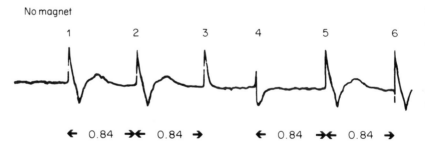

Fig. 12.7 Example 5. An electrocardiogram illustrating failure to capture the ventricles by a ventricular-inhibited (demand) pacemaker. (Courtesy of Medtronic of Canada, Ltd)

Example 6   In this electrocardiogram (Fig. 12.8) the pacing rate of the first three beats are regular, and there is an obvious pause between the third and the fourth beats. This is an example of another pacing dysfunction — *intermittent pacemaker output.* While capturing is normal, the output of the pacing impulses is erratic and irregular. Although the electrocardiogram of a pacemaker functioning in the fixed rate mode is used to illustrate this point, the same dysfunction can happen when this device is functioning in the demand mode.

Magnet

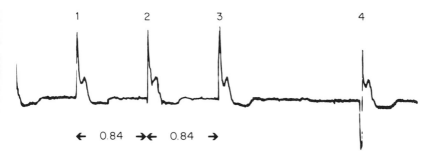

Fig. 12.8 Example 6. An electrocardiogram illustrating intermittent output of a ventricular-inhibited (demand) pacemaker functioning in the fixed rate (asynchronous) mode. (Courtesy of Medtronic of Canada, Ltd)

Example 7   Failure to sense is illustrated in Fig. 12.9. Beats 1, 2 and 3 are intrinsic beats (rate of 83 per minute) while A, B and C are pacing impulses and their signal decay. If this pacemaker had been sensing properly, the pacing impulses B and C would have been inhibited. They should come no sooner than 0.84 second (rate of 72 per minute) after the R waves of beat 1 and beat 2 respectively. There is another problem with this pacemaker: impulse C clearly falls outside the refractory period (from the Q wave to the

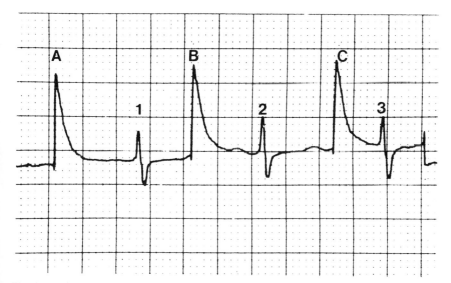

Fig. 12.9 Example 7. An electrocardiogram illustrating failure to sense and failure to capture by a ventricular-inhibited (demand) pacemaker.

upstroke of the T wave) of the intrinsic beat 2, but it fails to capture the ventricle. The regular pacing output of 72 per minute, however, indicates normal power supply. Pacing and sensing dysfunctions can occur alternately and intermittently; a very complicated rhythm is the result.

Example 8   If failure to sense is a problem, oversensing is also a cause for concern. In Fig. 12.10, beats 1, 2, 4 and 5 are paced beats, and 3 is an intrinsic beat. Sensing between 3 and 4, pacing, ventricular capture and power supply seem normal; but the delay between 2 and 3 is obvious. The clue to the malfunction of this device lies in the very rough and irregular baseline of the electrocardiogram. This is due to *interference by skeletal muscle myopotentials*. A summation of these skeletal muscle myopotentials must have been sensed by the pacemaker between 2 and 3 and inhibited its pacing function. Inhibition by skeletal muscle myopotentials can be a problem following suxamethonium administration and during postoperative shivering.

No magnet

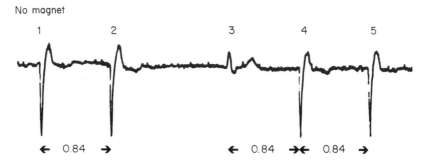

Fig. 12.10   Example 8. An electrocardiogram illustrating the inhibition of pacing function of a ventricular-inhibited (demand) pacemaker by skeletal muscle myopotentials. (Courtesy of Medtronic of Canada, Ltd)

Example 9   A different category of improper sensing is illustrated in Fig. 12.11. All six beats are paced complexes in this electrocardiogram. Note that the intervals between pacing artefacts 1 and 2, 3 and 4 and 5 and 6 are the same but longer than the intervals 2 to 3 and 4 to 5, which are normal at 0.84 second (rate of 72 per minute) each. Improper sensing between 1 and 2, 3 and 4 and 5 and 6 is obvious. On closer examination it can be determined that the pacing artefacts of beats 2, 4 and 6 are 0.84 second from the upstroke of the T waves preceding them. That is, with beats 2, 4 and 6, the unit has reset on the upstroke of the T waves instead of the R waves of the preceding beats — *T wave sensing*. With T wave sensing the pacing rate of the unit is only marginally slower than normal. It may not be a serious problem and need not be corrected unless the patient is symptomatic with the slow-down in rate. Abnormal *P wave sensing* can also occur. It is serious because it can inhibit ventricular pacing completely and leave the patient with an unsatisfactory endogenous ventricular rhythm.

From the foregoing examples, the diagnostic value of an ECG rhythm trace is obvious. It is also clear that the state of the power supply, the pacing

No magnet

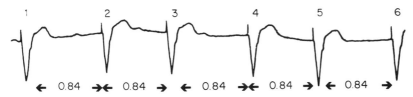

Fig. 12.11 Example 9. An electrocardiogram illustrating T wave sensing by a ventricular-inhibited (demand) pacemaker. (Courtesy of Medtronic of Canada, Ltd)

function and the sensing function of the pacemaker can be determined from a single trace only if the pacemaker is pacing and sensing in the same trace (example 1). In all other situations the state of the power supply, the pacing function and the sensing function may have to be determined separately. This can also be done at the bedside with the help of simple equipment.

Checking power supply

To check the state of the power supply, a timed 1 minute ECG rhythm trace is obtained with a magnet applied over the demand pacemaker to switch it to operate in the fixed rate (asynchronous) mode. A timed 1 minute rhythm trace is advisable because of the inaccuracy of the paper speed of most ECG machines. The number of pacing artefacts in 1 minute are counted. The rate of discharge of the pacemaker should equal that of the magnet rate specified by the manufacturer (usually 72 per minute). A rate 10 per cent (7 per minute) below the specified magnet rate is a definitive sign of exhaustion of one of the cells. An increase in rate or an irregular rate of discharge also warrants further investigation. This method of checking the state of the power supply can induce competition between the intrinsic and the artificial pacemaker rhythms (Fig. 12.12). The pacing stimulus may even fall on the T wave of an intrinsic beat (beat 5 in Fig. 12.12); but its energy level is low and is below the fibrillation threshold (Lown and Kosowsky, 1970a) except in the presence of hypokalaemia, hypoxaemia, acute myocardial infarction and digitalis toxicity, or during the administration of exogenous catecholamines (Bilitch, Cosby and Cafferky, 1967). This method of checking the power supply is contraindicated when these conditions are present.

Checking pacing function

When the intrinsic rhythm is faster than the preset rate of the pacemaker, as in example 3, pacing function is inhibited and should be checked by other means. This can be done by examining the ECG rhythm trace obtained when the demand pacemaker is operating in the fixed rate (asynchronous) mode. If pacing function is normal, competition between the intrinsic and the artificial pacemaker rhythms will be obvious (Fig. 12.12). Some pacing stimuli will capture the ventricle (beat 7 in Fig. 12.12); others, discharging in the refractory period of intrinsic beats, will not (beats 4 and 5 in Fig. 12.12). Effective ventricular pacing can be confirmed by slowing the intrinsic rhythm transiently by carotid sinus massage or by the administration of edrophonium. When the intrinsic rhythm is slowed, the pacemaker should assume total pacing function. Slowing the intrinsic rhythm should not be performed unless the ECG trace obtained with the pacemaker operating in the fixed rate (asynchronous) mode has demonstrated effective ventricular capturing.

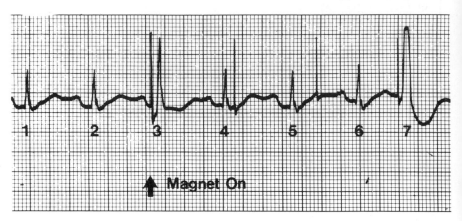

Fig. 12.12   Pacemaker arrhythmia. An electrocardiogram illustrating competition between the endogenous rhythm and that of a ventricular-inhibited (demand) pacemaker when it is switched on to function in the fixed rate (asynchronous) mode.

Checking sensing function

When the pacemaker is assuming total pacing function, as in example 2, its sensing function can be checked by the application of external electrical impulses across two ECG-type electrodes placed on the chest (Barold *et al.*, 1970): one over the apex of the heart and the other over the pulse generator (Fig. 12.13). With the patient monitored by ECG and using an external artificial pacemaker, electrical impulses (up to the maximum output of the external pacemaker) are applied across the two chest electrodes at a rate above that of the implanted pacemaker. Proper sensing is illustrated in Fig. 12.14, where pacing function is inhibited by the two externally applied electrical impulses (E). This method of checking the sensing function must be as brief as possible (no more than 2–3 seconds) because the patient's intrinsic rhythm may be non-existent.

The ventricular-triggered (standby or ventricular synchronous) pacemaker

This pacemaker is much less popular, but it can be assessed by the analysis of ECG traces in a manner similar to that described for the ventricular-inhibited device. When the intrinsic cardiac rhythm is slow or absent, the ventricular-triggered pacemaker is activated to discharge at a basic preset rate (usually of the order of 70/minute). Proper pacing function is confirmed by pacing

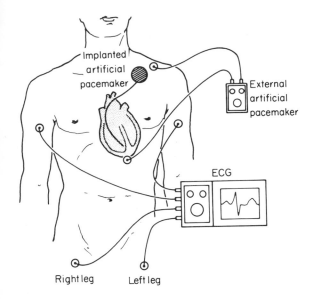

Fig. 12.13   Checking sensing function of a ventricular-inhibited (demand) pacemaker. Electrical impulses applied to the chest wall should be sensed by the pacemaker. Thus its pacing function will be inhibited.

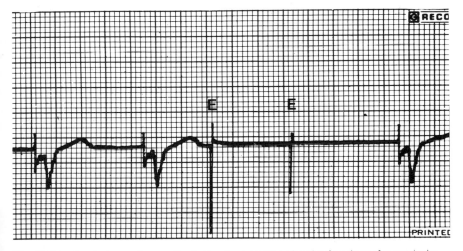

Fig. 12.14   An electrocardiogram illustrating the inhibition of pacing functions of a ventricular-inhibited (demand) pacemaker by external electrical impulses.

artefacts preceding electrically induced ventricular complexes. When the intrinsic rhythm quickens, this pacemaker, instead of being inhibited, is stimulated by the R wave of an intrinsic beat to discharge an ineffective stimulus in the refractory period, thus distorting the intrinsic ventricular complexes. Power supply can be checked by converting it to pace in the fixed rate (asynchronous) mode with a magnet. A 10 per cent slow-down in the magnet rate, or any increase or irregularity in the magnet rate, is a sign of the power source being depleted.

The atrial synchronous pacemaker

The characteristic of this pacemaker is its ability to follow the patient's normal atrial activity. Its function can be checked by obtaining an ECG rhythm trace and counting the peripheral pulse. When pacemaker function is normal, each intrinsic P wave is followed by a pacing artefact, a QRS complex and a palpable pulse. Pacing activity and ventricular response should follow closely the atrial activity when it accelerates with exercise. With the help of an external pulse generator, pacemaker function can also be checked by applying electrical impulses across two ECG-type electrodes on the chest wall: one placed over the right atrium and the other over the implanted pacemaker. The rate of discharge of the external pulse generator is set above that of the patient's intrinsic atrial activity and is increased in steps to over 125 per minute. When the pacemaker is functioning properly, every external electrical impulse is sensed by the atrial electrode, and a corresponding ventricular pacing stimulus is delivered independent of intrinsic P wave activity. Ventricular capture is confirmed by the appearance of a QRS complex and a palpable pulse. When the rate of discharge of the external pulse generator is above 125 per minute, the built-in blocking mechanism of the pacemaker wll be activated, and it will continue to pace at a fixed rate of 60 per minute. A failure of the power supply of this device is invariably followed by an inability to sense properly and to follow the changing rates of the intrinsic atrial activity or the externally applied electrical stimuli. The pacemaker then continues to discharge at a fixed rate of 60 per minute in the asynchronous mode.

The fixed rate (asynchronous) pacemaker

This pacemaker is the easiest to check. A timed 1 minute ECG rhythm tracing should be obtained and the peripheral pulse counted simultaneously. A 10 per cent slow-down in pacing rate (usually 70–75 per minute) and any increase or irregularity in pacing rates are indications of impending power failure. Sometimes power failure is accompanied by failure in its timing mechanism; a runaway rhythm with rapid pacing can occur.

This pacemaker assumes total pacing function and is designed for patients without endogenous ventricular rhythm. However, spontaneous sinus rhythm and normal atrioventricular conduction may return after pacemaker implantation in 20 per cent of the patients. If that is the case, competition between the intrinsic and the artificial pacemaker rhythms will occur. When competition is severe, the intrinsic rhythm can be slowed with propranolol, or the pacemaker can be changed to a demand-type device. More frequently intrinsic ventricular ectopic beats are the cause of competition. When this occurs, anti-arrhythmic agents can be used to suppress the ventricular ectopic focus.

The special purpose pacemaker

This generator is designed to be activated externally to convert supraventricular tachyarrhythmias by rapid pacing. It is less important to verify its function in the presence of normal sinus rhythm. If the pacemaker should fail during an attack, the arrhythmia can always be controlled medically or by external cardioversion.

Anaesthetic considerations

When pacemaker malfunction is suspected during preoperative evaluation, further tests can be performed to localize the problem in a well equipped pacemaker clinic. When malfunction is confirmed, it must be rectified: usually by replacement of the pulse generator or by reimplantation of its leads, which can be done at the beginning of the patient's planned surgical procedure under local anaesthesia.

When the function of the pacemaker is in order, general anaesthesia can proceed, and the principles described for patients with ischaemic heart disease should be followed (see Part III: 'Anaesthesia in Patients with Ischaemic Heart Disease'). During operaton and in the postoperative period, pacemaker function is subjected to interference by electromagnetic signals of biological origin or those from electrical equipment used in the operating theatre (Sowton, Gray and Preston, 1970; Smyth *et al.*, 1974; Simon *et al.*, 1975). These include skeletal muscle myopotentials, diathermy, the electrocautery, the peripheral nerve stimulator, the pulp vitality tester in dental surgery, radiofrequency equipment in neurosurgery and equipment driven by electric motors (e.g. orthopaedic saw and electric operating table). All current models have special shielding and filtering components to minimize malfunction from electromagnetic interference. However, as protection improves, the strength and the variety of electromagnetic signals also increase. There is no guarantee against interference from all sources in all occasions.

During operation and in the postoperative period, interference of normal pacemaker function by biological potentials and electrical equipment must be regarded as a possibility. Extra precautions in monitoring and to deal with interference are necessary.

Interference of pacemaker function

The ventricular-inhibited (demand) pacemaker

This commonly encountered pacemaker is most susceptible to electromagnetic interference. Extraneous electromagnetic signals can lead to its inhibition even when endogenous ventricular activity is absent. Newer models are designed to switch automatically, in the presence of a strong continuous interference, to operate in the fixed rate (asynchronous) mode.

When the interference is of short duration and intermittent but repetitive in quick succession, conversion to asynchronous function will not occur. All models can be switched to pace in the fixed rate (asynchronous) mode with the application of a strong magnet over the pacemaker externally.

The ventricular-triggered (standby or ventricular synchronous) pacemaker

Instead of being inhibited by extraneous electromagnetic signals, this device is triggered to pace at a maximum rate of 150 per minute (120 per minute for older models), which is consistent with a built-in refractory period of 0.4 second (0.5 second for older models). This rapid ventricular rate reduces the efficiency of the heart. It increases myocardial work to a degree not tolerated by most patients with ischaemic heart disease. When interference occurs, the pacemaker can be converted to operate in the fixed rate (asynchronous) mode with an externally applied magnet.

The atrial synchronous pacemaker

This pacemaker can be triggered by electromagnetic interference to pace at the maximum rate of 125 per minute. At a higher rate, its blocking mechanism will automatically switch it over to pace at a fixed rate of 60 per minute.

The fixed rate (asynchronous) pacemaker

This device is not sensitive to electromagnetic interference.

The special purpose pacemaker

The older model, which has a magnetic switch, is immune to interference. The newer model, which is activated by radiowave of a narrow bandwidth emitted from an external transmitter, is safe in most situations; but interference cannot be ruled out in all occasions. The manufacturer recommends that general precautions be exercised when electrocautery or diathermy is used in close proximity to the implanted receiver.

Special monitoring

The patient should be monitored by both ECG and continuous palpitation of a peripheral pulse. A pulse meter using the principle of digital plethysmography can be used instead, and the oesophageal stethoscope is another alternative.

The electrocardiogram is a useful monitor of the ongoing cardiac rhythm and the mode in which the pacemaker is functioning. However, most ECG monitors are easily overloaded by extraneous electromagnetic signals and their diagnostic function rendered useless. Simultaneous monitoring of the peripheral pulse is, therefore, important. A palpable pulse also serves to confirm that the electrical activity of the heart is followed by ventricular contraction and ejection.

Any pause, increse or irregularity of the peripheral pulse is an indication of interference with normal pacemaker function. Interference varies with the type and intensity of the extraneous signal. It can occur at unexpected moments. Continuous monitoring is mandatory.

Coping with interference

The first principle of coping with interference is prevention.

Biological potentials

The commonest interference of biological origin is skeletal muscle myopotentials (Ohm *et al.*, 1974; Redd *et al.*, 1974). This can happen with fasciculation following the administration of suxamethonium and with shivering during emergence. Precurarization may alleviate the problem associated with suxamethonium, but its effectiveness has not been confirmed. Shivering can be prevented by keeping the patient warm. Diazepam 5–10 mg, or methylphenidate 10–20 mg, can be given intravenously to stop shivering as indicated.

Electrical equipment

To minimize interference from electrical instruments, the following precautions should be exercised.

1. All electrical equipment must be properly grounded. Leakage current from ungrounded instruments will not only interfere with pacemaker function, but also cause electrocution.

2. The ground electrodes of all electrical surgical instruments and monitoring devices must be attached to the patient at a site as far away from the pacemaker as possible. This is to ensure that the path of the electric current travelling through the patient is directed away from the pacemaker.

3. ECG and other leads must be as short as practicable because long leads can act as antennae for indirect electromagnetic signals.

4. The use of bipolar forceps can reduce the level of interference from electrocautery units.

A strong magnet must always be available. In the face of interference, the magnet can be applied over the pacemaker to convert it to a fixed rate (asynchronous) device when appropriate. If the pacemaker is close to the field of surgery, a sterilized magnet can be brought into the field and taped into place with a sterile waterproof plastic drape. If endogenous rhythm should return when the magnet is in place, competition between endogenous and pacemaker rhythms will occur. At times this pacemaker arrhythmia can be severe and can interfere with cardiac output. When this is the case, the magnet should be removed, or an attempt can be made to slow the endogenous rhythm with edrophonium or propranolol (exercise care in the presence of haemodynamic instability).

When the magnet cannot be applied safely and yet interference is a problem, the use of electrocautery should either be abandoned or be limited to momentary bursts (2–3 seconds each) interrupted by long pauses for the pacemaker to regain normal function.

Other precautions

All pacemakers can be damaged by the 400 joule (watt-sec) discharge from a direct-current defibrillator (Technical Manual, Medtronic). If defibrillation is necessary, the paddles should be placed at least 12 cm (5 inches) away from the implanted pulse generator. After a successful defibrillation, pacemaker function should be evaluated as soon as possible.

References

Barold, S. S., Pupillo, G. A., Gaidula, J. J. and Linhart, J. W. (1970). Chest wall stimulation in evaluation of patients with implanted ventricular-inhibited demand pacemakers. *British Heart Journal* **32**, 783.

Bennett, M. A. and Pentecost, B. L. (1971). Reversion of ventricular tachycardia by pacemaker stimulation. *British Heart Journal* **33**, 922.

Bilitch, M., Cosby, R. S. and Cafferky, E. A. (1967). Ventricular fiibrillation and competitive pacing. *New England Journal of Medicine* **276**, 598.

Carleton, R. A., Passovoy, M. and Graettinger, J. S. (1966). The importance of the contribution and timing of left atrial systole. *Clinical Science* **30**, 151.

Chardack, W. M., Gage, A. A. and Greatbatch, W. (1960). A transistorized, self-contained, implantable pacemaker for the long-term correction of complete heart block. *Surgery* **48**, 643.

Chung, E. K. (Ed.) (1977). *Artificial Cardiac Packing — A Practical Approach*. Williams & Wilkins: Baltimore.

Kastor, J. A. (1978). Cardiac electrophysiology: hemiblocks and stopped hearts. *New England Journal of Medicine* **299**, 249.

Keller, J. W. Jr, Gosselin, A. J. and Lister J. W. (1972). Engineering aspects of cardiac pacemaking. *Progress in Cardiovascular Dieases* **14**, 447.

Lister, J. W., Gosselin, A. J., Nathan, D. A. and Barold, S. S. (1973). Rapid atrial stimulation in the treatment of supraventricular tacyhcardia. *Chest* **63**, 995.

Lown, B. and Kosowsky, B. D. (1970a). Artificial cardiac pacemakers (first of three parts). *New England Journal of Medicine* **283**, 907.

Lown, B. and Kosowsky, B. D. (1970b). Artificial cardiac pacemakers (second of three parts). *New England Journal of Medicine* **283**, 971.

Lown, B. and Kosowsky, B. D. (1970c). Artificial cardiac pacemakers (third of three parts). *New England Journal of Medicine* **283**, 1023.

McAnulty, J. H., Rahimtoola, S. H., Murphy, E. S., Kauffman, S., Ritzman, L. W., Kanarek, P. and DeMots, H. (1978). A prospective study of sudden death in 'high-risk' bundle-branch block. *New England Journal of Medicine* **299**, 209.

Ohm, O. J., Bruland, H., Pedersen, O. M. and Waerness, E. (1974). Interference effect of myopotentials on function of unipolar demand pacemakers. *British Heart Journal* **36**, 77.

Redd, R., McAnulty, J., Phillips, S., Dobbs, J. and Ritzman, L. (1974). Demand pacemaker inhibition by isometric skeletal muscle contraction. *Circulation* **49** and **50**, Suppl. III, III–241.

Ruben, S. (1969). Sealed zinc–mercuric oxide cells for implantable cardiac pacemakers. *Annals of the New York Academy of Sciences* **167**, 627.

Simon, A. B., Linde, B., Bonnette, G. H. and Schlentz, R. J. (1975). The individual with a pacemaker in the dental environment. *Journal of the American Dental Association* **91**, 1224.

Smyth, N. P. D., Parsonnet, V., Escher, D. J. W. and Furman, S. (1974). The pacemaker patient and the electromagnetic environment. *Journal of the American Medical Association* **227**, 1412.

Sowton, E., Gray, K. and Preston, T. (1970). Electrical interference in non-competitive pacemakers. *British Heart Journal* **32**, 626.

Tarjan, P. P. (1973). Engineering aspects of implantable cardiac pacemakers. In: *Cardiac Pacing*, pp. 47–71. Ed. by P. Samet. Grune & Stratton: New York, London.

Index

Adrenaline induced ventricular
  arrhythmias
  and droperidol 44
  and enflurane 39
  and halothane 37, 39
  and isoflurane 39, 40
  dose-response curve 39
Alpha-adrenergic agents in
  hypotension 113
Althesin 45–6
  circulatory effects 45–6
Anaesthesia
  regional, conditions for 99–100
  versus general 99–101
Anaesthetic
  agents, circulatory effects 32–66
    (*see also* specific agents)
  implications, general 2–4
  techniques 99–107
    artificial ventilation versus
      spontaneous respiration
      104
    choice of agents 101–2
    during emergence 101, 105
    during induction 100–101
    during operation 101
    endotracheal intubation 102–4
    from induction to operation 101
    laryngoscopy 102–4
    parenteral fluid requirements
      104–5
    pre-oxygenation 102
    regional versus general 99–101
Analgesia, postoperative 119–20
Analgesics
  narcotic, circulatory effects 49–52
    interaction with nitrous oxide
      33–4
    and propranolol 128
Angina pectoris, diagnosis 68
  atypical 68
  stable 68

  unstable 68
Anrep effect 26–8
Arrhythmias
  control before operation 73–6
  treatment during operation 114–16
  (*see also* specific arrhythmias)
Arterial blood
  pressure, direct measurement 86–7
  supply, coronary circulation 6–7
Artificial ventilation versus
    spontaneous respiration 104
Aspartate transaminase in myocardial
    infarction 70
Asystole following suxamethonium 46
Atherosclerosis of coronary artery 1
Atrial
  fibrillation and flutter 74, 115
  tachycardia 115
Atrioventricular block in digitalis
    toxicity, treatment 147
Atropine
  in bradycardia 130
  in hypotension 112
  in halothane-induced nodal
    bradycardia 36

Beta-adrenergic anatagonists 122–35
  (*see also* Propranolol)
  anaesthetic considerations 126–9
  assessment and preparation of
    patient 126–7
  during operation 126–7
  postoperative management 129
  bradycardia and hypotension,
    treatment 129–31
  interaction with anaesthetic agents
    128–9
  in protection of ischaemic
    myocardium 25
Blood
  flow, coronary (*see* Coronary blood
    flow)

173